BRITAIN—
Uneasy Ally

THIS BOOK HAS BEEN PREPARED UNDER THE AUSPICES OF THE CENTER FOR THE STUDY OF AMERICAN FOREIGN POLICY AT THE UNIVERSITY OF CHICAGO

BRITAIN—
Uneasy Ally

By Leon D. Epstein

THE UNIVERSITY OF CHICAGO PRESS

THE UNIVERSITY OF CHICAGO PRESS, CHICAGO 37
Cambridge University Press, London N.W. 1, England
The University of Toronto Press, Toronto 5, Canada

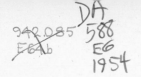

The Center for the Study of American Foreign Policy was established in 1950 under a grant from the Lilly Endowment and is now supported by a grant from the Carnegie Corporation. Its general purpose is to contribute to a better understanding of the principles, objectives, and probable results of American foreign policy and contemporary problems of United States foreign policy.

Dr. Epstein's book belongs to the third area of research. Previous publications are Robert E. Osgood, Ideals and Self-interest in America's Foreign Relations (1953), and Gerald Stourzh, Benjamin Franklin and American Foreign Policy (1954).

Hans J. Morgenthau
Director

June 1, 1954

I am indebted to so many individuals in Great Britain for their willingness to discuss Anglo-American problems that I must be content to extend my acknowledgment collectively. Without their frank and friendly assistance the research upon which this book is based could not have been completed. I do owe, in addition, a particular debt to R. Bassett and B. G. Roberts, of the faculty of the London School of Economics and Political Science, for their reading of the manuscript.

For encouragement to pursue this work I am indebted to my colleagues in political science at the University of Wisconsin and to Professor Hans J. Morgenthau, director of the Center for the Study of American Foreign Policy at the University of Chicago. The book has resulted, in part, from studies undertaken under a summer research grant in 1951 from the Graduate School of the University of Wisconsin and during the tenure of a fellowship in 1952-53 from the Fund for the Advancement of Education designed to broaden my qualifications for college teaching. However, I assume full responsibility for the work, and neither the sources of funds nor the individuals named above are associated in any way with the views expressed herein.

Some of the material contained in chapter v originally appeared as "The British Labour Left and U. S. Foreign Policy" in the American Political Science Review, XLV (December, 1951), 974-95.

At every stage of this work I have depended upon the critical advice and the sympathetic patience of my wife.

Madison, Wisconsin   L. D. E.
December 1953

TABLE OF CONTENTS

The intention is to analyze British responses to American foreign policy in the postwar years 1945 through 1952. References to subsequent events are only parenthetical. Not only does this time period have the advantage of coinciding with the tenure of the Truman Administration but it includes the critical postwar events around which patterns of opinion first developed in relation to the new American assumption of global responsibility. While treating "American foreign policy" of this period as a constant for purposes of analysis, it is possible to agree with the criticism, British as well as American, that the policy was not a constant at all in the usual sense of the term. A major complaint against the United States was that it did not adopt a definite and clear-cut line but only improvised, rather unpredictably, from time to time. Most literally, Britain might be viewed as responding to several different postwar policies rather than to a single and distinctive American position.

Certainly that was the case with respect to the changing and uncertain American attitude toward China. And it also applied to the American policy about which the British were usually most anxious: the commitment to defend Europe and the West against aggression. An American decision to this effect could not be taken for granted in the earliest part of the postwar period; then, the remnants of Rooseveltian optimism about Russia were so combined with a back-to-normalcy spirit that the United States appeared less ready than the British government to oppose Soviet aggrandizement. Later, though American hostility to Russia became firmly established, there was still occasional cause for Britain to doubt, at critical moments, how deeply and firmly the United States was willing to be involved in the economic and military defense of Europe.

Yet, in spite of all that might be said about its sporadic qualities, American postwar policy did develop in a shape designed to check the power of the Soviet Union. It was in the role of principal anti-Communist nation that the United States usually appeared to postwar Britain (and to the rest of the world). The manner in which this international leadership developed, including its fits and starts, became the overwhelming object

1

of British attention. This attention increased with the growing national awareness that, for better or for worse, Britain was dependent on American economic and military power.

It is the public concern with American policy that provides the book with its subject matter, and there is no emphasis, as in a diplomatic history, on official pronouncements.[1] Nevertheless, it is appreciated that official British policy is itself a major influence on public opinion. To cite the most general illustration, national attitudes were undoubtedly affected by the fact that the Foreign Office (and its peripheral unofficial spokesmen) accepted Britain's need for close American ties—and had, indeed, appreciated that need for at least a generation. Or when the British government disagreed with American policy, as on the recognition of China, this also influenced, though in a different way, the public response to the position of the United States. While such currents cannot be overlooked, the investigation relates mainly to unofficial attitudes. These are assumed to affect, though not themselves to determine, the commitments of the British government and at the very least to affect the spirit and manner in which such commitments are carried out. This is said despite the acknowledgment of the counterinfluence of governmental policy and without denying that the exigencies of Britain's international situation may be much more decisive than public opinion in the formulation of foreign policy. Such exigencies ruled against the adoption of alternatives to the American alliance. But that did not preclude dissatisfaction with the alliance, or with its terms, from indirectly influencing the extent to which a British government could go along with American policy.

The media for the study of British attitudes are conceived as broadly political rather than strictly governmental. Sources include parliamentary debates, party and union conferences, partisan books and pamphlets, and newspaper and magazine editorials. Emphasis is placed on the argumentative and polemical rather than on the academic or scholarly reaction to American policy. There is a concentration on the political channels through which British opinion was

---

1. The postwar development of official British policy toward the United States as well as the rest of the world has been described by M. A. Fitzsimons, The Foreign Policy of the British Labour Government: 1945-1951 (Notre Dame, Ind.: University of Notre Dame Press, 1953).

expressed and mobilized,[2] and therefore the work depends on written materials to a very large extent. The views of the man in the street are not sampled. Although opinion polls, when available, are used for illustrative purposes, no other effort is made to present the attitudes of the ordinarily inarticulate and politically passive mass of the population. To do so might be an important project but essentially different from the one undertaken here.

Nonquantitative methods were employed in gathering the data upon which interpretation is based. The process has the traditional academic claims to objectivity. The canvass of newspapers and magazines was on a scale large enough to cover most of the principal conveyors of political opinion, at least on a national basis. Scottish and provincial papers were checked less thoroughly but sufficiently to indicate that no major regional bias in international commentary had been omitted. Editorial lines in the quality press were more carefully studied, befitting their seriousness, than were those of the popular papers, but the latter were also surveyed, especially during critical periods in Anglo-American relations. As will be noted in the text, the few publications ordinarily assumed to be leading opinion-makers were drawn upon most frequently. It is not thereby implied that such journals were typical of the whole public, or anything approaching it, but only that they represented substantial segments of the articulate community—that is, the community with which this work is concerned. In this connection a study of written sources is somewhat simplified in Britain, as compared with the United States, by the acknowledged ascendancy of a national press largely centered in the capital.

Similarly, the House of Commons provides a most convenient focal point for the analysis of political opinion. The importance of individual members of Parliament may be much less than that of congressmen so far as the enactment of legislation is concerned, but (perhaps partly for that reason) the Commons commands relatively greater attention as a national forum. Parliamentary debates have, in consequence, been used more often than any other single source of opinion. Not only were the

---

2. This orientation is different from that of Henry L. Roberts and Paul A. Wilson, Britain and the United States (New York: Harper & Bros., 1953). Their work is a report on problems of Anglo-American co-operation as seen by the quasi-official participants in a joint conference sponsored by the Council on Foreign Relations and the Royal Institute of International Affairs.

foreign-policy and defense discussions in the House of Commons, and a few in the House of Lords, especially significant, but the give and take of oral question time also furnished a variety of views on international affairs. It need not be assumed that members of Parliament addressing the subject of Anglo-American relations always spoke for their constituencies, or for large numbers of followers, to assign some weight to their status as articulate public figures.

Both in and out of Parliament an attempt was made to observe a wide range of political opinion, including some that was expressed in relatively minor journals and pamphlets. The reports of the major party conferences and of the Trades Union Congress were valuable in this respect, but even more so because of the light they cast on the lines of political conflict, notably within the Labour movement. It was at the annual conferences that there could be observed, most clearly, the relationship between general political outlooks and the several attitudes toward the United States. On this interpretative matter, written sources were most usefully supplemented by personal investigations in Great Britain in 1952 and early 1953. It was possible to observe, at first hand, parliamentary debates as well as the annual meetings of the Trades Union Congress, the Labour party, and the Conservative party. Numerous other political meetings, some in connection with an important by-election, were also attended. Informal discussions were arranged with politicians in both major parties and with British journalists and scholars interested in the general field of investigation.

Broadly speaking, this work treats British responses to American policy at two different levels. The first might be described as national, where the most striking feature was a sharing of more or less similar attitudes by the bulk of the British community. The second level is based on political orientations rather than nationality and is meant to show the diversities instead of the similarities in British attitudes. For this purpose the term "ideology" is used to indicate the deep-going basis upon which political outlooks were founded. It is not contended that ideological factors were more important than those of nationality in determining British views of American leadership, since any particular political conspectus probably operated within boundaries set by the national consciousness. No doubt, this was true of all British political groups except the Communists. But, within those boundaries, different ideologies did make for significantly different approaches to American foreign policy. The

ideological categories, indicated by the chapter headings, are related to
evident alignments between and within the major political parties. In dis-
cussing these alignments, the fact that each party contained disparate elements is allowed for. Yet there is a certain amount of generalizing that
may violate the nuances of British politics. In part, this results from
treating the parties, organized primarily around domestic issues, as
vehicles for the expression of foreign policy. The justification for doing
so lies in the general relationship between domestic and international attitudes. Nevertheless, there remain individual politicians who have not
conformed to any such basic relationship within their own party, or even
within a readily identifiable wing of their party.

Despite this difficulty, the breakdown of opinion by political groups
is most appropriate for this analysis. There is virtually no case for the
alternative of studying British attitudes according to regions or economic
pressure groups, either of which might be significant in an analogous study
of American opinion. On the other hand, a good deal is to be said for a
breakdown of the community along the lines of economic, social, or educational status. Of course, that would involve finding ordinarily inartic-
ulated opinions (assuming their existence) and exploring such opinions
by special interviewing techniques. Investigation of that sort has already
been noted as beyond the province of this work.

The part of the book mainly concerned with the various ideological
approaches to American foreign policy consists of chapters v through ix
plus chapter xi. Devotion of the largest proportion of this discussion
to the attitudes of the left results not only from their volubility but also
from the conviction that the hostility within the Labour party to American
leadership is the single most important political factor in Britain's relations with the United States.

Existing differences between the approaches of the various political
groups are touched upon in almost all parts of the work, although often
subordinate in importance to the broader national outlook. Chapter ii
is exceptional in that it is entirely devoted to social and cultural considerations. Generally, no hard-and-fast line is drawn between the two
levels of analysis, and thus chapters iii and iv, dealing with reactions
to American economic policies, include the variations as well as the
general theme. The same is true, though less evidently, when the conflict over Far Eastern issues is discussed in chapter x.

Although this organization deliberately subordinates the chrono-
logical order of events to a topical arrangement, the many changes in
British attitudes (and in American programs) over the seven-year period
are taken into account. This is done in almost every chapter, with the degree of attention varying with the significance of the temporal change.
Also the historical sequence is partly observed by placing the Far Eastern
topic toward the end of the book and by following it with the chapter devoted to Bevanism. The latter is separated from the earlier and underlying discussion of left-wing ideology, because Bevanism, as a political
movement, could be most meaningfully understood against the full background of general British attitudes, especially toward the Far Eastern
conflict.

In connection neither with Bevanism nor with other responses to
American foreign policy is British opinion divided into pro-American
and anti-American camps. One reason is that attitudes toward America
and Americans do not always coincide with attitudes toward American
foreign policy. There is even some truth in the quip that socialists like
Americans but dislike American policies, while Conservatives dislike
the individual American manner but like the policies. Actually, the two
views are not that disconnected, and it is possible to observe an inter-
action between responses to social and cultural Americanism, on the one
hand, and responses to American foreign policy, on the other.

But there is a more fundamental reason for avoiding the descriptions
"pro-American" and "anti-American." The convenience, admittedly
tempting for an American, is deceptive and misleading. It cannot be
assumed that all, or even a large share, of those insisting on the importance of preserving good relations with the United States either like
the idea of American leadership or many prominent aspects of it. To
call "pro-American" those who have accepted harmony with the United
States as a matter of necessity is to do violence to the language and to
speak as though the British international approach were determined almost entirely by attitudes toward the United States. In reality, it is more
the other way round. [British conceptions of their own national interest
are vital in conditioning responses to American foreign policy.]

The several points of view are presented as natural phenomena—as
interpretations of national interests as they are understood by Englishmen of various political persuasions. But since these interpretations

are based on national, and often political, perspectives different from
the author's, there can be no pretense to complete detachment. It is
fair to note at the outset that in this work the general direction of postwar American foreign policy is assumed to have been justified. And, of
special relevance to much of the study, American policy is viewed in a
perspective that is nonsocialist[3] as well as American. Thus, in spite of
the fact that it is not the author's purpose to discuss or judge American
Administration measures on their merits, it may often seem that there
is an implicit defense of those measures. Such an impression, though
perhaps unavoidable, would nevertheless be unfortunate. While believing
generally in the policy of strength toward which the United States has
tended in postwar dealings with the Soviet bloc and while also accepting
the overseas aid and alliances characteristic of that policy, there remains,
in the author's mind, much room for debate concerning particular measures
adopted by the American government. For example, one would not have to
take an exclusively British position to find fault with American trade and
tariff policies or to dispute the efficacy of the Truman Administration's
position in relation to Communist China. By avoiding, in the discussion
of British responses to various American policies, the large and vexing
questions concerning the validity of the criticism, the writer does not
assume that all American decisions have best served the Western cause
or even the cause of the United States.

On the other hand, it can be granted that this study, because it does
assume the desirability of the general direction of American policy, tends
to judge unfavorably that portion of British criticism which derives from
sources basically hostile to the exercise of power against Communist
states. In other words, there is a conscious bias against those who find
American policy generally unacceptable and who would seemingly destroy
the terms upon which Anglo-American co-operation is based. The writer
emphatically believes that continuation of that co-operation is in the interests
of both nations.

In concentrating only on British responses to American policy, it is

---

3. The word "socialist" is used here in a narrower sense (to indicate
a belief in the virtues of public ownership of the means of production)
than is often the case in the British Labour party, where many right-
wingers describe themselves as socialists even though they appear
not at all anxious for a drastic alteration in the capitalist system as
it now exists in Britain.

hoped that something may be added to an understanding of one kind of problem involved in maintaining close relations between the two nations. The very idea of this kind of study results from the new realization that much of the burden for satisfactory Anglo-American relations now rests on the United States. This is only one of the tasks which have stemmed from the rapid and sudden shift in America's role in world affairs. Previously it was the British, among others, who needed to win our favor as a prospective ally. Then we were interested only as a matter of curiosity in what the British (and other Europeans) thought of us. Now, in Walter Lippmann's words, the American problem has become "not whether we will join the allies, but whether the allies will stay joined with us."[4]

4. Public Opinion and Foreign Policy in the United States (London: Allen & Unwin, 1952), p. 33.

II / THE UNITED STATES IN BRITISH PERSPECTIVE

The American does not fit easily in the British scheme of things. The European is a foreign neighbor. The Canadian, the Australian, and the New Zealander are members of the same political house. And so, with a different status, are the Imperial subjects. But the American is none of these. He is never, like the Continental, called a "foreigner." Nor is he of the Commonwealth or the colonies. The American is a special breed with whom there are significant ties, but ties that are indefinite and confused.

Nothing is simplified by speaking symbolically of the relationship as that of an aged father with a strong grown-up son.[1] This generation knows enough psychology to appreciate that there is no bond more complex emotionally than that of parent and child. No more readily than the formerly well-to-do father in relation to his rich but not always tactful son can the British nation accept with unadulterated gratitude the leadership of Americans. For within the memory of men still living, and thus well within the historical consciousness of almost all the present generation, the British were the top dogs of Europe and of the world. Their superiority was of such import and duration that finally, in the recent past, there was no need to boast after the manner of new rivals for world power. National self-confidence was in the bones. It was the heritage of British success over the centuries of modern history. Specifically linked to this national tradition was the belief in the crucial quality of British strength. The essence of the balance-of-power consciousness was that the decisions of British statesmen either preserved the peace or, in war, made one side or another victorious. Such a traditional self-confidence has not died with the mixed fortunes of a few recent decades. Or, at least, it has died hard. There has been no ready or happy transformation of the national attitude to the acceptance of second place in an Anglo-American alliance. There must, from the British standpoint, be a flaw somewhere in a situation in which the Americans, newcomers in world politics, made the vital decisions

---

1. This figure of speech was skilfully employed by Crane Brinton, The United States and Britain (Cambridge: Harvard University Press, 1945), pp. 244-45.

for Britain as well as for themselves.

One flaw the British often thought they discovered was that American predominance rested on undeserved wealth. It has always been hard, as Raymond Aron remarked, for any nation "to accept the fact that the richest and strongest country in the world is also the most virtuous."[2] But it must have been especially difficult for the nation which only so recently lost economic precedence to the United States and which in the postwar period displayed an unmistakable feeling for times past—"when the going was good." More conspicuous among the upper and middle classes, the feeling was sufficiently pervasive to be counted as part of the British state of mind. Sometimes it was merely nostalgia. Other times it took the form of a troubled dissatisfaction with the world. So Churchill's cry from the heart: "It does seem indeed hard that the traditions and triumphs of a thousand years should be challenged by the ebb and flow of markets and commercial and financial transactions in the vast swaying world which has sprung and is growing ever larger around us, and that we have to watch from month to month the narrow margins upon which our solvency, and consequently our reputation and influence and livelihood depend."[3]

On occasion the note has been more plaintive and mixed with the resentment of the once-wealthy toward the new rich men of the world. Englishmen were reminded of their nation's less secure status, economically and otherwise, by the apparent need for their statesmen to visit American makers of foreign policy. Attlee and Churchill journeyed to Washington, not the President to London.[4]

Although how the British felt about this relationship is mainly to be observed in responses to particular American policies, the study does begin with an examination of the attraction and the repulsion, not of policies, but of the American way of life. The prominence of the United States in British consciousness has been social and cultural as well as military and economic, and the more general factors are not simply results of govern-

2. New York Times Book Review, January 7, 1951, p. 29.

3. British Information Services, official text of speech delivered in London, June 11, 1952.

4. The importance of the British assumption of the burden for keeping Anglo-American relations on an intimate basis was treated by W. T. R. Fox and A. B. Fox, Britain and America in the Era of Total Diplomacy (Princeton: Princeton Center of International Studies, 1952), p. 29.

mental relations.

In the last decade things American have become obtrusive in Great Britain.[5] The influence of Hollywood, which has long provided the bulk of Britain's film entertainment, is incalculable but tremendous. American films have made everyone aware of the advertised material standards of American life. English newspaper correspondents, in the United States, have filled in the details. They have told their countrymen how Americans build their houses, drive their cars, eat their steaks, and train their successful Olympic athletes. British concern for these stories was just what might have been expected of a people without enough houses, cars, steaks, or successful athletes. The British were almost always interested, frequently envious, and sometimes resentful.[6] But in any case it was an American standard that was set before British eyes. For material things to be attractive to the mass of the population, they had to resemble the American product. Even in a local beauty contest Britain was exhorted by a popular newspaper to show that it too had female lovelies to rival California's best. And, on the other hand, when Britain clearly did have something better than America, notably in jet airliners, the national joy was understandably boundless.

In addition to the impact of America through the films, the press, and consumers' goods, Americans themselves became familiar in Britain. First, there was the immense disposition of American servicemen during World War II, when Air Force personnel and Army service troops remained in Britain in substantial numbers for three years, while entire armies stayed a few months en route to the Continent. The second wave, growing in volume, consisted of postwar tourists, who, like American soldiers, were undis-

---

5. Measuring the increased American prominence is difficult. What has been shown, by content analysis, is that the London *Times* in the postwar period devoted an increased percentage of its editorial attention to the United States (compared with other geographical units) than was typical in the previous half-century (Ithiel de Sola Pool, Symbols of Internationalism [Stanford University: Stanford University Press, 1951], p. 69).

6. Antagonism apparently inspired by such material considerations was reported to have reached a high point in 1947, when acute British shortages were in sharpest contrast to American abundance (not yet distributed through the Marshall Plan) (Fred Vanderschmidt, What the English Think of Us [New York: R. M. McBride, 1948], p. 2).

tinguished for modesty in proclaiming the virtues of the United States. Finally, there was the return of the American Air Force, reportedly some thirty thousand strong plus about eight thousand dependents. More than either wartime troops or tourists, this last wave brought its own way of life. In the southeast of England, where the Air Force was heavily concentrated, entire American communities were created—as islands of high salaries, large cars, and big portions of meat. These accouterments of American well-being were unavoidable irritants to Englishmen, already troubled by the novelty of having another nation's troops on their soil during a period of nominal peace.[7]

Common Grounds?

The use of the same language in Britain and in America provides the most obviously common ground. Although it is occasionally claimed, in excessive fondness for the paradoxical, that the common language contributes mainly to misunderstanding because of the different ways in which the two peoples use, or misuse, it, nevertheless the English tongue is one of the principal terms in which a mystique of Anglo-American kinship is stated. The prime example is afforded by the oldest of the important promoters of transatlantic friendship, the English-speaking Union. Its expressed purpose is "to draw together in the bond of comradeship the English-speaking peoples of the world," and it propagates this faith in the Commonwealth as well as in Britain and the United States. While its activities in the United States are not conspicuous, in Britain the Union not only dispenses hospitality to English-speaking visitors but also carries on a rather broad program of education in various aspects of Anglo-American relations.[8] Always, in its publications, the organization stresses mutual friendship and understanding; and in Britain the Union has come to be recognized, in the words of the London Times, as one of "the foundations of

7.   Undercurrents of opposition to various influences attributed to American troops apparently existed, but only rarely did they appear in print. One example was a lurid portrayal by a small-town paper of the ill effects of Air Force personnel on the mores of the local community's younger generation (Essex Chronicle, August 1, 1952, pp. 1-2).

8.   The English-speaking World is the principal written medium. Quotation as to the Union's purpose is from the official prospectus.

that Anglo-American friendship on which the very continuance of civilized
life may depend."[9]

Almost necessarily the program of the English-speaking Union has
been limited to the relatively small numbers willing and able to maintain
transatlantic ties. But well outside the bonds of the Union, the fact of common language has been used as a method of stating, and even of justifying,
an especially close relationship with the United States. The device has
been a favorite of Winston Churchill, who struck the phrase the "fraternal
association of English speaking peoples" in his famous advance toward
Anglo-American unity at Fulton, Missouri.[10] The tie of language has suited
many who, like Churchill, wished to stress the solidarity of their country
and the United States and yet not exclude the Commonwealth nations from
the frame of reference.[11] No other label would do so well. In omitting
the rest of the world, common language does so without invidious distinction. Nothing is overtly implied to the discredit of non-English-speaking
peoples on the score of race, national origin, wealth, or even political institutions.

Yet the significance of the common language may often be exaggerated
as a factor in establishing identification. This is not to belittle the usefulness of English in facilitating communication between Britain and America
and in fostering individual friendships, but it is to question whether language
itself operates to make two national communities more like one in their outlook on the world. Probably there are more potent associations concealed
beneath the nicety of the phrase "English-speaking." One of these, the tradition of a common Anglo-Saxon origin, is no less important for the fact
that it has become almost an unmentionable in a world sensitive to intima-
tions of racial superiority. While it is true that references to "a common
racial origin from which the American nation drew its sturdiest charac-
teristics"[12] have been rare in postwar accounts by British travelers in the

---

9. March 10, 1948, p. 5.

10. New York Times, March 6, 1946, p. 4.

11. Examples of "Anglo-Americanism": 418 H. C. Deb. 2087-92 (February
    8, 1946), 430 H. C. Deb. 341-46 (November 14, 1946), and 499 H. C.
    Deb. 1910-18 (May 2, 1952).

12. Cecil Roberts, And So to America (New York: Doubleday & Co.,
    1947), p. 531.

United States, still there is ample evidence of a depth of feeling, drawn partly from the knowledge of actual American cousins.

What remains in America that is distinctively English in origin is almost always noticed as opposed to that which is either peculiarly American or of Continental derivation. For instance, relatively unsophisticated Englishmen, exposed to a cross-section of American servicemen, often express a preference for the southerners, whose names are Anglo-Saxon, whose complexions are familiar, and whose manners are leisured. In short, the American southerner seems more "English" and seems so even to many in Britain who have been critical of American race relations. It is also noteworthy that, when a British visitor has been surprised by the alien nature of American life, he should conclude that this is because the Americans are now "essentially a different race in which the Anglo-Saxon strain has been heavily diluted and is scarcely perceptible."[13] The American of Eastern European descent, it may be observed, has not been Anglicized in the process of his Americanization and acquisition of the English language. An adverse reaction to the mixture of American national origins might occur more frequently as non-Anglo-Saxon features of American life become more conspicuous—for example, through the increasing public participation of citizens of Slavic, Italian, or Jewish origin.

If the importance of Anglo-Saxon kinship should diminish, there would remain the consciousness of commonly derived political institutions. In some general way the American heritage of political freedom is regarded by Englishmen as their contribution to American life and so as a basis for Anglo-American solidarity. On this score the unity of British and American purposes may be stated without inhibitions, as in these words of the postwar ambassador, Sir Oliver Franks: "We are heirs to a great estate, that heritage of freedom handed down to us by the preceding generations. From the struggles and sacrifices of the past we have acquired a personal sense of what freedom means."[14] This affinity is expressed in various other terms of reference, such as the mutual success in parliamentary government, the "liberal civilization"

---

13. Michael Robertson, Beyond the Sunset (New York: Falcon Press, 1950), p. 7.

14. Saturday Review of Literature, XXXIV (October 13, 1951), 59.

linking Britain and the United States, or more broadly the "humanism which distinguishes Western thought."[15] In so far as the communion is accepted, no difference over the aims of foreign policies can be admitted. When the defense of "common values" is in the forefront of British consciousness, there is only room (though importantly) for differences as to the means for accomplishing that defense.

In contrast to the recognition of similarity in political faith, there have been tendencies, since the war, to emphasize philosophical differences between the two nations in matters only slightly less fundamental. Socialist doctrine has been chiefly important in this respect, and its particular role needs a separate discussion.[16] But a general issue is raised by nonsocialists who have occasionally found the United States committed to first principles different from their own.[17] The crucial element has been the widespread reluctance, in postwar Britain, to accept the American equation of capitalism and democracy. Business enterprise did, it is true, have its staunch defenders and probably the tacit support of a majority. But if one were to try to summarize British attitudes toward capitalism in a term descriptive of the whole community, the word would be "ambivalent."

Although, in later postwar years, Britain was not definitely turned toward socialist objectives, the national economic outlook appeared strikingly different from the American. The difference rested on a deeper basis than distinctions in the degree of enterprise owned or controlled by the respective governments. There was, by the 1940's, a

---

15. This theme has frequently been put in intellectual terms: Norman Angell, The Steep Places (New York: Harper & Bros., 1947), p. 12; Manchester Guardian Weekly, LIV (March 8, 1946), 122; Kenneth Lindsay (446 H. C. Deb. 458 [January 22, 1948]); Lewis Einstein, "Anglo-American Relations and Security," Fortnightly, CLXVI (July, 1946), 42-48; Max Beloff, "North America: 1948," Fortnightly, CLXX (December, 1948), 357-62; and Spectator, CLXXVI (February 22, 1946), 183-84.

16. See chap. v.

17. Typical of the British view just after the end of the war were these comments from the London Times: "The frontier mentality, with its desire to exploit fresh riches, does not take kindly to any brake on expansion. It is individualistic rather than collectivist in its temper, and there has been a perceptible shift from that emphasis on human values which marked the philosophy of the United States during the slump and during the Roosevelt supremacy" (October 13, 1945, p. 5).

rooted British view toward profit-seeking that ran counter to prevailing American trends of thought. It had become deeply alien to the British way of life to believe that it was of the essence of national well-being to engage in aggressive business competition. As a matter of national temper, Englishmen recognized a contrast to the American economic verve—of which they often disapproved.

Another current of differentiation flowed from the widespread, and sometimes quite genuine, British repugnance to American race relationships. Doubtless the facts of segregation and maltreatment were, in a few quarters, more highly publicized for specific anti-American purposes than was justified by their news value, but adverse publicity would have had no point unless there was a considerable body of opinion ready to be appalled at what was read of American attitudes toward the Negroes.[18]

Among the British, whose confidence in the humanitarian quality of their own race attitudes was mostly unchallenged by domestic experience, doubts were easily raised as to what sort of fellow-democrats they had to deal with in the champions of white supremacy. The recent American progress in raising the status of the Negro was not widely known in Britain, and, even if it were, it could not very well have destroyed the prevailing picture of discrimination. That picture, unfortunately, was strengthened every time an Englishman visited the United States, expecially if he traveled to the national capital and points south. No amount of explanation about things-not-being-as-bad-as-they-were could blur the shock of meeting or hearing a southerner's articulate Jim Crow philosophy.

No doubt these elements potentially destructive of a common feeling with the United States may be overplayed. Divisive factors did have to compete against the tried and tested ties of language, origin, and liberty. There was also the fact that in two world wars Britain became accustomed to being on the same side as the United States. It was not surprising that in the spring of 1949, without at the moment any acute threat of war, 72 per cent of those interviewed in a British opinion sample were either

---

18. Some were ready to find in American discrimination a kind of compensatory evil for the totalitarianism of the U.S.S.R., as in the case of the extreme Labour Left member of Parliament, Tom Driberg (463 H.C. Deb. 494 [March 23, 1949]).

favorable or strongly favorable to the signing of a treaty of alliance with
the United States. Actually only 12 per cent were in some degree unfavorable, while 16 per cent were in the sampler's category of "unde-
cided."[19]

A minor matter may also be noted as illustrative of the special
nature of the American bond. It was a mark of remiss gentility openly
to attack the United States as a nation. The polite press almost never
did so. And it was another badge of the dishonor of the popular press for
it to indulge in anything that was even by implication sensationally anti-
American. By 1952 the British Communists had made so much of their
"Yanks, go home" campaign that flagrant anti-Americanism was regarded
as undignified and un-English. Even the more significant critics of American policies, like the Bevanites, were placed in the position of having to
explain that, no matter how unfavorable their comments, they were not
really "anti-American." Aneurin Bevan sought to absolve himself in the
House of Commons with this variant of the some-of-my-best-friends-are-
Americans approach: "I have never had any anti-American feeling. I can
tell hon. Members opposite that I have more friends in America than I
have on the other side of the House."[20]

The Materialist Curse

Although open and general anti-Americanism was bad manners in
in the British community, many aspects of American life were not immune
from criticism by polite Englishmen. The leading illustration was the recurrent objection to what the British regarded as the excessive materialism
of American life. This criticism had the respectability of a long and dis-

---

19. Survey by Research Services, Ltd., International Journal of Opinion
    and Attitude Research, III (summer, 1949), 288-89. Incidentally
    the percentage of Conservative voters strongly favoring the alliance
    was significantly higher than the Labour figure.

20. 496 H.C. Deb. 986 (February 26, 1952). Sometimes the intrusion
    of personal acquaintance into British discussion of America took
    an even stranger form, as in these remarks of a Labour Member
    of Parliament: "I think it is utterly wrong to refer to American
    bankers or any Americans as thugs or moneylenders or anything
    of that kind. I am personally acquainted with some of those Ameri-
    can bankers and I know that suggestion to be utterly false" (443
    H.C. Deb. 779 [October 28, 1947]).

tinguished lineage. It had been standard, in the nineteenth century, for
notable men of letters to refer to an American wilderness of money-
getting that provided inferior cultural advantages. This was a theme of
Matthew Arnold's essays on America; whatever else he found admirable
in the United States, he was sure that life in Anglo-European circumstances was more favorable for cultural pursuits.[21] Doubtless the British
acceptance of this view was fortified in the twentieth century by the volun-
tary residence in England of America's most cultivated and respected
authors, Henry James and T. S. Eliot.

What the British observer had in mind when he visualized American
materialism was never more vividly put than in a well-known passage,
written forty years ago, by G. Lowes Dickinson. In essays not generally
unfriendly to the United States, Dickinson described the American as
"masterful, aggressive, unscrupulous, egotistic, at once good-natured and
brutal, kind if you do not cross him, ruthless if you do, greedy, ambitious,
self-reliant, active for the sake of activity, intelligent and unintellectual,
quick-witted and crass, contemptuous of ideas but amorous of devices,
valuing nothing but success, recognizing nothing but the actual. . . ."[22]

Although this response belonged to the highly cultured Englishman,
who characteristically disdained American education and culture, it
would be a mistake to regard the general stereotype as held only by intellectuals.[23] In one way or another, the concept of the American as highly
materialistic permeated the British community. For example, it was
discovered by the British Broadcasting Corporation, in conducting a
survey preliminary to its 1952 campaign to counteract various unfavorable impressions of the United States, that its listeners thought that Americans hustled too much, that they were "uncultured" and did not "really
appreciate the finer things of life," and that money was far too important
to them.[24] The B.B.C.'s first program in its American series was de-

---

21. Civilization in the United States (Boston: De Wolfe Fisk & Co.,
    1900), pp. 172-77.

22. Appearances (Garden City, N.Y.: Doubleday, Page & Co., 1914), p. 140.

23. The widespread acceptance of this stereotype was commented on by
    Saul K. Padover, who attributed much of it to the ignorance of United
    States history ("America and Europe," Social Research, XVII
    [December, 1950], 403-16).

24. Statements contained in a memorandum of the B.B.C. Further Edu-
    cation Section.

voted to the question, "Is America more materialistic than we are?"

English critics occasionally offered explanations for American materialism, and these explanations were as revealing of European-mindedness as the stereotype itself. For example, Bertrand Russell, in one of his more mellow commentaries, stressing the good effects of American buoyancy of spirit and rejecting the view that the United States was crassly materialistic, declared nonetheless that Americans were without the Europeans' traditional and religious humility before facts and that they lacked an aesthetic sense because of an excessive preoccupation with utility.[25] Or when as sympathetic an observer as D. W. Brogan called attention to American material competitiveness, he explained that it was the result of the absence in American life, from the beginning, of any real stability or security.[26] It is just this sense of order in society which the Englishman, like other Europeans, has felt to be missing in the United States, where individuals were able to strive for material success uninhibited by the traditional forms which so often in Europe were equated with civilization.[27]

Finding in America a society whose principles of behavior were settled in an environment unlike his own in its possibilities for individual material betterment, the Englishman often found the strangeness of American hustling peculiarly unattractive. The American standard was said to be the unsavory "test of worth by money."[28] Whether the European should feel superior to this aspect of American life is obviously a highly subjective question. So, for that matter, is the query whether Americans were really as materialistic as Englishmen believed, or whether the belief itself was not mainly a psychological device compensating Britain for its own inferior stock of material possessions at a time when Americans had so much and were apparently able to acquire more.

Regardless of these moot points, the durability of the stereotype was real enough. In the postwar years it was especially prominent, although

25. "The Political and Cultural Influence," in The Impact of America on European Culture (Boston: Beacon Press, 1951), pp. 3-19.

26. The American Character (New York: A. A. Knopf, 1944), p. 6.

27. See, e.g., Harold Nicholson, "Marginal Comment," Spectator, CLXXIX (September 26, 1947), 395.

28. Patrick Gordon-Walker, Restatement of Liberty (London: Hutchinson & Co., 1951), p. 258.

the picture of the American hustler was not always drawn unfavorably.
Sometimes the hard-working, enterprising American youth was upheld as
an example for Britons.[29] However, even such comment pointed up the
difference between the American and the British ways of life, and in any
case it was decidedly a minor note in the chorus of reaction against American materialism. More typical was the attitude of the popular British
writer, Beverley Nichols, whose book on America stressed the unpleasant-
ness of what he thought was the dog-eat-dog atmosphere of American business. Nichols, while one of the most superficial of observers, was interesting for the context in which he discussed American competitiveness.
He was sure that in this respect American society represented the past
that had already died in Europe and especially in England and would in
time disappear even in America.[30] By this method of assuming that he
was of a society that had been through all this before, Nichols almost
managed to convey a sense of wise superiority to the material aspects of
American life.

One of the most striking reactions was the concern with the impact
of American mass culture on the British mind. American literature as well
as films were viewed as the vulgar products of the materialist civilization
to the West. What they represented—the potential Americanization of
Britain—was alarming, especially to the purveyors of English culture.
Where possible, as in radiobroadcasting, American methods were successfully resisted. The trouble was that many Yankee products did become
popular among ordinary Englishmen. There was, one critic said, "an
enormous encroachment by the United States on all that Matthew Arnold
implied by 'culture' in its widest sense."[31] Literature, treated as a com-
modity (it was explained) in the United States, was simply exported to
Britain like other goods. In addition to American products, as such, the
American influence on British media also constituted a source of complaint. For instance, the term "American-style comics" referred to any
comic book, regardless of its national origin, which stressed sex and

---

29. As in Audrey Whiting, "Who Said These Yanks Are Soft?" Daily
    Mirror, August 19, 1952, p. 5.

30. Uncle Samson (London: Evans Bros., 1950), p. 8.

31. Geoffrey Wagner, "The American Invaders," Tribune, October 19,
    1951, p. 14.

violence.[32] These themes were considered American inventions.

In all this there was strong evidence of rear-guard action by the cultural aristocracy, including many intellectuals even (or perhaps especially) of the left. This aristocracy, in Britain as on the Continent, did not pretend to furnish culture to the masses, and the exploitation of that market by typically American media was only confirming evidence of the sacrifice of art to business in the United States. But it was not proper, in a democratic age, to speak of the degradation of the culture primarily because of the low standards of the masses. Certainly this was impossible for the intellectuals of the left. Instead, the fire was directed at American materialism—a stereotype ready and waiting. Hollywood, as the chief target, became the symbol of dollars against art.

How much this low opinion of American culture vexed relations between the two countries is difficult to estimate. It might be assumed that Englishmen resented having to accept the leadership of a people conceived as so excessively materialist as to be their cultural inferiors. But, for Anglo-American relations, there may also have been an advantage in the British consciousness of superiority in the "finer things of life." Except among a few, there was often a satisfaction, even an eagerness, in contributing to the cultural edification of Americans. This was in the tradition, if not the exact purpose, of Cecil Rhodes. It was appropriate, in a period when Britain's material contributions were overwhelmed by the United States, that Englishmen should feel that their nation could play the part of Greece to the American Rome.

The Charge of Immaturity

The attitude of advantageous wisdom was abundantly displayed in the prevailing British image of Americans as the peculiarly immature people of the modern world. The frequency of British comment on the youthful aspects of the American character was marked and undiminishing. This could be noted in various ways, but it was made especially clear in an opinion research organization's study of the British view of America:

---

32. The matter of American-style comics has more than once been raised in Parliament (see, e.g., 444 H.C. Deb. 2355-59 [November 28, 1947]).

Key point in this picture is the conception of the American who does not grow up. This is expressed differently according to whether the writer is favorably or unfavorably disposed toward his subject; if he likes Americans they frequently acquire the good qualities of youth and childhood, if he dislikes them he describes the less pleasing qualities of adolescence. Often there is a mixture of the two.[33]

So the relatively critical Englishman described American youthfulness in terms of arrogance, conceit, crudeness, wastefulness, and lack of social discipline. The more friendly view was that the youth was strong, generous, enterprising, dynamic, and optimistic. But in either case the American was decidedly different from the British model.

What there was of this stereotype before World War II must have been fixed in the public mind by the wartime experience of American troops in England. American military personnel away from home not only displayed the very few inhibitions normal in such circumstances but also provided the British with a sample of what was literally the youth of America. Although it is perhaps correct to attribute the extensiveness of the stereotype to the nature of the wartime contact, it would be wrong to think that it was based only on such a distortion in British experience. Rather it had roots in the nature of American and British temperaments.

An entirely sympathetic and discerning observer like Graham Hutton, who spent the war years in the Midwest for the Office of British Information, was struck by the same qualities of American youthfulness that impressed Englishmen at home. In Hutton's balanced accounting of midwesterners, they emerge "with all the effervescent, illimitable, and often undisciplined vigor of young people who refuse to count the cost, who take great risks, gamble, venture all, and cannot believe in bad luck or bad times." These aspects of American youthfulness obviously had their attractive side for Hutton, but with the commendable zest and zeal went "the crude extremisms and the dogmatic self-assertion; bragging, boasting, and intolerance; the unamenability to discipline, whether of parental, national, or local governmental origins; the individualism and self-centeredness but also the kindliness; and, paradoxically but naturally,

---

33. Mass-Observation, "Portrait of an American?" International Journal of Opinion and Attitude Research, I (June, 1947), 96. The persistence of this view of the American is testified to by another study by Mass-Observation, "Report on Middle-Class Attitudes to Russians and Americans" (unpublished memorandum No. 3015, July, 1948).

youth's temperamental and mercurial sensitiveness."[34]

While this mixture of reactions to American youthfulness was fairly representative, there was a not very well-concealed sense that to be grown up was a better thing. Certainly this was conveyed by the very word "immaturity," which instead of the term "youthfulness," was empasized by British members of Parliament when they were carefully interviewed in a survey of their reactions to the United States. One member of Parliament suggested that "for America to 'mature' meant it would become 'more British.'"[35] Probably this was more bluntly stated than usual. But even when "youthful" and "immature" were applied to Americans by friendly British critics, they implied shortcomings (though imbedded in a crown of youthful virtues). If American prodigality made for a commendable generosity, it was also thought to lead to wasteful, uncontrolled, and unpredictable behavior. And if American energy and vigor brought about great productive efforts plus heroic military ventures, they were also associated with impetuous or headstrong conduct.[36]

Here the stereotype was readily transferred from an application to individual Americans, or from Americans as a people, to the foreign policies of their government. What the British considered errors of American judgment were thus ascribable to the youthful inexperience of the American nation. This kind of comment was more frequent among those who disliked imputing evil intentions to the United States and so drew on American immaturity for criticism that was patronizing but not hostile. The mercurial in the American temperament was used to account for what was regarded as the changeableness of American policies.

---

34. Midwest at Noon (Chicago: University of Chicago Press, 1946), p. 164. A similar point was made by Adam de Hegedus after his trip to the United States, Strangers Here Ourselves (London: Gollancz, 1949), p. 223.

35. Marjorie Bremner, "An Analysis of British Parliamentary Thought concerning the United States in the Post-war Period" (unpublished Ph.D. dissertation, University of London, June, 1950), p. 310.

36. Doubtless this is translatable, in foreign-policy terms, into the charge that American policy was too "changeable," which was one of the findings concerning British attitudes in Henry Lee Munson, European Beliefs regarding the United States (New York: Common Council for American Unity, 1949), p. 100.

Or, in a more critical spirit, it was said that the impatience of a youthful people might lead to a "kicking-out" at the world's problems instead of trying to solve them in the mature British way.[37] Crudeness, irresponsibility, impetuousness, brashness, and rashness—all applied to phases of American policy—were not terms of endearment, but neither were they words which necessarily indicated a wide gulf over policies themselves.[38] Rather they reflected the British assurance that such a young people were bound to make mistakes for want of "experience and technical expertness."[39] So it was more in sorrow than in anger that Chester Wilmot discussed American shortcomings in his much-heralded history of World War II. The failure of Allied policy, especially of the American, to take account of postwar political possibilities while fighting the war was caused (among other factors), Wilmot remarked, by the "immaturity" of American conceptions.[40]

Whether or not American conduct, individually or nationally, was immature is, like the allegation of materialism, decided from respective national vantage points. What matters here is that the Englishman was appparently just as confirmed in his conception of American immaturity in relation to his own adulthood as the American was certain that the English, like other Europeans, were old and tired (if not actually senile) in contrast to the American's own vigorous manhood. What else is relevant is that out of their preoccupation with American immaturity the English were able, as with the assumption of cultural leadership, to feel superior to the Americans in a way that could not be measured and challenged. Occasionally this thought was rather starkly revealed in an Englishman's discussion of the Anglo-American alliance: "The Americans provide the hustle, the resilience, and strength of their capitalist economy and we provide diplomacy, interpretation, conciliation, wisdom,

---

37. Morgan Thomson, Glasgow Forward, January 5, 1952, p. 5.

38. Much of the time American impetuousness has been treated as a short-run vice, as in the manner of Cyril Falls, "The United States and the Defence of Europe," Illustrated London News, CCXVIII (January 6, 1951), 14; Robert Waithman, The Day after Tomorrow (New York: Scribner's, 1951), p. 222; or the Economist, CL (February 23, 1946), 281-82.

39. Spectator, CLXXXVIII (February 29, 1952), 252-53.

40. The Struggle for Europe (New York: Harper & Bros., 1952), p. 714.

and poise."[41] In another instance the "tremendous experience and wisdom" of the British in political matters were put beside American material strength. Pride in British experience came close to suggesting,
in rasher moments, that it was brains that the nation had to add to the
raw and headstrong American power.[42]

"Tyranny of the Herd"

What has been said concerning the compensating pleasure which
Englishmen might seek from their view of American materialism and
immaturity is not meant to belittle the genuineness of alarm concerning
aspects of the American state of mind. While, for example, there lurked
some feeling of superiority to the strenuousness of American campaigns
against subversives, this did not mean that any recognizable section of
the British public, except presumably the Communists, derived satisfaction from what were considered threats to American freedom of
thought. In the first place, this tended to break down the broad ideological identification of British and American democracy. Second, and
more immediately significant to British proponents of Anglo-American
unity, was a fear of a political atmosphere in which Americans could
not freely express their opinions because of a possible Communist label.
Whether this was the situation may be arguable, but there was enough
publicity to that effect to trouble those Englishmen already aware that
much of their fate rested upon the intelligence of the process by which
American policy was determined.

As early as 1949 the Manchester Guardian Weekly, spokesman for
the nonsocialist tradition of British liberalism, could write of the "stu-
pidities of the Communist witch-hunt" and of the anxiety of liberals outside America watching "these manifestations of a spiritual totalitarianism
as dangerous in its way as that of Moscow."[43] What the Manchester
Guardian had to say continued to reflect, throughout the subsequent campaign inaugurated by Senator McCarthy, a sensitivity to American political behavior characteristic of those in Britain who, on the whole, as-

41. Viscount Hinchingbrooke,"The Course of Conservative Politics,"
     Quarterly Review, CCLXXXVIII (January, 1950), 8-9. See also
     Vernon Bartlett, 459 H.C. Deb. 652 (December 9, 1948).

42. 494 H.C. Deb. 307 (November 20, 1951); ibid., col. 119 (November
     19, 1951).

43. June 16, 1949, p. 9.

sumed the burden of defending the United States against attacks from the
left. Virtually all other champions of the American alliance, whether
Liberal, moderate Labour, or Conservative in politics, did not fail to
make some debit entry on the score of "witch-hunting" in otherwise
friendly accounting of American policies.[44]

Senator McCarthy was not the only object of concern, although "Mc-
Carthyism" did eventually become the highly advertised symbol of what
the British considered wrong with the American climate of opinion. The
McCarran Acts of 1950 and 1952 also attracted special comment. At
first, this was at the level of anxiety over the first act's effect on the freedom of international intellectual exchange. Here the Manchester Guardian
was perhaps sharper in its criticism of an official American policy than
it usually permitted itself. Aspects of the law were said to be "repugnant
to civilized intercourse." A case was presented, in the form of a letter
from a distinguished scientist, to support this view.[45] The example,
while not appealing to popular imagination, was of sufficient import to
embarrass the American symbolization of freedom within a wide intellectual circle. But what transformed the application of American immigration laws to the level of broad public attention was the hubbub in
all varieties of newspapers over the threat to exclude Charlie Chaplin
from returning to the United States. The legal niceties as well as
Chaplin's record were overlooked in the British public's assumption that
the action was ridiculous, unfair, and oppressive.

Still the Chaplin case was an exception in the breadth of British
interest that it provoked. Ordinarily, while making allowance for the
opportunity provided enemies of the Anglo-American alliance for exploitation of any kind of case (such as that involving seamen under the
McCarran Act of 1952), the direct effects of restrictive American legislation were likely to be marked only in that part of the community which
was itself mainly interested in the free exchange of ideas. However, that
sector of the body politic, considering its virtual unanimity in condemnation of American practices, was very significant indeed. For in Britain
the intelligentsia especially in political discussion was a good deal more
secure as well as more influential than in the United States. In this re-

---

44. For a Labour example see Maurice Webb, Reynolds News, September
    28, 1952, p. 4.

45. March 13, 1952, pp. 9 and 13; ibid., December 20, 1951, p. 9.

spect there were significant differences between the American and British environments, and these differences, not always fully appreciated, afford much of the explanation for the fact that British intellectuals, and European intellectuals generally, have found American practices affecting freedom of thought so alien and thus so appalling.

This discovery is not new. It is at least as old as Alexis de Tocqueville's fear of the tyranny of the American democratic majority in the shape of oppressive public opinion. The continuity of criticism has been recognized by an occasional British visitor to postwar American university life, as by the discerning Max Beloff.[46] What was usually noticed by the European observer, fresh from an environment where liberty had an aristocratic and so an older basis than equality, was that the Americans, as part of the price of their wholehearted equalitarianism, had embraced the spirit of conformity. Diversity of opinions as well as eccentricity of behavior were subjected to the overwhelming pressure of a public norm—or so it seemed to the Englishman, whose educational system, as well as his culture, was founded as the preserve of the privileged or talented few and not the concern of the less sophisticated mass of ordinary men. Perhaps many European intellectuals would agree with the American scholar, Louis Hartz, that the absence of this real conservative tradition in the United States was "the ironic flaw in American liberalism."[47]

In no area has the reaction been so sharp as in the strictly academic field where popular pressures, especially in state-supported schools, represented a strange element to the British intellectual. It is doubtful whether this specific reaction, any more than the more general attitude to American conformity, was peculiar to the postwar period, but there is no question that it was more extensive. Probably the statement that "orthodoxy, the absolute equivalent of Americanism, had become the driving force behind American education"[48] would have been as likely an observation by an Englishman in the past if he then had had as much reason to be concerned

46. "Tocqueville and the Americans," Fortnightly, CLXXVI (September, 1951), 577-78.

47. "American Political Thought and the American Revolution," American Political Science Review, XLIV (June, 1952), 336.

48. J. E. Morpurgo, "Hollywood: America's Voice," in The Impact of America in European Culture, p. 56.

over the nature of the American mind. A critic of such stature as Bertrand Russell has, in fact, remarked on the historical roots of the American "tyranny of the herd."[49] And indeed Russell knew from personal experience, before the postwar anti-Communist campaign, how public feeling, well outside strictly political views, could be brought to bear on teaching appointments. The ouster of Russell in 1940 from the City College of New York, on religious and moral grounds, was an almost classic instance of the relationship between American attitudes and American schools.[50] The very idea that the public should play a part in the elimination of unpopular teachings was deeply repugnant to the tradition of academic independence as it was cherished in Britain.

This repugnance was undoubtedly maximized, in the postwar period, by the attention directed to the American campaign against left-wing ideas in general. The campaign itself was well publicized in the quality newspapers, and there were continued signs of disapproval. None was quite so impressive as the astoundingly long correspondence in the Manchester Guardian Weekly on the general subject of democracy and teachers in the United States. The correspondence was initiated by Bertrand Russell, whose interest, of course, was of long standing. From November 1, 1951, when Russell's own comments appeared, through the following March, the Guardian ran a series of letters devoted to incidents of pressure for conformity in education in the United States.[51] The fact that British concern was not just the Guardian's became obvious from the volume of letters, with various views, which were received and printed. This was not the kind of thing that would have occurred among a people unworried for the democratic soul of their ally. And the worry, while reaching an especially high pitch with the apparent growth of Senator McCarthy's influence after November, 1952, had its origins in fears accumulated throughout the postwar years.[52]

---

49. Op. cit., p. 17.

50. An account of the affair was given by John Dewey and Horace Kallen (eds.), The Bertrand Russell Case (New York: Viking Press, 1941).

51. November 1, 1951, p. 6; November 22 and 29, 1951, p. 7; January 17 and February 7, 1952, p. 7; and February 23, March 6, 20, and 27, 1952, p. 13 (in each instance).

52. The Senator's increasing prominence in British consciousness during 1953 was clearly reflected by Clement Attlee's widely publicized question about who was more powerful, President Eisenhower or Senator

By suggesting that British criticism of American practices springs
from a different, though not necessarily a stronger, tradition of liberty,
there is no intention of excluding another and more obvious explanation
of the abhorrence of antisubversive campaigns in the United States.
British concern was undoubtedly maximized by the absence of anything
like the American belief in the necessity for drastic action against Communists. [The fact that most Englishmen themselves refused to take Communists so seriously made the American campaign, in their eyes, un-
necessary as well as undesirable.] The idea that there was an advantage,
in anti-Communist results, sufficient to justify open attacks on a variety
of suspects was something the British rejected because of their greater
tolerance of communism, in particular, as well as because of an intellectual tolerance in general. This tolerance cannot be assumed to have
prevented responsible authorities from removing Communists from
critical positions, but such removals were likely to have been accomplished quietly and without public pressure.

Alien Government

Among the American habits which their own historical experience
conditioned the British to consider foreign and dangerous, the operation
of the entire political system of the United States deserves special attention. The sheer inability to comprehend American political practices
was part of the reason for the British distrust of government in the United
States, but incomprehension was not the result only of a lack of knowledge.
More important was the block to any real understanding and appreciation
of American government which was imposed by the British assurance that
their own system was so natural, logical, and mature that any fully developed
nation desiring to institutionalize democracy would adopt at least a reasonable facsimile. After all, the Commonwealth nations have done so. Yet here
was the United States "living under an eighteenth-century constitution"[53] and
trying to operate a rigid formula that embalms an old-fashioned "Whiggery."[54]

McCarthy (515 H.C. Deb. 1065 [May 12, 1953]). Attlee's parliamentary remark was, of course, only one of a great many indications of
a steeply mounting British concern over McCarthy's activities.

53. Geoffrey Gorer, The American People (New York: W. W. Norton & Co.,
1948), p. 122.

54. Wyndham Lewis, America and Cosmic Man (New York: Doubleday &
Co., 1949), p. 166.

The use of such phrases by British men of letters (not so much recently by British political scientists) is testimony to their common currency. That the view of the Constitution as a strait jacket was sadly out of date did not remove the conception from British consciousness. Usually, however, the case against the American form of government was more highly particularized. It was aimed at that separation of executive and legislative powers which was at odds with the British assumption that an effective government must rest on the cabinet's enjoyment of the continuous confidence of a parliamentary majority. Since in the United States it is entirely possible for the Congress and the President to be of different minds, or even of different parties, the American system has not only seemed strange but seriously imperfect by British standards. In the ordinary course of American domestic affairs the British were not likely to be anxious about the results of this "imperfection." The effect on foreign policy of a presidential-congressional deadlock was the disturbing element. Although experience in this connection was not unhappy after World War II, the latent possibilities remained in the British mind. They were fixed there by the tremendously important break between President Wilson and the Senate over the Treaty of Versailles and the League of Nations.

That unfortunate event was what commentators, at least since the time of Walter Bagehot, had prepared the educated British public to expect of the American system. In his most famous work, Bagehot himself, making an introductory statement with the troubles of President Johnson fresh in mind, gave what was to be the standard invidious comparison:

> My great object was to contrast the office of President as an executive officer and to compare it with that of a Prime Minister; and I devoted much space to showing that in one principal respect the English system is by far the best. The English Premier being appointed by the selection, and being removable at the pleasure, of the preponderant Legislative Assembly, is sure to be able to rely on that assembly. If he wants legislation to aid his policy he can obtain that legislation; he can carry out that policy. But the American President has no similar security.[55]

Bagehot was ready to grant that the possibility of legislative-executive battles was not serious when there was not much to fight about, as in the United States before the Civil War, but in a nation with real problems the system would, he thought, be an awful one indeed.[56]

---

55. The English Constitution and Other Political Essays (New York: Appleton & Co., 1906), p. 52.

56. Ibid., p. 87.

With this general outlook goes a special dislike for the American Congress. Not improbably this was intensified by the fact that British opinion, in the instances of Wilson's, Roosevelt's, and Truman's struggles with Congress, was policy-wise on the side of the President. Agreement with presidential purposes, most notably in foreign policy, emphasized what would, in any case, be British objection to a legislative body whose functions differed so much from those of the House of Commons. The true measure of this objection may be taken from comments in sources generally friendly to the United States and usually to its foreign policy as well. The Manchester Guardian provided a good example when it said that the congressional system "is the cross the United States has to bear."[57] For the moderate Spectator, the fault was that the congressional power prevented the government of the United States from speaking with full authority in international affairs.[58] And the Economist restated the essence of the Bagehot argument: "The division of power between President and Congress, the possibility of different parties controlling the one and the other, the lack of a Cabinet responsible to the legislature, the working of the party system, are all weighted against the present pursuit of long-term national or international objectives."[59] These were fixed ideas, and the "lack," not merely the absence, of responsible cabinet government was foremost in the catalogue of unfavorable comparisons.

The structural aspects of the constitutional system were not all that troubled the British in the field of American government. From the familiar vantage point of the aristocratic tradition of British leadership (if not of political participation), there was detected a demagogic element in the politics of the United States. It was not uncommon to speak of "the agitations and caprices, which distract the purposes of any democratic government, but to which American political life is particularly prone."[60] The agitations and caprices were those of domestic political considera-

---

57. LV (July 19, 1946), 26.

58. CLXXVI (January 18, 1946), 55-56.

59. CLII (May 24, 1947), 786.

60. Sir Harold Butler, "The Two Giants," Fortnightly, CLXVIII (December, 1947), 407. See also Brian Tunstall, "Some Broader Aspects of Western Strategy," World Affairs, IV (April, 1950), 187.

tions, whether of the disdained category of economic or racial pressure groups, for instance, or of the despised class of partisan election campaigns.[61] Most of these supposed American sins were usually related to the opportunity for evil afforded by the congressional power, but the influence of group pressures on policy decisions was also fancied as a special quality of the American political character. For the British public at large, as well as the academic stratum, the experience of the postwar Palestine crisis conveyed a picture of the American government adjusting its policies with primary regard to the demands of a nationality bloc within the United States. The New York "Jewish vote" became a symbol of the level at which American foreign policy was determined.[62]

It is not conceivable that the Englishman really believed that his own governmental system somehow eliminated the effectiveness of interest groups. Nevertheless, he saw American pressures operating more clearly, and so more impressively, on and through congressmen than he could see British groups pressing their interests at a different but not necessarily less influential political level.

Another manifestation of American behavior that disturbed Englishmen was the violence of political language.[63] The hyperbole of American campaigning, although much of it had become familiar, still had a capacity for frightening the British nearly to the stage of believing that their postwar ally was about to be torn apart by internal dissension. The words of political abuse in the United States were not very gentlemanly by British standards, but, since those standards were not so rigid as they once were,

---

61. For an example of one of the many British complaints on American elections as distracting elements in policy-making see Spectator, CLXXX (January 2, 1948), 1.

62. Occasionally, in the heat of animosity toward the United States over the Palestine issue, there was a coupling of anti-Semitism with anti-Americanism, as noted by H. D. Willcock, "Public Opinion: Attitudes towards America and Russia," Political Quarterly, XIX (January-March, 1948), 68. For a sampling of general criticism of the United States on the Palestine issue see Ernest Bevin's speech (443 H.C. Deb. 1901-20 [February 25, 1947]) and parliamentary addresses by other members of Parliament (ibid., Vol. 445, cols. 1278-86, 1299-1307, 1345-53, 1408-14 [December 11, 1947], Vol. 448, cols. 1288-90 [March 10, 1948], and Vol. 460, cols. 1000-1008 [January 26, 1949]).

63. Kenneth Harris, Travelling Tongues (London: John Murray, 1949), p. 102, commented on his English reactions to this phenomenon.

it is doubtful if rudeness alone was the cause for criticism. Just as important, and perhaps increasingly so, was the rhetoric of American politicians.[64] The bombastic style of oratory has had no recent fashion in Britain, and Englishmen were bound to regard as most unsophisticated the noisy platitudes of American campaigning. With this style they equated a low level of statesmanship, since generally the British measured parliamentarians in terms of polish and urbanity in the use of the language. This was never illustrated, on the positive side, any more clearly than in the almost universally favorable response to Governor Stevenson upon the release of his first major campaign speeches.

Distrusting America's political types, as well as its constitutional system, Englishmen were terribly impressed with American difficulties in evolving and maintaining a coherent foreign policy, or any kind of foreign policy whatsoever. The thwarting of international programs, based on intelligence and knowledge, was assumed to be the bitter fruit of the American structure. Bad results, from the British point of view, were almost always attributed to the system, and there was a definite reluctance to connect anything to virtues inherent in American political arrangements. On the contrary, whatever the British deemed good was supposed to have arisen in spite of the system. So the Economist, thoroughly pleased with the 1952 presidential nominations, found those results only fortuitous. The conventions themselves remained a "clumsy chaos," and, rather than seeing any advantage in the nominating machinery, the Economist simply observed that "God moves in a mysterious way His wonders to perform."[65] Here, it ought to be added, the learned journal was true to the tradition of Walter Bagehot, its nineteenth-century editor. Bagehot had disposed of the example of Lincoln as a case in favor of the method of selecting a President by saying that "success in a lottery" was no argument for lotteries.[66]

The General Relationship

The suspicion of the American political system is of a piece with the

---

64. With his usual shrewdness, D. W. Brogan touched on the point in "America through British Eyes," Saturday Review of Literature, XXXIV (October 13, 1951), 55.

65. Vol. CLXIV, (August 2, 1952), p. 265, The same general tone was struck by the London Times, July 28, 1952, p. 7.

66. Op. cit., p. 100.

general British attitude toward other distinguishing features of life in the United States. Charges of materialism, immaturity, and intolerance also form part of the British pattern of thought, and that pattern, in a context of responses to American foreign policy, amounted to the feeling that the United States was not an entirely responsible nation. With such, the British could not completely identify, nor could they completely trust the policies the United States evolved. Perhaps this was no more than the distrust one nation always feels for the folkways and so for the policies of another, but the nature of British suspicion, centering as it did upon a firm belief in American irresponsibility, was of special import. Among its results, as already observed, was the desire of the British to provide the ingredients they felt lacking in the unsophisticated American mind.

Obviously the tutorial role would be more credible and more satisfying the more nearly equal the Anglo-American partnership appeared to be. Equality, therefore, was a very precious conception for just those Englishmen who clearly recognized the British need for the strength of America in world affairs. It was not merely paradoxical that the realistic appraisers of Britain's postwar dependence on the American power, including sea power, should be the most eager to have the relationship as near to equality as possible. Surely Winston Churchill was among the Englishmen who treasured the idea of partnership because, among other things, it afforded the opportunity for giving advice to the less experienced Americans.

In some respects this aspiration for joint policy-making was a residue from times past, and especially from the historical environment of the years just before and during the first World War. Then it was Britain, still a power of the very first rank, that wanted to add the strength of the United States to its own. What was now clung to by way of a British contribution to the alliance was a very pale replica of the older concept of parity if not superiority. But, however much the contribution had diminished in material terms, the feeling was still at the root of the British acceptance of the American connection. The Times expressed the virtually official character of the outlook:

> Britain has much to give, by way of counsel and initiative, to the shaping, still tentative and often uncertain, of a world policy, political and economic, "at the summit" in America; and it is today as always the special feature of their special bond that, whatever the balance of power between them, they can, and should, talk together as free men.[67]

---

67. May 13, 1948, p. 5.

Consultation with American leaders was the minimum expectancy, with British statesmen free to point out American mistakes and try to have them corrected.

Whatever suggested subordination has been deeply resented—though in a special way by the British left, which saw enforced inequality as confirmation of its own unfavorable views of the American alliance. But most of the rest of British opinion could be genuinely offended by the absence of consultation. [Occasionally the cat was let out of the bag: "As the balance of strength between the United States and this country has changed to the British disadvantage, so American policy has become less restrained, less comradely in matters of vital interest to the whole Commonwealth."[68] Or there was the petulant note that "we also have the right to be heard in the affairs of the alliance."[69] What emerged clearly, regardless of the language, was the breadth of public resentment concerning a second-fiddle role. Any reminder, like the appointment of an American admiral to the North Atlantic command, was unhappily received.[70]

In such a climate of opinion the assertion of British policy was a psychological necessity. Who could best stand up to the Americans was a political issue. British national pride required, as the very moderate Clement Attlee said, that the country hold its own position in the world and "not be regarded as a mere tool of any other country."[71] This anxiety, lest Britain be considered unimportant, was a symptom of a growing national inferiority complex, resulting from the very rapid decline in Britain's status relative to the United States.[72] [The desire to stand up to the United States became especially meaningful politically in 1952 and 1953, when any assertion of British initiative was hopefully taken as a sign of the nation's recovery from the worst of the postwar years.]

---

68. *Economist*, CLXI (November 17, 1951), 1165.

69. *Manchester Guardian Weekly*, November 15, 1951, p. 8. A similar complaint was made by the London *Times*, May 11, 1951, p. 7.

70. The reaction of Churchill, the "former naval person," was especially noteworthy (486 H.C. Deb. 2017-36 [April 19, 1951]).

71. 495 H.C. Deb. 842 (February 5, 1952).

72. The British did not want to feel, as Raymond Aron described his fellow-Frenchmen, involved in "an alliance whose policy she does not direct but whose dangers she shares" ("French Public Opinion and the Atlantic Treaty," *International Affairs*, XXVIII [January, 1952], 8).

During much of the postwar period economic-aid programs seemed more important to Britain than did any other aspect of American policy. Even when this was not the case, the consciousness of economic dependence influenced British views of whatever else the United States was doing. The description of the development of this consciousness is fundamental in approaching general British responses to American leadership.

Termination of Lend-Lease

At the very beginning of the postwar period the British public suffered a nearly traumatic experience concerning the halt in the shipment of lend-lease supplies. In the forefront of British thought at that time was the nation's economic sacrifice in the common cause of World War II. National impoverishment was regarded as no fault of the British people but rather as the result of their early and wholehearted contribution to the prosecution of the war. Financial help from the richer American partner was considered only a matter of right. That the United States recognized no such right was most discomforting. The way in which the American attitude was conveyed did nothing to make the adjustment any easier. The unexpected announcement of the end of the lend-lease system, in the same month as the achievement of victory against Japan, caused a shock both intense and prolonged. Whether with or without reason, the British had expected the continuation into the postwar period of what they counted as the fair American method of filling the gaps in their highly mobilized economy. Britain had been receiving food and civilian goods, as well as war material, and the cessation of lend-lease shipments constituted an economic crisis of the first magnitude. In 1945 Britain had neither its old prewar income from foreign investments nor yet any appreciable share of its industry reconverted to the manufacture of civilian goods. The end of lend-lease seemed to leave Britain no way to pay for imports of food. Thus the nation's situation was made naked and apparent by the American termination of a wartime economic partnership.

Labour had been in power only one month when the blow struck.

Prime Minister Attlee's official statement was a model of restraint, but it did not completely conceal his disappointment. There had been hopes, Attlee said, that "the sudden cessation of this great mutual effort, which has contributed so much to victory, would not have been effected without consultation, and prior discussions of the difficult problems involved in the disappearance of a system of so great a range and complication." Britain, he added, was now put in "a very serious financial position."[1] It was no wonder that prominent members of the government were described as "very downcast" by the news from the United States.[2] In fact, there is every reason to agree with a source then close to the Prime Minister that the announcement of the end of lend-lease gave the new Labour government one of its blackest hours.[3]

In some quarters the reaction was tempered by an expression to the effect that the American policy could not really be so harsh as it seemed on the surface. There was also, in the conservative and independent press, a note of regret that the United States should have taken unilateral action instead of continuing the wartime partnership into the era of postwar economic relationships.[4] Even in these essentially soft criticisms, the complaint was made that Britain had been "cut off overnight" while its forces were "still flung across half the world" and its ships were "still in the Allied pool."[5] More significant was the reminder that Britain deserved better treatment. The value of Britain's contribution in the year it stood alone against Hitler was evoked as an imponderable to put in the balance against strictly material considerations.[6]

Much of the moderate British reaction to the American shift from lend-lease to a commercial basis was summarized by the Economist: "It would be difficult to find anyone in Great Britain who does not think the country is being very harshly treated by being dealt with as if its

---

1. 413 H.C. Deb. 956 (August 24, 1945).

2. R. F. Harrod, The Life of John Maynard Keynes (London: Macmillan & Co., 1951), p. 596.

3. Francis Williams, Socialist Britain (New York: Viking Press, 1949), p. 143.

4. See Daily Telegraph, August 25, 1945, p. 2; Daily Mail, August 25, 1945, p. 2; and Spectator, CLXXV (August 31, 1945), 187-88.

5. Manchester Guardian Weekly, LIII (August 31, 1945), 110.

6. News Chronicle, August 24, 1945, p. 2.

poverty in foreign exchange were the result of its own improvidence rather than of the agreed allocation of tasks during a common struggle."[7] This view rested on the fact that Britain had, during the war, concentrated almost entirely on the production of war goods rather than on the manufacture of goods for export. Perhaps this had originally been dictated by necessity, but in any case it had become part of Allied policy. The British looked upon themselves as having made an economic sacrifice greater, in proportion, than that made by the United States.

A closely related theme was the reference to the early stage of the war, before 1941, when Britain had to liquidate its overseas investment in order to pay for war materials, especially those purchasable under American cash-and-carry arrangements then in force. The largest of the daily tabloids told its readers: "Americans may now be reminded that we stood alone a whole year before Lease-Lend came into operation, and that during that period we spent every penny we had in fighting America's battle as well as our own. Our money was spent mainly in America which thereby became richer as we became poorer."[8] In some such simplified form the reaction to American economic policy reached the level of popular consciousness. When public opinion was surveyed not long after the end of lend-lease, 35 per cent said their feelings toward the United States were less friendly than the year before; the cause most frequently cited was the "discontinuance of Lease-Lend Food supplies." The attitude was that the Americans had let Britain down.[9] At the very least, the United States was believed guilty of conduct unbecoming an ally.

Among spokesmen of the socialist left the United States did not escape with such a vague indictment. Rather, the ending of lend-lease, usually called the "abrupt ending," was interpreted as "the beginning of that policy of economic world domination which [had] to be expected from America as soon as the war ended and which [would] replace the pre-war isolationism."[10] It was also suggested that the termination might have been a "calculated blow against the new Government directed

---

7. CXLIX (September 1, 1945), 289.

8. Daily Mirror, September 14, 1945, p. 2.

9. British Institute of Public Opinion, poll of September 29, 1945.

10. Socialist Commentary, September, 1945, p. 165.

from Wall Street."[11] These criticisms, belonging to the specifically socialist distrust of the actions of a capitalist nation, persisted over a very considerable period of time. The termination of lend-lease gave the left an especially satisfying confirmation of its suspicion, and the unpopularity of this American policy made it a useful reference point for broader criticism of the United States.

In fact, this was true not only in 1945, when the termination itself was a prominent issue, but throughout much of the postwar period. The cut-off of lend-lease became a standard item in the attack on the United States. The British public was not allowed to forget especially in 1946 and 1947 that, whatever else the Americans might have done or were doing, they had prematurely "restored the dollar sign" on aid to Britain and struck the "most grievous blow ever dealt by one ally against another."[12]

While there was little talk of lend-lease termination during the period of general satisfaction with Marshall aid, the wound of 1945 was reopened by the Bevanite revival of criticism of the United States in 1951 and 1952. Aneurin Bevan himself recalled that the ending of lend-lease had been a "grievous and unjust blow to the prospects of British recovery."[13] In the general argument against American economic policy made by Harold Wilson for the Bevanite group, the "abrupt withdrawal" of aid was discussed in the context of Britain's plight in having lost export markets, especially during the war, to the United States.[14] The Americans, in this portrait, re-emerged as the direct beneficiaries of Britain's sacrificial wartime losses. The termination of lend-lease served as a dramatic sign of selfish American policy toward Britain. This was not, in all probability, the potent critical weapon that it had been in 1945 and early 1946, but the Bevanites were aware, in harking back to the event, that there remained in the British mind a conviction of American unfairness.

---

11. Tribune, August 31, 1945, p. 2.

12. Norman Smith (430 H.C. Deb. 332 [November 14, 1946] and 443 H.C. Deb. 199 [October 22, 1947]).

13. In Place of Fear (New York: Simon & Schuster, 1952), p. 128.

14. In Place of Dollars (Tribune pamphlet [London, September, 1952]), p. 5.

That this conviction should not have been completely obliterated by subsequent policies, especially the Marshall Plan, is testimony to the strength of the original reaction. Whatever might be said pro or con for the termination of lend-lease, there can be no question that the tactics of termination were such as to maximize hostility toward the United States. The American action simply flew in the face of Britain's assumption that it was entitled, as the most faithful of allies, to lend-lease in the immediate postwar period. In destroying that assumption, the United States also destroyed the general British idea that postwar economic need was compatible with partnership rather than dependence. Perhaps that idea could only have been a fiction, but for British self-respect it might have been a very useful fiction.

Loan Agreement

That the United States would not deal with a needy Britain as an equal seemed to be confirmed by the negotiations and the terms of the Anglo-American Loan Agreement of 1945-46. Not only, in this relation-ship, did the United States treat Britain on the basis of commerce rather than comradeship; what was worse was that the acute British dependence, following the end of lend-lease, appeared to be used to obtain interna-tional trade concessions for the American benefit. It was bad enough, in the British view, to have to repay with interest the billions of dollars that should have been freely forthcoming, but it was terribly onerous, in an hour of need, to have to agree to the American insistence that at a future date the sterling balances held by Britain's creditors should be convertible into dollars and that various departures from strictly Empire trade practices should be made. The latter provisions meant that the staunch champions of Imperial Preference found the loan agreement en-tirely objectionable—in fact, so much so that they opposed its acceptance. However, their opposition was part of a larger case against American trade policy and, as such, can be more usefully discussed in the next chapter. At any rate, the Empire trade school's reaction to the terms of the loan was out of the ordinary. The general public was not concerned with the detailed terms or their dubious workability. What made the loan widely unpopular was the bare fact that it carried Ameri-can-imposed conditions of any sort.

Nevertheless, the Labour government felt it had no choice but to accept the loan agreement. Its spokesmen were sure that the price of doing without American aid was too great. The terms of the agreement, the government made plain, were not what had been expected. The Chancellor of the Exchequer said as much: ". . . our representatives first proposed at Washington that, to enable us to restore the gravely disturbed balance of our economy, gravely disturbed, as I have emphasized, in the common cause of us all, we should receive some form of grant-in-aid, or, failing that, an interest-free loan." This preferred policy had to be abandoned by the British, the Chancellor remarked, because it was learned that Congress would never approve that kind of arrangement.[15] Lord Keynes, who had been a principal British negotiator in Washington, said virtually the same thing in his defense of the agreement. "I shall never cease to regret," Keynes added, "that this is not an interest-free loan."[16] Given the state of American opinion, the best possible bargain had been struck, but no one pretended that it was a good bargain. Furthermore, no one thought that the Americans could not, and should not, have offered more and better.

British unhappiness with the terms of the loan was reflected in the rather curious line of party conflict in the House of Commons. Labour, of course, had a commanding majority and even with a few dissidents had the votes to obtain parliamentary approval. The Conservatives, who in most circumstances after the war were to become more favorably disposed than Labour to American policies, found this one quite unattractive. Their leader, Winston Churchill, advised the Conservatives to abstain from voting, and he did so himself. Not all of his party followed suit. Some joined the handful of left-wing members of Parliament in voting against the agreement.[17] Many of these, along with the abstainers, probably appreciated the editorial sentiment of the Tory Daily Mail: "We believe that the loan is necessary, but we agree that the Coalition Government, or a Conservative Government headed by Mr. Churchill, could have obtained better terms."[18] This notion tended to mitigate outright Conservative criticism of United States policy in favor of condemnation of

---

15. Hugh Dalton (417 H.C. Deb. 427-28 [December 12, 1945]).

16. 138 H.L. Deb. 784 (December 18, 1945).

17. The vote was 345 for accepting the agreement and 98 against, indicating a very large number of abstentions (417 H.C. Deb. 736 [December 12, 1945]).

18. December 14, 1945, p. 2.

the Labour government for being unable to strike a good bargain.

Even Lord Beaverbrook, speaking for the right and more especially for the sanctity of Empire trade, directed his vigorous complaints not at the United States but primarily at the Labour government for its weakness in accepting the agreement.[19] Lord Beaverbrook was almost unique in suggesting that Britain could do without American aid. Not many were ready to go that far, although, on the right, there were cries about the economic surrender of Britain for the benefit of the United States[20] and talk of the "financial enslavement of the once proud and strong Britannia."[21] That brand of highly nationalist, or imperialist, sentiment may be regarded as extreme, but it was not entirely without an audience.

Strong sensitivity concerning American encroachment on British independence was also present at the other end of the political spectrum. The language of the socialist left was different, to be sure, but it too drew the picture of a Britain put upon by American policy. Tribune, the paper which became the voice of Bevanism in the Labour party, called the loan "a savage bargain" in an editorial which was its first really blunt post-war criticism of America.[22] In the words of Jennie Lee, the wife of Aneurin Bevan, the American Administration consisted of "hard-faced business men."[23] The loan was the instrument of "big business," which was said to be "riding high" in the United States.[24] Although the left's hostility to the loan did run along lines (to become familiar in other contexts) of a special antithesis of a capitalist America to a socialist Britain, it was mixed with the purely national juxtaposition of the interests of the two countries. To the extreme left as well as the extreme right, this clash of interests appeared to have been starkly revealed by the terms of the loan agreement. Perhaps it did not seem so very different to the

---

19. Lord Beaverbrook's Daily Express intermittently complained about the loan agreement for two years. See especially the editorials of December 7 and 8, 1945, July 12 and 16, 1947, and September 20, 1947.

20. Robert Boothby, "The Loan Agreement," National Review, CXXVI (February, 1946), 118-25.

21. George Glasgow, "Foreign Affairs," Contemporary Review, CLXVIII (October, 1945), 248.

22. December 14, 1945, pp. 1-2.

23. 417 H.C. Deb. 666 (December 13, 1945).

24. Reynolds News, December 16, 1945, p. 2. For a similar tone see New Statesman, XXX (December 15, 1945), 397-98.

main elements of British opinion, but moderate critics, like the government spokesmen, were much more restrained.

Typical press opinion consisted of faint praise instead of open condemnation. "The loan is accepted," one newspaper said, "less as a boon
than as an alternative to something which could almost certainly be worse,
and as one of the necessary conditions of continued Anglo-American co-
operation."[25] The best that the leading Conservative organ could say was
that the terms were "not unduly onerous."[26] Another paper, while admitting the loan's necessity, was more grudging in its reminder of the
injustice of forcing Britain "to assume a 50-year burden of debt payments
to America simply and solely because we threw our assets without stint
into what was at one time a single-handed struggle against tyranny."[27]
This note was more often sounded as British discussion of the agreement
continued. Relief that there was to be any loan at all, which was prominent in the press when the agreement was first announced, turned increasingly to misgiving as the offending conditions became better known.[28]
And when, after parliamentary approval, the American Congress debated
the loan at some length, British misgiving turned to incredulity that the
United States should hestitate to approve terms that already seemed
stacked in America's favor.

American consideration of whether Britain was a good business risk
offended the same British attitude as had the termination of lend-lease.
There remained in 1946, as there had been in August, 1945, the British
sense of deserving aid and specifically deserving it from America. For
the United States not to consider at all the British "right" to help was
still deeply offensive. Or, to borrow the measured language of the
Economist, the British found it "aggravating" that their reward for losing
a quarter of their total national wealth in the common cause was "to pay

---

25. Glasgow Herald, December 15, 1945, p. 4.

26. Daily Telegraph, December 7, 1945, p. 4.

27. News Chronicle, December 13, 1945, p. 2.

28. E.g., the Daily Herald, usually reflecting the views of the Labour
    government, at first simply welcomed a "good agreement" (De-
    cember 7, 1945, p. 2) but a few days later shifted to the defensive
    line by stressing Britain's need for the loan even if the terms were
    not easy or generous (December 11, 1945, p. 2). See also the
    parliamentary discussion after the agreement had been approved
    by both nations (425 H.C. Deb. 1611-46 [July 19, 1946]).

tribute for half a century to those who have been enriched by the war."[29] The use of such language by the Economist, perhaps the most genuinely international-minded of British journals, was an index to the weight of British resentment of the loan agreement. Ordinarily the charge of American enrichment during the war was not made by the genteel press.

There is not much doubt that the Anglo-American Loan Agreement created, as did the end of lend-lease, a permanent source of ill-feeling. Some of this came to the surface in 1947, when, under the conditions of the agreement, sterling was made convertible for a brief and nearly disastrous interval. Although nonconvertibility was re-established with American consent, the incident served to recall, in British minds, the lack of wisdom as well as the harshness of the American terms. Attention was also called to the fact that what benefit Britain could derive from the loan had been partially dissipated by the inflationary rise in American prices.[30] "We have had a shabby deal," was the less polite language of the leading tabloid.[31] Helplessness in the face of getting less than originally expected only added to British grievances concerning the loan agreement. Those grievances, it should be emphasized, rested not so much on any particular provision but more significantly on the further realization of the misfortune of national dependence on America.

Marshall Aid

To the unhappy frame of mind associated with the need for American economic aid, the very favorable British reception of the Marshall Plan constituted a large and significant exception. Both at the time of the plan's inception and during the course of its operation, American aid was looked upon as generous and enlightened. The grand scale of financial assistance and especially its method of presentation marked off the Marshall Plan from the previous postwar American economic policy. For the British, whose economy in 1947 and 1948 still showed almost all the obvious marks of the war, the sponsorship of the European Recovery Program meant a just if belated American recognition of the difficulties created by wartime

---

29. CXLIX (December 15, 1945), 850. Much the same thing was said by the independent and moderate Spectator, CLXXV (December 14, 1945), 559.

30. Economist, CLIII (August 9 and 23, 1947), 228-30 and 305-6.

31. Daily Mirror, July 3, 1947, p. 2.

sacrifices. To be in need of American aid might remain annoying, in and of itself, but the Marshall Plan provided relatively few reminders of the humiliating aspects of dependence. What was there about the Marshall Plan that so reduced the curse accompanying the relations of giver and receiver?

In the first place, the promise of the ERP was that it would so restore the British economy that in three or four years the state of dependence would be ended. Britain and Europe were to be aided not in the form of relief but rather for the purpose of rebuilding productive machinery. Economic independence was the goal of the program, and in this it was almost impossible to detect an unattractive American motive. "The most unsordid act in history"—formerly applied to lend-lease—became a much-repeated British epithet for the plan.[32] In so far as European economic independence was in America's self-interest, it was so only in the long run and in such a way that the American and the European interests simply coincided. This seemed, in Britain, to be a very enlightened self-interest. America, said Ernest Bevin, had given Europe a great opportunity and out of no motive "other than the valuable human motive of helping Europe to help herself, and so restore the economic and political health of this world."[33]

Another important reason for British approval of the Marshall Plan was that it was widely considered, at its inception, to be a kind of peace program as well as a huge scheme of financial assistance. Secretary of State Marshall's implication that Russia and Eastern Europe could participate in the plan was interpreted as an American move to end the rift between East and West, and as such it caused rejoicing in Great Britain. It was taken as an attractive departure from previously projected American anti-Communist policies and especially from the Truman Doctrine, which had been announced only three months before Secretary Marshall's famous offer of June, 1947.[34] Since for various reasons, to

32. Used, for instance, by a government spokesman (453 H.C. Deb. 230 [July 6, 1948]) and by the Economist, CLIII (December 27, 1947), 1033.

33. 446 H.C. Deb. 402 (January 22, 1948).

34. Roughly the same satisfaction with the Marshall Plan as an economic bridge over the East-West ideological gulf was voiced by such evidently nonsocialist sources as the London Times, June 12, 1947, p. 5; the News Chronicle, June 13, 1947, p. 2; and the Manchester Guardian Weekly, June 12, 1947, pp. 2-3.

be explored later, hope for a reconciliation with the U.S.S.R. lingered longer in Britain than in the United States, there was a welcome in many quarters, in addition to that of the socialist left, for an American policy that was not based on a hard-and-fast hostility to the Soviet Union. And the Marshall Plan, almost miraculously, appeared to rest on just the opposite belief that it was possible to work with Russia to achieve European economic recovery. This possibility was cause for applause from the Times, to cite the most noteworthy of many examples: "The first condition for European recovery—the achievement of a specifically European conference attended by the Powers of the eastern as well as the western part of the Continent—seems within sight of fulfilment."[35]

That American generosity was stretched out to the East as well as the West in a grand gesture of good intentions doubtless added to the popularity of the Marshall Plan. Russia, it was earnestly hoped in Great Britain, would not fail to take advantage of the American offer. If any Englishmen wished otherwise, their voices were not heard. The most that was said was that Britain and Western Europe should go ahead even if Russia refused to join the arrangements. So general was the wish for Russian participation that even the strongly right-wing, anti-Communist Daily Mail, in editorializing that the plan might have to proceed without Russia, said that if Russia should join "no one would rejoice more than the British people."[36] This was no exaggeration in view of the chorus of approval given the inclusion of Russia and Eastern Europe in the blanket invitation for the submission of recovery plans. The newspaper voice of the Labour party had gone so far as to indicate that, until it became clear that Marshall did include the East, there was grave question whether the plan was desirable.[37] Another Labour paper, often suspiciously far to the left, had used the stronger language that it wanted no part in any plan which was "simply another move in an East-West struggle."[38]

The broad and inclusive nature of the American offer cut the ground from under this suspicion. The subsequent refusal of Russia to co-operate did not change the evidence that the United States had of-

---

35. June 24, 1947, p. 5.

36. June 20, 1947, p. 1.

37. Daily Herald, June 7, 1947, p. 2.

38. Reynolds News, June 15, 1947, p. 4.

fered its help to all of Europe. Indeed, the Russian action was considered entirely unreasonable by virtually all shades of British opinion. The result from the point of view of the reception of the American policy was doubly fortunate. The United States received full credit for having made the inclusive offer, and Russia received the brunt of the responsibility for refusing. If originally the American policy had been contrived to secure that effect, it is difficult to believe that the onus could have been more neatly fixed on the Communist power. Nothing could have made America, in British eyes, look more helpful and peaceful than to have extended its broad offer. A few cynics might have remained to say that America did not really mean to give any aid to Russia or that, whatever Marshall's and the Administration's intentions, Congress would never have approved the European Recovery Program if it had extended help to Communist countries. But the fact was the offer had been made, Russia had turned it down for flagrantly bad reasons, and the United States Administration did not have to face the embarrassment of trying to fulfil its broad and not very realistic proposals.

Often it has been suggested that, by accepting the American offer, Russia could have won much European opinion to its side, especially if the United States then refused to follow through with aid to all alike. Perhaps from the Kremlin's view there were overwhelming reasons against trying this tactic. At any rate, the Communists and other defenders of Russia in Great Britain (and Europe generally) were put in the very difficult position of opposing a plan so obviously beneficent in its intentions. The lie could always be given to an attack on the Marshall Plan as a strictly capitalist scheme by referring to the original terms of the proposal. This was of special importance in the British Labour movement, where hostility to Russia had long been suspect and where American policies in this respect had been most distrusted. Now, however, the United States looked patently co-operative and the Soviet Union did not. The rift was widened between the Communists, on the one hand, and the British unions and even the socialist left, on the other.[39] This

---

39. A notable instance of the wedge driven by the Marshall Plan between British Labour and the Communists was provided by the vexed relations of the Trades Union Congress with the Communist-dominated World Federation of Trades Unions. The break by British Labour from the WFTU was undoubtedly expedited by the unpopularity of the WFTU's attitude toward the Marshall Plan (80th Annual Report of the Trades Union Congress [London, 1948], pp. 175-89, 439-41).

triumph for the anti-Communist cause, it ought to be noted, was achieved
by an American policy that was not ostensibly anti-Communist at all.
Americans who have felt almost constantly outmaneuvered by Communist
propaganda might take some comfort from this very considerable victory.

The anti-Communist aspect of the Marshall Plan's development was
not entirely unappreciated in Britain. It was hardly, however, so much
in the forefront as to trouble most of the socialists whose sensibilities
might have been offended at this point.[40] There were few voices anywhere
in the Labour party, except among known fellow-travelers, that sounded
the critical note that the Marshall Plan was part of America's anti-Russian
strategy. Among nonsocialists, as time went on, the cold-war component
was increasingly recognized, but this came to be the cause for support
rather than criticism.[41] However, it was almost never a principal
British commendation of the European Recovery Program that it was
designed to check communism. The "nonpolitical" character of the plan
was what was praised.

Closely related to this theme of the Marshall Plan's acceptability
in Britain was the satisfaction that no troublesome conditions were attached.[42] The United States appeared to seek no advantage for itself in
return for aid. Socialists could note that there was no attempt to impose
capitalism on a reluctant Britain and that, specifically, nationalization
was not to be prevented.[43] And Imperial-minded Conservatives were able
to point out, as did one member of Parliament who had voted against the
Anglo-American Loan Agreement, that the Marshall aid agreement had
nothing affecting the Empire "to which serious objections" could be taken.[44]

---

40. Occasionally there was a socialist who remained worried about the
    possibilities of American political intentions but who still could not
    oppose what, on the surface, was only economic aid. See, e.g., the
    socialist soul-searching of F. Fairhurst (453 H.C. Deb. 301-4 [July
    6, 1948]).

41. By the Economist, CLIII (September 15, 1947), 787-88; Spectator,
    CLXXX (January 16, 1948), 63-64; and Time and Tide, XXXVIII
    (June 21, 1947), 648.

42. Sir Stafford Cripps made this clear when he spoke for the European
    Economic Co-operation Agreement (453 H.C. Deb. 48-49 [July 5,
    1948]).

43. Harold Wilson (453 H.C. Deb. 328-29 [July 6, 1948]).

44. Robert Boothby (453 H.C. Deb. 252 [July 6, 1948]).

Besides being a matter of particular concern to socialists and avid champions of Empire trade, the fact that there were "no strings attached" was
also a source of more general gratification.[45] Britain was being treated
as a self-respecting nation and not as an indigent.

With such a combination of favorable factors, it is no wonder that
parliamentary approval was overwhelming. There were only twelve
negative votes in the House of Commons when the European Economic
Co-operation Agreement was approved in mid-1948. Of the twelve, half
were recognized Communists or fellow-travelers, whose opposition could
be taken for granted. The other six belonged to a die-hard, right-wing
opposition to anything less than a predominantly British Empire policy
in economic affairs.[46] Theirs was the attitude of complete independence—to be insisted on even when American aid carried no specifically
onerous conditions. American generosity was acknowledged, but, it was
argued, Britain should make its own way with the Empire and without
help from America.[47] This brand of protest against accepting Marshall
aid was joined from time to time by Lord Beaverbrook's Daily Express,
so that it was never completely submerged even in the period of the
Marshall Plan's operation.[48] Although for the most part this was a quiet
opposition without any anti-American tones, on its fringe a rare attempt
was made to treat the European Recovery Program as part of a pattern
of American blows against the British Empire.[49]

Generally, this kind of criticism of the United States was insignifi-
cant during the operation of the Marshall Plan. The years of the ERP
coincided with what it is fair to call the "era of good feeling" in British
postwar attitudes toward the United States.[50] From 1947 to mid-1950

45. Spectator, CLXXIX (October 17, 1947), 483-84, and Manchester
    Guardian Weekly, July 1, 1948, p. 8.

46. 453 H.C. Deb. 338-42 (July 6, 1948).

47. Beverley Baxter (453 H.C. Deb. 264-73 [July 6, 1948]).

48. The Daily Express editorialized as late as July 26, 1950, p. 4,
    against accepting Marshall aid.

49. Most strenuous was the right-wing periodical, National Review,
    CXXXI (July and August, 1948), 8-9 and 89-92, which said that
    "the more loan we get the more we shall be struck down" and spoke
    of "hauling down the flag."

50. In April, 1950, Mass-Observation found, on the basis of a sample of
    five hundred Londoners, that feelings about America had "quietened
    down considerably over the past two years" (Some Notes on the
    Americans [Mass-Observation Report No. 3236]).

Marshall aid was by far the most prominent of American policies, much more so than any military programs. The plan's success was a matter of agreement in the major political parties. Non-Labour sources stressed the contribution of American aid more than did the Labour government, which preferred to claim a large share of credit for its own efforts to achieve British recovery. But this was only a difference in emphasis and not in general point of view. There is no question that the Marshall Plan created a fund of good will toward the United States throughout the non-Communist public. So substantial was this fund that it could be drawn upon later, in 1951 and 1952, as a counter to the less popular military programs with which the United States was being identified by that time. Thus Anthony Eden, defending Anglo-American co-operation in 1952, called forth the evidence of the Marshall Plan to confute the current charges of "dollar imperialism":

> It was Marshall Aid that rebuilt a war-shattered Europe. And never forget that aid was offered to every European country, east as well as west of the Iron Curtain—to the Soviets and their satellites, as well as to the free nations of the west. The Americans, so far as I know, are the only people who have ever taxed themselves for foreigners in peace time.[51]

Similarly, at public meetings, the standard reply to all hostile criticism of the United States was that American taxpayers had been so generous as to give Britain thousands of millions of pounds of Marshall aid.

No doubt such references were strong testimonials to the good feeling that came in the wake of the Marshall Plan. However, as has been suggested, this favorable attitude had a special basis, particularly in the British expectancy that the Marshall Plan would put an end to the need for further aid. The United States was providing Britain with a new start in the postwar period. Dependence itself could not, and was not, made any more attractive. Nor could the fear be completely wiped out that the United States might take advantage, in the future if not in the present, of British need for economic assistance.

Pressure for Integration

Even in the favorable environment of Marshall aid, there was one policy irksome enough to the British to serve as a reminder that to receive aid from the United States subjected the nation to American pressure.

---

51. British Information Services, official text of speech delivered over the B.B.C., April 5, 1952, p. 2.

That was the American belief, first expressed in conjunction with the European Recovery Program and subsequently with the European defense program, that Britain should move in the direction of integration with Western Europe. Awareness of any real American pressure was probably not widespread, and certainly the popularity of the Marshall Plan was not significantly diminished by any difference in opinion over economic integration. Yet the difference was real enough. The American desire that the recipients of Marshall aid should form a kind of economic federation was clearly at odds with the British preference for independent economic policies. Since the war, as is well known, Britain has insisted on standing apart (in varying degrees) from all schemes for integration with the Continental countries.

Often, in the case of the Schuman Plan, for instance, this meant resisting mainly Continental overtures. It was not always that the undoubtedly existent American desire for European integration was in the forefront. When it was, however, there came into play the complex of British reactions to "advice" from the nation on which it was dependent. This was observable in 1949 and 1950 when Paul Hoffman, speaking for the United States Administration, indicated that American help was based on the expectancy that Britain and Western Europe would create something like a single large market. Since the idea itself was regarded in Britain as unworkable without a common European political authority, which was neither wanted nor thought likely of accomplishment, the American proposal was dismissed as failing to appreciate the problem.[52] It was pointed out that the United States was trying to apply its own successful federal experience to an altogether more complex situation. The thirteen states had created their single market before modern industry was developed, and what kind of parallel, it was asked, was that for the problem of combining the highly developed and competitive industrial establishments of Western Europe?[53] "America is not Europe; and the eighteenth century is not the twentieth," the Economist remarked in its discussion of the "impossibly naive" American cry for European federation.[54]

---

52. Economist, CLVII (November 5, 1949), 985-87, and CLVIII (February 25, 1950), 416-17.

53. The same feeling that America was trying to impose its pattern on Europe was reflected in the Edinburgh Scotsman, February 8, 1950, p. 6; Spectator, CLXXXVII (November 30, 1951), 728-29; and Manchester Guardian Weekly, November 3, 1949, p. 8.

54. CLXI (July 7, 1951), 3-4.

In addition to complaining about a lack of sophistication in the American case for integration, the British found a variety of reasons for opposing any such program. That the Americans overlooked these reasons was cause for resentment, since the United States thereby seemed to override strictly British concerns.[55] Pressure for amalgamation with the Continent threatened many interests. Socialists disliked getting too closely involved with the more nearly free-enterprise system of the Continent.[56] Labour also suspected a design to bring lower-paid Continentals into competition with British workers.[57] And the British generally did not like the idea of being considered simply as Europeans. The ties to the Commonwealth and Empire were frequently evoked, sometimes in the most unlikely places,[58] as the basis for resisting federation with the Continent. Furthermore, the British did not find the politics of Europe, especially what they regarded as the instability of French politics, very appealing. At any rate, the British knew "in their bones," as Eden said, that European federation was something they just could not join.[59]

Whatever the reasons, the British resistance to economic integration was undeniably great and their resentment of American pressure correspondingly high. Perhaps it was especially high because the United States, in its argument for European federation, seemed to be rejecting Britain as a prime Atlantic partner in favor of treating the country as part of a European whole. How provoking the American policy had become at one point was revealed by the customarily unsubtle language of Foreign Secretary Ernest Bevin: "I get a good deal of talk from the United States, but, then, we are not integrating the United States with Europe. I wonder what sort of arguments I should get if the United

---

55. Continued British dislike of American pressure for integration was displayed in articles by William Clark, Denis Healey, and Robert Boothby (men of diverse political attachments) in "Aspects and Problems of European Union," Twentieth Century, CLII (September, 1952), 210-32.

56. M. Edelman (473 H.C. Deb. 242 [March 28, 1950]) and Tribune, September 10, 1948, pp. 1-2.

57. The strength of British working-class nationalism was clearly illustrated by the refusal of the National Union of Mineworkers to allow Italians to be brought to work in the undermanned British coalpits. The rationale is found in Tribune, March 6, 1952, pp. 3-4.

58. As in the New Statesman, XXXIV (August 23, 1947), 143.

59. Reported in the Manchester Guardian Weekly, January 17, 1952, p. 8.

States were in the Council of Europe and I was trying to put something over on their consitution."[60] The trouble was that the United States did offend national sentiment by seeming, in Bevin's language, to "put something over" on Britain, and it was likely to be so during any period of economic dependence. In that circumstance the United States, in advancing European policies, appeared to be exerting pressure rather than making suggestions.

The Humiliation of Dependence

Discomfort over Britain's economic relationships with the United States grew through the years of postwar aid. The relative acceptability of the Marshall Plan approach was not enough to offset the fact that dependence itself became more humiliating as time went on. Perhaps the grounds for that feeling had been prepared by the termination of lend-lease and the conditions of the loan agreement. In any event, it appears doubtful that British self-respect, while the nation received aid six or seven years after the war, could have been sustained by an acknowledgment of a "right" to be helped. The sense of wartime economic sacrifices did remain meaningfully in British consciousness, but not as a basis after 1950 to claim American aid. The announcement, in 1950, of Britain's economic recovery and consequent ability to do without Marshall aid was cause for considerable congratulation. It is no wonder that feelings were drastically different when, shortly afterward, it appeared that the nation's defense program was going to require American help in one form or another. Whether it was the defense program or something else, the British, in 1951 and 1952, had to face the "threat" of economic dependence.

That this was a threat not only to national self-respect but more particularly to the working-out of a separate foreign policy had been intermittently suspected. While only the socialist left, and the extreme right-wing imperialists, had ever said, in early postwar years, that receiving aid necessarily meant subordination, there was a wider fear that it might lead in that direction. The Times, for example, in admitting the need for Britain's "weaknesses and embarrassments" to be alleviated by American aid, insisted as early as 1947 that "unreserved cooperation with the United States" was not an adequate substitute for an independent foreign

---

60. 473 H.C. Deb. 322 (March 28, 1950).

policy.[61] Although this suspicion that independent foreign policy was difficult to achieve while requiring American aid was temporarily pushed into the background during the period of Marshall aid, it was nevertheless discussed in muted fashion by a few irreconcilable socialists. But only the Communists played consistently on the theme, since little occurred between 1947 and 1950 to remind socialists of the extent of their "dependence on America."[62]

Yet by 1950 even among the plainly grateful, there was a desire to be "free" from American help. The nearly official voice of the Times put it this way: "There can be no doubt at all that the weight of this country's counsels would be immeasurably greater—and indeed that the British attitude to many questions would become more simple and objective—if Britain were not in fact receiving aid from the United States purely for her own domestic economic needs."[63] The phrase "purely for her own domestic economic needs" was of considerable import. It reflected the special opprobrium attached to further economic dependence as such and the need to distinguish arms aid from the stigmatized category. This need was characteristic of British opinion in 1951 and 1952. John Strachey, Labour's former war minister (to take a quite different segment of opinion from that of the Times), wrote of "the special case of rapid rearmament—which after all America is urging on us" as a possible exception to his emphatic: "We must not take any more American help."[64] Clearly, this exception was difficult to make. It was not entirely apparent that arms aid was really distinguished from an economic subsidy, especially when the aid was in the form, not just of military equipment, but of American funds that helped to fill Britain's notorious dollar gap. "Mutual security" must have looked to the British

---

61. January 1, 1947, p. 5.

62. Devaluation, subsequent to American advice, was one of the things which seemed a reminder of dependence to the shade of opinion exemplified by New Statesman, XXXVIII (September 24, 1949), 319. A few British socialists did not need anything specific to fortify their pessimistic views of the motives of American aid even during the Marshall period, as, e.g., William Warbey, Can Britain Recover? (Fabian Research Series, No. 127 [London, June, 1948]), pp. 12-15, 22.

63. November 14, 1950, p. 5.

64. "Tasks and Achievements of British Labour," in New Fabian Essays, ed. R. H. S. Crossman (London: Turnstile Press, 1952), p. 207.

much like "European co-operation," regardless of the difference in immediate purpose.

Consequently, in objecting to continued American aid in 1951 and 1952, the Bevanites undoubtedly seized a responsive theme. They urged that one of the misfortunes of Britain's large rearmament program was that it made it necessary to rely on American assistance and so to be tied to American policy. Whether any part of their case was, in fact, established need not be admitted in order to appreciate the play on the British suspicion of the consequences of dependence. The Bevanites could put their appeal in simple nationalist terms, as was done in November, 1951: "If we accept dollar aid now to maintain a rearmament programme that is beyond our means to support, so far from helping ourselves to try and achieve economic independence we shall be placing ourselves in a position of dependence on the Americans worse than we have ever been in before."[65] Rather than making any favorable distinction for arms aid over previous forms of aid, the Bevanites claimed that the arms program was worse for Britain. The European Recovery Program had been acceptable, it was argued, because it was designed to get Britain on its own feet. The new assistance "would place us more fatefully at the mercy of American decisions."[66]

Through 1952 the Bevanites kept up a steady barrage along this line. Continued American aid meant British obedience to American policy. This was one of the chief principles of the Bevanite economist, Harold Wilson, in his pamphlet, In Place of Dollars. "The first aim of Britain's economic policy," he argued, "must be to achieve independence of aid from abroad at the earliest possible moment. Without that freedom there can be no independent foreign policy, for, more and more, American aid is being voted on conditions which involve British acceptance of American strategic decisions, and control not even by Congress, but by the Pentagon, headquarters of the United States chiefs of staff."[67] This appeal was not much more sensational than usual in its reference to the horrors of dependence on American aid. Tribune went further when, under the heading of "Declaration of Independence" and "We Don't Want Those Dollars," it said that the danger to Britain, greater than at almost any time since 1940, was "a creeping decay and a mortal surrender of British

65. Michael Foot (494 H.C. Deb. 155 [November 19, 1951]).

66. Tribune, November 16, 1951, p. 2; ibid., March 21, 1952, pp. 1-2, 5-6.

67. Op. cit., p. 3.

independence."[68]

This strong language was nearly a monopoly of the Bevanites, and its strident rejection of dependence on America would appear to have gone well beyond the public's desire for economic self-reliance. The general sentiment was real enough, however. In the 1951 general election campaign, political speakers, regardless of party, won cheers by declaring their independence of America.[69] The Conservative government, in 1952, and particularly its chancellor of the exchequer, R. A. Butler, popularized the slogan of "Trade, Not Aid." And in a by-election contest a Conservative spokesman claimed in behalf of his government: "For the first time England is not living on charity. You and I can now stand up proudly and say we are paying our way."[70] At the same time, Labour was prepared to admit no such Conservative achievement of independence but claimed instead (as had the Conservatives with respect to Labour when it was in power) that any government success was owed in large measure to American aid. "Part of Mr. Butler's balance comes from payments from the United States of America," said Mr. Attlee.[71] To be dependent was a very considerable accusation.

By 1952 the British nation was weary with the humiliation of anything that looked like economic aid. It wanted a program that would end the suspicions attached to dependence on the United States. Some, particularly the Bevanites,[72] argued that this could be done by cutting the rearmament program. Others prescribed different remedies. But on the desirability of doing something to establish the feeling of independence there was much more unity than division. The Times represented this general attitude when it declared that it was indispensable that Britain should speak with the United States "on terms of independence."[73] What was required was public certainty that the government adopted Allied policies as an independent partner and not as an economic dependent.

---

68. September 26, 1952, p. 1.

69. New York Times, October 14, 1951, Sec. 4, p. 3.

70. E. C. H. Leather (speech reported in Bucks Free Press, October 31, 1952, p. 7).

71. Speech at High Wycombe Town Hall, October 31, 1952.

72. See chap. xi.

73. November 17, 1951, p. 7.

As an accompaniment of the anxiety about the debilitating political
effect of American aid, there was a recurrent vogue for trade policies
designed to establish British economic independence. These policies
were frequently at odds with American ideas of international trade. Occasionally in Anglo-American disagreements over trade policies it was
believed that the United States was heedlessly pursuing its own interests
so that Britain could not become self-sustaining on the basis of trade.
And, at worst, it was suspected that the United States was deliberately
preventing the accomplishment of British independence.

Imperial Preference

The first and most lasting of the clashes in trade policy was between
the Imperial Preference system and American multilateralism. In fact,
open disagreement may be traced to the last years of World War II, when
(particularly at the Bretton Woods Conference) the United States pressed
for a postwar international economy threatening the existence of an Empire financial bloc.[1] At that time and later the American opposition to
discriminatory trade agreements was seen as an attack on British Commonwealth arrangements for mutual tariff concessions. This system of
Empire trade had been enlarged in the 1930's and was widely credited,
notably among the Conservatives, who had initiated it, as a cause of
Britain's economic revival from the interwar depression. In any case,
Imperial Preference was widely accepted as a foundation of the British
economic structure. Only a handful of the waning Liberals, traditional
upholders of free trade, were openly opposed to the Empire system.

That Imperial Preference could have grown sufficiently so that it
alone could have obviated the British need for postwar American aid
was not widely accepted. Such an attempted solution would have required harsh sacrifices by Britain as well as by other Commonwealth

---

1.   Significant reference to British reactions at the time of the Bretton
     Woods Conference may be found in R. F. Harrod, The Life of John
     Maynard Keynes (London: Macmillan & Co., 1951), p. 574.

nations, and there was hardly any promise of clear-cut success. But
many Englishmen undoubtedly looked to a greater development of Empire
trade for a future British prosperity, and any American attempt to apply
straight multilateral principles to Commonwealth nations appeared as a
but slightly disguised blow to British interests. It was stoutly insisted
that Britain had as much right to regard the Commonwealth of Nations
as a single economic unit as had the United States so to regard its forty-
eight components. The British champion of Imperial Preference could
only imagine an American thinking otherwise because of blindness or the
crass desire to take Commonwealth markets from British manufacturers.
Either way, American trade policy was not viewed in a kindly light.

Although the general public approved of Imperial Preference, the
defense of the system against American multilateralism was mostly
undertaken by Conservatives and particularly by a few Empire-conscious
publicists. Imperial Preference was symbolically the substitute for Tory
imperialism of another day. Empire trade was a kind of economic Union
Jack—the means by which British greatness, as in the past, was to be
sought in overseas development. Whether realizable or not, the ideas
of the Imperial Preference school had an obvious attractiveness. Britain
alone, it was said, could be nothing but an American dependency. With
the Empire, and especially with the Commonwealth nations, Britain cut
a much more considerable figure in the world. And potentially, the argument ran, the economic development of the Empire consequent on increased trade would make Britain prosperous and once again a world
power.

The prospect of a revived and transformed twentieth-century Empire
accounted for the fervor of the Imperial Preference school. "The British
Empire and its development is now, and will be for evermore," Lord
Beaverbrook proclaimed, "the ark of the covenant."[2] Consequently,
every postwar move to reduce Imperial Preference in exchange for American tariff concessions was, for Lord Beaverbrook, a betrayal of a sacred
trust as well as a bad bargain. By definition any British retreat from
Imperial Preference, whatever the supposed advantages to British trade
elsewhere, marked a success for "American attacks on the Empire system."[3]
Lord Beaverbrook's case, it must be emphasized, was only against closer

---

2.   Daily Express, January 1, 1946, p. 2.

3.   Ibid., November 18, 1947, p. 2; ibid., September 25, 1950, p. 4.

economic links with the United States; on matters of general foreign
policy he championed Anglo-American co-operation—but by a Britain
that was economically strong and independent on the basis of Empire
trade and development.

This position was typical not only of Lord Beaverbrook and his Daily
Express but of most postwar proponents of Imperial Preference.[4] Much
of the time, in fact, the strictly economic criticism of American policy
was also limited, partly in favor of attacks on the Labour governments
of 1945-51[5] and partly in deference to the admitted need for American
partnership in foreign policy. This did not prevent some open hostility
to the United States especially at the time of the Anglo-American Loan
Agreement[6] and over a longer period from ultranationalist sources.[7]
But outright attacks on the United States by Empire Preference advocates
became very rare as the postwar menace of Russia loomed larger and
larger. Yet the championship of the imperial interest against American
trade policy was no less staunch, and it was probable that there remained a considerable resentment of the United States that did not find
its way into print.

Intellectually the leader of the Imperial Preference school was

---

4. This was the view of the Tory National Review, which, for instance
    (CXXIX [November, 1947], 353, 364, and 366-67), combined strong
    criticism of the American position on Imperial Preference with a
    defense of the Marshall Plan against its Communist opponents. There
    was, in such a source, an ambivalence with respect to the development
    of American policy, since the National Review was as much in favor
    of the increasingly firm American stand against communism as it
    was against American economic hegemony based on multilateralism.

5. Ibid., CXXXIII (October, 1949), 303.

6. An all-out onslaught on American economic policy was launched by
    an interesting independent writer, R. P. Schwarz, "The Anglo-Ameri-
    can Agreements," Fortnightly, CLXV (January, 1946), 81-88,
    and "A Post-Mortem on the Loan," ibid., CLXVIII (October, 1947),
    251-58. Schwarz found the loan agreement entirely one-sided,
    an act of American imperialism on the one side, and of British ap-
    peasement on the other.

7. The most consistently hostile of right-wing sources was Truth, which
    regularly through the postwar period opposed anything that looked like
    a derogation of British sovereignty in favor of American policy. This
    meant opposition by Truth to British "surrender" on matters of trade
    and also to the "humiliation" of having American air bases on British
    soil (see, e.g., CXXXIX, 213 [March 8, 1946], 238 [March 15, 1946],
    362 [April 19, 1946], 457 [May 17, 1946], and CLII, 203-4 [August
    29, 1952]).

Leopold S. Amery, a highly respected and distinguished former Conservative minister. His ideas were well beyond the commitment of his party, and he operated from a more or less independent, elder statesman's position. As such he was franker than might otherwise have been the case. His arguments are worth examining as a way of understanding the imperialist's grievance against the United States. In Amery's view the United States had, in its own apparent interests, been trying to force Britain to return to the free-trade ideas of 1849-75—to the very ideas it was in British interests to have abondoned. This meant an American attack on the sterling-area arrangements as well as simply on Imperial Preference. The Atlantic Charter, the Lend-Lease Act, Bretton Woods, the loan agreement, and the postwar trade and tariff conferences, were all considered in the American design to break up the economic unit centered on Great Britain. Why, Amery asked himself, did the United States persist in its animosity to the preference system when it was, in the postwar period, anxious for European customs unions? His answer was a drastic indictment of American intentions:

> The real motive, conscious or sub-conscious, is the desire of American exporting and financial interests to maintain a one-sided world hegemony by keeping the rest of the world broken up into small economic units incapable of ever competing on equal terms with American production, and dependent on American finance to redress a continuously adverse balance of payments. More particularly, it is to be feared, does this ambition extend to the economic, and eventually political, domination of the widely scattered and individually weak members of the British Commonwealth. . . .[8]

In some quarters the attack was softened a little by the remark that the United States was not really acting in its own long-run best interests.[9] It was argued that the United States would really be better off, along with the rest of the world, if there were a strong sterling bloc with which to deal. The idea was to get Americans to see that this was the real truth of the matter. In part of the postwar period Englishmen had some reason to believe progress had been made in the direction of American enlightenment. Especially was this view held during the years of Marshall aid.[10]

8. "Non-discrimination and Convertibility," World Affairs, II (January, 1948), 21.

9. E.g., in the Economist, CLIV (May 8, 1948), 751-52, which of course did not represent the Imperial Preference school of thought; and in the writing of L. S. Amery's son, Julian Amery, "Imperial Preference and the Conservative Party," National Review, CXXXII (January, 1949), 42-53.

10. Voiced by Robert Boothby, a chief parliamentary champion of Imperial Preference (473 H.C. Deb. 257-65 [March 28, 1950]).

However, suspicions were readily revived whenever an international conference was held pursuant to the General Agreement on Tariffs and Trade of 1947. Both in 1949 and in 1950-51 there was bargaining which resulted in mutual tariff concessions among the twenty-three participating countries and, specifically, from the British view, in a reduction and in some cases a suspension of Commonwealth preferences.[11] That American and other nations' concessions might have more than compensated Britain in direct economic benefits was no answer to the imperialist argument. The very conception of GATT was dreadful to the champions of an imperial economy, for it involved British acquiescence in the view that the Commonwealth was not so much a "national" unit as, say, the United States.

Conservative opposition to GATT was by no means limited to the articulate fringe which Amery represented. As early as 1948 a large portion of the Conservative party in the House of Commons, led by a prospective cabinet member, Oliver Lyttelton, opposed the Geneva Tariff Agreement's limit on Imperial Preference and any "premature" subscribing to principles of nondiscrimination.[12] Similarly in 1950, with respect to the Torquay tariff conference, there was strenuous Conservative criticism of the Labour government's policy on Empire trade. The Americans, it was charged, wanted to have Imperial Preference abolished so that they could "prise open the markets of the Dominions and Colonies for their own mass-produced goods."[13] Still there was hope that the American attitude might change, and, in any event, a future Conservative minister reminded the Labour government, the Conservatives would not consider themselves necessarily bound by arrangements reached at Torquay.[14]

Dislike for GATT continued among Conservatives after they came to power in late 1951, and it coincided, in the next year, with an accumulation of wider public sentiment in favor of turning to an Empire solution for Britain's economic problems. Closer Commonwealth economic co-operation was talked about in Labour circles,[15] and there was

---

11. A useful summary of GATT activities was published in the London *Times*, October 17, 1952, p. 7.

12. 446 <u>H.C. Deb.</u> 1210-1334 (January 29, 1948).

13. 478 <u>H.C. Deb.</u> 861 (July 28, 1950).

14. A. T. Lennox-Boyd (478 <u>H.C. Deb.</u> 870-73 [July 28, 1950]).

15. The case for state planning of Commonwealth development was made as an alternative to becoming America's "49th state" by a Labour member of Parliament, R. Adams (496 <u>H.C. Deb.</u> 567-79 [February 22, 1952]).

an occasional indication that Bevanism was moving in that general direction in search of an alternative to American economic aid.[16] But the
most meaningful revival of an imperial program was in the Conservative
ranks and in the form of a concerted attack on GATT.

At the party's conference in October, 1952, there was considerable
rank-and-file enthusiasm for complete withdrawal from GATT. However,
L. S. Amery's suggestion to that effect was not voted on by the conference.
The Conservative leaders may have agreed with Amery that GATT and
Empire were irreconcilables, but they had no desire to be committed to
withdrawal from GATT on the basis of the agreement's sixty-day notice
procedure. That would have meant a drastic break with the United States,
and a difficult one to justify so long as American tariffs were not rising.
On the other hand, there was almost unanimous approval, by both the
conference and the leadership, of a resolution urging the government to
seek an amendment to the articles in GATT that "were injurious to Empire trade and development."[17]

What was mainly sought was the release of the Commonwealth
countries from GATT's rule against the establishment of new tariff
preferences. But, before approaching the GATT organization on this
point, the Conservative government had first to secure the agreement of
the other Commonwealth countries. This, as it turned out, could not be
obtained at the Commonwealth Economic Conference of December, 1952,[18]
and therefore Conservative policy became a pale replica of the party's
desire. Failure of the Commonwealth to agree to further Imperial Preference was a hard blow to the apostles of the Empire system, but it was
not a final one. Amery and his supporters did not readily surrender,
especially when they knew that increases in American tariffs, if they
occurred on a large scale, would tend to move the Commonwealth toward
Empire Preference. It was the essence of the imperialist case that the
United States could not be depended upon, in the long run, as a market
for British or Commonwealth goods.

In the meantime, however, Imperial Preference looked like a lost
cause. Although championed with customary fervor, its point was at

---

16. Harold Wilson (496 H.C. Deb. 604-16 [February 22, 1952]).

17. 72d Annual Report of the National Union of Conservative and Unionist
    Associations (London, 1952), pp. 50-55.

18. London Times, December 12, 1952, p. 6.

least temporarily blunted. Furthermore, American multilateralism could be only indirectly blamed as long as increased Empire trade was frustrated by the Commonwealth nations.

East-West Trade

While the favorite right-wing alternative to economic dependence on the United States was Imperial Preference, elements of the left were attracted by the idea of East-West trade—specifically of an increased exchange of British manufactured goods for raw materials and foodstuffs of the nations behind the Iron Curtain, The idea rested in part on a customary belief that the economies of Western and Eastern Europe were complementary and that political barriers to East-West trade were unnatural interferences with a free and mutually beneficial flow of goods. The strictly complementary nature of the two economies, it might be recognized, was modified by industrialization in Russia and the satellite countries, but the general conception of reciprocal needs retained some of its hold on British economic consciousness. Like Empire trade, East-West exchange was accepted as a desirable thing by almost the whole of the British community. However, just as Imperial Preference was usually advanced primarily by the group most concerned with the Empire as such, so East-West trade was most vigorously championed by those devoted to the principle that increased trade with Communist nations would improve chances for peaceful political relations with the Soviet Union. Although this essentially political aim motivated many of the active propagandists, the appeal to the British public was more apparently in terms of direct economic benefits.

In the pressure for East-West trade, Communists and fellow-travelers were unquestionably active. But support for the general point of view ran deep in the Labour movement. Many not under direct Communist influence looked to trade with the Soviet bloc as the road to Britain's economic salvation as well as to European peace. The root of this outlook often appeared to be a loose, and not necessarily Marxian, economic determinism. Perhaps it was only a leftist variety of free-trade doctrine. Elimination of East-West trade barriers, it was argued, would make for a more prosperous Europe and so reduce the economic causes of war. For the believers in the primacy of economic causes, there could be no better basis for East-West trade than the promise of peace in the wake of European prosperity. Certainly this was felt by many Englishmen in the early postwar years, when it underlay, for example, the desire for Russian co-operation in the Marshall Plan and Foreign Secretary Ernest Bevin's advocacy of economic agreements as the prelude to international settlement. Political factors were not always ignored, in this outlook, and it was sometimes granted that there were genuine political difficulties. But they were to be overcome by **trade** agreements.

Desire to increase British trade with Eastern Europe was present throughout the postwar period, even among those prepared to admit that there were obstacles of Soviet design. So, during the period of Marshall aid, when almost no Englishman regarded the failure to achieve East-West co-operation as anyone's fault but the Communists', Britain was expected to persist in trying to increase trade with Eastern Europe. Any success was greeted with the kind of satisfaction voiced by the main Labour party organ in late 1948: "Here's a good piece of year-end news. Final negotiations for an Anglo-Polish trade pact are almost completed."[19] Perhaps by this time there was little real confidence in "closer trading fellowship with Eastern Europe," but the hope at least was still present.

The fact that this "fellowship" came to very little was not, at first, attributed to any specific American policy. During the Marshall Plan period it was only rarely that a non-Communist charged the United States with "using her tremendous economic power to erect an economic iron curtain between the agricultural East of Europe and the industrial West."[20] However, there was a vaguer notion that the American interest in waging the cold war worked generally against East-West exchange. Even the European Recovery Program, at its inception, was examined for restrictive provisions.

Fears, which in the late 1940's were mainly under the surface, blossomed in 1951. One precipitating cause was the congressional provision, known as the Battle Act, that required the American government to cut off mutual aid to any nation that refused to agree to restrict exports of strategically important goods to the Soviet bloc. Previously, it is true, there had been British submission to American pressure for a partial blockade of China, but the Battle Act was more troublesome in its wide application to all Communist countries. The act attempted to prohibit

---

19. Daily Herald, December 31, 1948, p. 2.

20. D. J. Williams (467 H.C. Deb. 1659 [July 21, 1949]).

the shipment of a large number of products related to arms (as well as the arms themselves) and also sought to restrict, but not embargo, a wide range of goods economically useful to the Soviet bloc. The President was allowed considerable discretion in applying the terms of the act, and its operation caused less British hardship than was first feared.[21] Nevertheless, the act was always disliked for its obvious motivation: to use a threatened suspension of American aid as a limitation on trade with the East. The Economist, although itself clearly opposed to the shipment of strategic materials to the Soviet bloc, denounced the Battle Act as giving the United States "a right of veto against its allies."[22] The spirit of equality was infringed, and Congress was said to treat Europe and Britain in the relationship of patron to client. Moderate British opinion singled out this aspect of the act as especially objectionable, but economic warfare against the Soviet Union, on any basis, would have been unwelcome. The British attitude toward East-West trade was based more generally on economic rather than on cold-war considerations. Thus an embargo on the shipment of goods to the Soviet Union, which went beyond a block on arms exports, seemed too sharply in conflict with Britain's economic interests to be readily accepted.[23]

The critical reaction of the Economist to the Battle Act was really relatively mild. In this it was typical of the large middle section of British opinion that favored close economic relations with the United States and hoped for increased British exports to America.[24] Eastern Europe was, in that quarter, only one of several hoped-for markets. But to the few who thought of increased East-West trade as an alternative to the expansion of exports to America, the Battle Act appeared to be worse than a mere affront to British dignity and business.[25] It was a block to

21. The effects of the Battle Act were reviewed in the Economist, CLXV (November 1, 1952), 309.

22. Ibid., CLXI (August 25, 1951), 431.

23. The London Times, July 30, 1951. p. 5, indicated the difficulty of a nation which "must trade to live" in bringing its export policy into line with the United States.

24. The tone of the Spectator was similar in deploring the method of the Battle Act (CLXXXVII [August 31, 1951], 258).

25. As a prime example there was the way the Battle Act rankled the New Statesman (XLIII [April 19, 1952], 451-52) in light of that journal's long-standing concern for an expansion of East-West trade (XXXVII [March 19, 1949], 265, and XL [July 8, 1950], 32-33).

left-wing hopes for improved economic and therefore political relations with the Soviet area. The consequent frustration was exploited by the highly publicized Moscow trade conference of 1952, which gave the appearance of a Communist desire for trade and seemed to blame the United States for having imposed difficulties. Whether the Communists told them so or not, there is no question that followers of the Labour Left readily supposed that curtailment of East-West trade was American policy rather than British (or Russian).

At times the trade issue served as a useful propaganda weapon against the United States in wider areas of the Labour movement. This was true in late 1951 and through 1952 when the desirability of increasing East-West trade became especially popular in British unions, largely because of economic recession in the textile industry and elsewhere. In the Trades Union Congress of 1951 a motion for "developing trade relations with all nations" and putting "an end to America's interference" received considerable support, although it was defeated by the pressure of the TUC leadership.[26] But a year later the story was rather different. By that time most of the unions were committed, in one form or another, to a program of more East-West trade. The need for it was regularly discussed at union conferences in the spring and summer of 1952.[27] Consequently, at the TUC meeting in September, 1952, a resolution was accepted which urged, this time without specific anti-American language, the promotion of East-West trade. The TUC expressed its belief that "extensive trading relations with China, the U.S.S.R., and other eastern countries would make a substantial contribution towards improving the present international situation which is causing grave concern to the people of all countries." The call was to "governments, regardless of their political systems, to act together without further delay to discuss the possibility of extending trade and removing artifical barriers."[28]

Such hopes of trade with the East were bound to rise with the slightest Russian encouragement (or even absence of discouragement). Given the traditional outlook of the Labour movement, the hopes were always likely

---

26. 83d Annual Report of the Trades Union Congress (London, 1951), pp. 423-31.

27. E.g., at the annual conference of the Confederation of Shipbuilding and Engineering Unions, as reported in the London Times, August 14, 1952, p. 4.

28. 84th Annual Report of the Trades Union Congress (London, 1952), p. 529.

to be incorporated in conference resolutions, regardless of their suspicious sponsorship. This could occur even when many responsible
Labour leaders gave no sign of believing that the Soviet bloc seriously
intended to increase the volume of East-West trade—beyond, that is, the
purchase of British machinery and other goods related to arms production. Generally, it did not seem to matter that East-West trade was, if
anything, less realizable than Imperial Preference as a means to an independent British prosperity. American opposition to trade with the Russian
orbit, whether expressed by the Battle Act or the Chinese embargo, remained a convenient target for attack by the left, especially by that section
of the left which was evidently unconcerned about the consequences of
quasi-military aid to the Soviet Union and its partners. And such an attack had a formidable potential if coincident with the British business
community's desire for expanded foreign markets.

German and Japanese Competition

The turn to Imperial Preference and East-West trade, and so against
American trade policies, was stimulated in the late postwar period by the
revival of German and Japanese competition in British overseas markets.
Imperial Preference, in particular, commended itself as a method of
keeping Japanese products out of the Empire; and East-West trade, in
general, stood as a substitute for the loss of markets to German and
Japanese manufactures elsewhere in the world. The contra-American
twist to the British reaction to German and Japanese revival derived from
its association with American policies. This was unavoidable in view of
the American predominance in both Japanese and German occupation
authorities (but especially in the Japanese), and because of the evident
concern of the United States that West Germany and Japan should become economic going concerns. The latter, while undeniably reasonable,
happened to conflict with the British desire to minimize German and
Japanese business competition (and prospective military strength).

In the case of Germany the compound of British uneasiness was
heavily military as well as economic. The rise of German competition,
notably in European markets, raised the specter of German hegemony on
a broader front. So it was that any policy of the United States favorable
to Germany—however much it may also have been justified as favorable
to general European economic welfare—appeared, in frightening ways,
to be at the expense of Britain and the rest of Western Europe. More

specifically, to the British, what strengthened Germany seemed often to weaken Britain in relation to a revived Continental power. Naturally, this feeling increased markedly after 1951, when West Germany's economic power and prosperity were already established facts. However, a suspicion of America's German policy went back some years, even to the time of Marshall aid when American administrators intervened in the Organization for European Economic Co-operation to raise the aid allocation for what was then German Bizonia.[29] That somehow America was apt to help Germany more than the rest of Europe persisted through much of the period of postwar economic help. Consequently, when German competition was a very appreciable factor, say, in 1952, the Americans could appear, in a rather foggy way, to have been responsible. Although it was not stated that West German recovery should have been prevented, the fact that the recovery was of a competitor made it entirely unattractive to the British. On the Left it was made to seem more than simply an unfortunate result of American policy; rather it was presented as a kind of plot, or "German-American financial condominium over the Western Continent."[30] This, while not in itself very plausible, looked more sinister when it was linked, as it was after 1950, to American proposals for German rearmament.

The British reaction to the Japanese revival was more purely economic in its nature. Japanese rearmament, based upon a rebuilt industry, might be menacing, but not so clearly as Japanese trade competition in textiles and pottery goods. The potency of this competition had been fixed in British minds by the experience of the interwar period. Unemployment, especially in textiles, had then been widely attributed to the loss of overseas markets to the Japanese. It was not surprising that misgivings as to the American policy of encouraging the revival of Japanese textile manufacture should have been expressed very early in the postwar occupation, long before there were any other outstanding differences between American and British policies in the Far East.

Early in 1947, for instance, there came a note of warning from a principal newspaper concerned with the welfare of Lancashire's cotton trade.[31] Consciousness of the British stake in America's policy

29. Economist, CLV (September 11, 1948), 407.

30. New Statesman, XXXVI (December 4, 1948), 475.

31. Manchester Guardian Weekly, January 30, 1947, p. 3.

in Japan was apparent from this time on. Parliamentary qualms were expressed in mid-1947, not only by representatives of areas directly affected by textile competition, but also by Anthony Eden speaking more generally for the effect on British prosperity.[32] Over and over, members of Parliament, of various parties, continued to deplore a policy which would cause Japan to become economically viable largely through the export of textiles.[33] No amount of understanding for the American desire to cease supporting the Japanese economy could blur the realization that the inevitable effects were hostile to British interests. The fact that Britain lacked a respectable argument against the revival of Japanese industry did not always preclude a condemnation of "passive acquiescence in the dominating policies put forward by the Government of the United States."[34] Nor did the frustration over the practical absence of British authority in Japan deter parliamentary complaints about the economic policies of the occupation.[35]

The inevitability of Japanese competition turned British attention to one thing which sufficient international pressure might accomplish: raising of the labor standards of Japanese industry. It was a large part of the British case that Japan had undersold British textiles in the interwar period because of the low wages paid in Japanese factories. The unfairness of Japanese competition was thus a commonplace in union discussions of the problem.[36] There was no confidence that "sweated labor" was really abolished in Japan. "The old evils of cheap exports based on terribly low living and working conditions" were still a menace.[37] The Japanese peace treaty of 1951 seemed to the British to lack adequate safeguards against such evils, and therefore misgivings were voiced along with reluctant approval of the treaty. Thus the Manchester Guardian

32. 437 H.C. Deb. 1742-56, 1881-93 (May 15-16, 1947).

33. A Conservative member of Parliament stated this view (446 H.C. Deb. 569-76 [January 23, 1948]).

34. John Paton, Labour member of Parliament (457 H.C. Deb. 121 [October 27, 1948]).

35. Examples of this frustration abound in parliamentary discussion (457 H.C. Deb. 1092-1113 [November 4, 1948], 470 H.C. Deb. 2615-21 [December 13, 1949], and 473 H.C. Deb. 1415-38 [April 6, 1950]).

36. 82d Annual Report of the Trades Union Congress (London, 1950), pp. 431-36.

37. Spectator, CLXXXVI (April 27 and June 8, 1951), 542 and 737.

Weekly said that "the threat of Japan's low labor standards hangs over the West and it is reasonable to try to meet it in advance."[38] How to meet it was still the question, and the hopes for doing so by enforcing international labor standards or fair-trade agreements were not entirely satisfying. Nor did the British have full confidence in Japanese unions to fix standards comparable with those of the West.[39]

While the Japanese peace treaty was being discussed, in 1951, the chorus of protest against American policy in connection with the Japanese industrial revival reached a crescendo. Now more than ever the United States was identified with the Japanese threat to British exports, since the treaty was in so many ways an American policy that Britain and Europe had been persuaded to accept. The protest may be examined by taking the arguments of Anthony Greenwood, a Labour member of Parliament for a textile constituency, who was not marked as "Bevanite" in his attitude toward the United States. Greenwood put the charge this way: ". . .there is a suspicion among many people in this country, particularly in Lancashire, that America is anxious to build up the Japanese textile industry because that would help to give Japan a viable economy without competing with America and at the same time—and this is important— provide an outlet for American raw cotton."[40] The circle of American selfish intention would seem to have been complete, but Greenwood six months later added another count to Lancashire's indictment of the United States. An American policy of limiting relations between Japan and the Chinese Communist government would, he said, bar a large export of Japanese textiles to the natural Chinese market and so force more of the Japanese goods into cutthroat competition with British textiles.[41] None of this quite added up to the belief that the United States was deliberately trying to ruin British trade, but it certainly said that American interests were such as to work in that direction. The parliamentary spokesmen for the pottery industry, it might be added, felt this as strongly as the representatives of textile areas.[42]

38. July 19, 1951, p. 8.

39. Ibid., January 10, 1952, p. 9.

40. 491 H.C. Deb. 514 (July 25, 1951).

41. Letter from Anthony Greenwood, Manchester Guardian Weekly, January 24, 1952, p. 7.

42. 491 H.C. Deb. 1359-66 (July 31, 1951). The same debate also reflected an anxiety about Japanese shipbuilding competition (cols. 1373-74).

Actually the conflict of British interests with the Japanese revival did not cause all the troubled members of Parliament to vote against approving the peace treaty. Virtually the only open opposition came from the Bevanite contingent, which had other reasons to attack Anglo-American policy at that stage. Nevertheless, misgivings were widespread, and many were voiced that were not voted.[43] At various times there were prominent Conservatives as well as Labour members who worried about the prospective effects on the British economy.[44] Not all of them seemed anxious to blame the United States for the unwelcome return of Japan to textile and pottery competition. The eventuality of that return was often granted, and safeguards against its worst effects were looked for. Yet, as in the case of Germany, it was the United States which was identified with the revival of a competitor and which seemed to champion the interests of the ex-enemy nation more than the interests of its British ally. The appearance made it possible for severe critics to suspect the worst: that evil American influences, able to control German or Japanese industries, were intent on using them for purposes detrimental to Great Britain.

American Tariffs

British grievances about the American relationship to Japanese and German revival were off the main line of British response to the postwar trade policy of the United States. At the center of attention, especially in its effects on the yearnings for Imperial Preference or East-West trade, was the problem of trade with the United States itself. On the increase of British sales in America there rested the case for multilateralism instead of Empire protectionism and also a part of the economic argument against the necessity for further development of trade with the Soviet bloc. Exports to the American market, to close the much-publicized "dollar gap," were widely accepted throughout the postwar period as the principal aim of British trade. It was indeed what the

---

43. Some Labour members of Parliament who were definite enough in criticism of the peace treaty because of its connection with a revived industrial Japan nevertheless did not vote against their party's commitment to the treaty (a commitment made when Labour had been in office). Thus the "nay" vote of 33 probably understated the amount of real opposition. There were 83 who did not vote (494 H.C. Deb. 879-1008 [November 26, 1951]).

44. Among them was the future Conservative chancellor of the exchequer, R. A. Butler (491 H.C. Deb. 489-94 [July 25, 1951]).

American Administration advocated as the means for Britain to achieve economic independence. To this policy there were two very different kinds of British attitude. There was the view, most prominent among the intellectual descendants of the old free-trade school but evidently accepted by much of the public, which welcomed American trade prospects and hoped for the best with respect to the willingness of the United States to countenance the large-scale importation of British goods. On the other hand, there were those who viewed Britain's economic future in different terms to begin with and never had faith in the expansion of trade with America. For the latter, any sign of an increase in American tariffs was confirmation of their own unfavorable prophecies, while, among the hopeful ones, an American policy that made British sales in America more difficult was a disconcerting blow to the existing faith in the possibilities of transatlantic trade.

Since Britain was so thoroughly committed, even if not entirely by choice, to American trade policy, it is not surprising that there was a widespread conviction that the United States should adopt a liberal tariff policy. Depending on the source of comment, it was either demanded or implored that the United States make it easier for Britain to compete in American markets. The fact that American tariff policy from the end of the war until 1952 was almost uniformly bent in a liberal direction did not preclude the British from urging further liberalization.[45] The firm believers in principles of multilateral trade saw salvation in a very much greater reduction in American tariffs. "The one thing which must happen," it was said by a spokesman of the free-trade school, "is that America should make it possible to pay for exports in the future by lowering her tariffs and in other ways being more willing to accept imports into the United States."[46]

America was looked to as the "promoter of freer commerce" and the reviver of "the principles to which nineteenth-century Manchester gave its adhesion."[47] In fact, a more liberal policy toward imports was described as the "American obligation in the long run"[48]—a duty owed

45. To cite one of many examples, News Chronicle, January 13, 1947, p. 2.

46. W. Roberts (438 H.C. Deb. 2275 [June 19, 1947]).

47. Manchester Guardian Weekly, November 3, 1949, p. 9.

48. The London Times, September 7, 1949, p. 5; ibid., September 26, 1948, p. 5.

Britain and the rest of the world if, together with America, they were
to survive. During the Marshall aid period, when most of the left as well
as the right was dedicated to the prospects of economic co-operation with
the United States, the American obligation to reduce tariffs was regularly
referred to as the prerequisite for subsequent British independence
of American assistance.[49] Exports to the United States would have to become sufficient in volume to fill the dollar gap that was temporarily
plugged by Marshall aid. And, while the role of the British in manufac-
turing the goods for export was not neglected, "really far-reaching reductions in the American tariff" were viewed as equally essential.[50]
This, the British appreciated only too well, would be decided by Americans themselves and in a tangle of conflicting domestic economic pressures which made the outcome extremely uncertain.

What a great deal of economically informed British opinion contemplated for the United States was a role rather like that of late-nine-
teenth-century Britain. After all, America was now the great creditor
nation. Why should it not act as Britain had in its day—buy freely from
the rest of the world and invest heavily overseas, thereby creating an
international market for her own goods? How, it was asked, could the
United States expect to sell abroad unless it were willing to buy more
from its potential customers? The Economist, for instance, was sure
that America must behave as had nineteenth-century Britain, despite the
admission that there were special difficulties in the way of America
doing so.[51] It was patently impossible for the United States to follow
Britain's lead in exporting manufactures and becoming dependent on
the rest of the world for food. America, it could be seen, was a continental, not an island, economy. Yet, granting all this, the British
judgment, except when turned to Imperial Preference or East-West

49. The left-wing Tribune was no exception to the British chorus in
    favor of a more liberal American tariff policy (September 2, 1949,
    p. 2), since at this period Tribune (and most of those later
    to become Bevanite critics of America) was most hopeful of gen-
    erally liberal, if not socialist, developments in American policy.

50. This was the phrase of R. P. Schwarz, previously cited as an un-
    usually frank critic of American trade policy, who now differed
    from the majority of British economic commentators only in the
    heavier emphasis he placed on reductions in the American tariff
    as the most important single contribution to a solution of Britain's
    dollar problem (Fortnightly, CLXXII [December, 1949], 368).

51. CLV (July 3, 1948), 4-5.

exchange, was that America had to provide the long-term solution to the problems of international trade. At times, increased American overseas loans and investments might figure in the solution recommended by Britain. But never was an expansion of American imports from abroad excluded from the challenge to the United States.[52]

Naturally the actual economic difficulties, besides the political ones, in the way of the United States becoming a large importing nation were used by the critics of the prevailing reliance on American markets. It was argued, in fact during the operation of the Marshall Plan, that it was insane for Britain to try to export enough to America to bridge the dollar gap. That could only be done by becoming "coolies" in order to produce goods cheaply enough to undersell American products.[53] This, to be sure, was an argument that discounted, a priori, an Anglo-American solution of Britain's trading problem and treated as irrelevant any liberalization of the American tariff.

However, only a minority advanced this view, and seldom with any pertinacity. Rather, even to those well aware of difficulties in expanding American trade, there usually seemed no other course but to try. There were not many whose hopes for Empire or East-West trade were so great as to encourage the belief that Britain could really survive without also selling more to the dollar area. Except, then, for extreme doctrinaires of the imperial right and the fellow-traveling left, the entire British community felt it had a very large stake in what the United States did with its tariffs. This may be observed in the anxieties of 1952, when, really for the first time since the war, there were tangible signs of a possible reversal of the tariff liberalization embodied in reciprocal trade agreements and in the General Agreement on Tariffs and Trade. The fact that the signs were not very large ones makes the extent of British alarm all the more striking.

What happened was that, by the spring of 1952, American manufacturers, in relatively large numbers, had appealed to the United States authorities to raise tariffs against a variety of competing foreign manufactures, including British-made bicycles and motorcycles. In the most notable instances the tariffs were not actually raised, but the specter of American protectionism had become apparent. The British government

---

52. Economist, CLVI (June 11, 1949), 1073-74, and Manchester Guardian Weekly, September 1, 1949, p. 8.

53. R. H. S. Crossman (468 H.C. Deb. 261-71 [September 28, 1949]).

protested.[54] In the press there was scorn for the American champions of free competition who ran to their tariff commission for relief against British competitors.[55] The Manchester Guardian, sensitive as always to an attack on free trade, devoted a long and detailed editorial to the various growing pressures in America for upward tariff adjustment and for restrictive quotas on imports.[56] Throughout the British business community there ran a kind of shudder at what might yet come.[57] The president of the Board of Trade appealed to the American Chamber of Commerce, in London, that Britain wanted to pay its own way and therefore wanted America to allow an expansion of British trade. More than simply keeping tariffs from going up, he insisted that the United States must further reduce the barriers to trade with the outside world. This meant simplifying customs procedures as well as cutting tariffs.[58] Or, on other occasions, the United States was chided for the "Buy-American" Act, which impeded British sales to American governmental agencies.

The magnitude of the American tariff question in British eyes may be appreciated by realizing that the very considerable discussion of the question in 1952 was without any parallel in the United States. What seemed in America a comparatively trivial issue of tariff relief for a handful of manufacturers, hardly worth any editorial attention, was in Britain a likely threat to the nation's economic future. Similarly, during the 1952 presidential election campaign there was, relative to the American public's indifference to the tariff question, appreciable British concern for the effects of an incoming Republican Administration on the reciprocal trade agreements program of the Democrats. A return to Smoot-Hawley protectionism was not envisioned, but even a slight move in that direction had, for the British, the mark of disaster upon it. An increased duty on bicycles, for instance, not only would have been bad in itself for British trade but, as a portent of future American policy, would have been taken as a much more serious calamity.

---

54. Reported in Manchester Guardian Weekly, April 24, 1952, p. 2.

55. Spectator, CLXXXVIII (April 25, 1952), 534.

56. June 19, 1952, p. 9.

57. See, e.g., the speech of Sir Frank Nixon, retiring president of the London Chamber of Commerce, as reported in the London Times, April 30, 1952, p. 4.

58. London Times, July 23, 1952, p. 4.

Facing the Economic Colossus

The hypersensitivity to agitation for American tariff increases was typical of the British state of mind in relation to economic policies of the United States. The slightest lurch of the American giant seemed capable (and probably was) of upsetting the delicately balanced British economy. If it was not the tariff, then the bugbear was some other American policy, like a large-scale stockpiling of raw materials adversely affecting the prices of British imports.[59] Or looming over everything else was the danger of an American business depression, which Englishmen had good reason to believe would spell their own economic doom even if the United States could weather the storm. It was pretty generally understood that a relatively mild American recession caused a disproportionately large decline in United States imports from the sterling area.

Realization that favorable American economic policies were necessary in order for Britain to establish a position based on "Trade, Not Aid" was almost as troublesome as dependence on aid itself. In either case, the nation appeared at the mercy of the United States. That situation nourished the extremes of opinion, where the good faith of American intentions was directly challenged. The United States, either by opposing Imperial Preference or East-West trade or by encouraging Japanese and German industrial revival, was charged with responsibility for Britain's existing vulnerabliity. In this drastic imputation of evil, the imposition of obstacles to the sale of British goods in the American market only completed the closing of the economic ring against Britain. To be sure, this view was exceptional but was important as an extreme symptom of a more widespread, and nonpathological, resentment of Britain's plight in an international economy dominated by the United States.

No matter how much the British were aware that the national welfare required their own hard work, they were also impressed that nothing would avail if American economic forces, blunderingly or deliberately, should be set against them. In these circumstances, British hostility toward the colossus looming over their lives was understandable. It was the concomitant of the economic dependence which had become a fixture of postwar relations between Britain and the United States.

59. American stockpiling was also blamed for actual shortages of raw materials in British industry (482 H.C. Deb. 1475-1511 [December 15, 1950]).

Furthermore, this hostility bedeviled British attitudes toward more than American aid and trade policies. The fear of being treated as a satellite, originating in large part from Britain's economic position, set much of the mood for the reception of American foreign policy in general. Attitudes accompanying dependence on the American economy were easily transferred to broader international matters in which it also appeared that the United States had the power to call the tune for Britain.

Among the various ideological approaches to American foreign
policy, that of left-wing socialists merits primary attention even though
it has represented only a minority within the postwar Labour party and
thus a relatively small portion of the whole British community. The
reason for beginning with an examination of the Labour Left's perspective is partly because of the intrinsic importance of its highly adverse
reactions to the United States and partly because it provides a useful
basis for comparing the more favorable orientations of other and larger
political groups.

The phrase "Labour Left" is meant to include socialist critics who
operated within the Labour party but in varying degrees of opposition to
the postwar policy of their official leaders. As a group, it was often
amorphous until 1951, when it assumed overt form as the Bevanite wing
of the party.[1] Until then neither Aneurin Bevan himself nor all his subsequent supporters were openly identified with left-wing criticism on
foreign-policy issues. However, the existence of a socialist opposition
was evident enough in early postwar years, both in the shape of an
abortive rebellion against Foreign Secretary Ernest Bevin and in the
pamphleteering activities of "Keep Left" members of Parliament. In
addition, there were always the journalistic lodestars, Tribune and the
New Statesman, each attracting a variety of socialist ideologists. The
personalities changed a little, but continuity was clearly observable both
in the point of view and in its verbal champions. Almost always the keynote was objection to British acceptance of American hegemony.

Spokesmen of the Labour Left were mainly "intellectuals" in the
broad sense that the term has been used in British politics. The category did include some of the university teachers (and former teachers)
who were active in the postwar Labour party, but "left-wing intellectuals"
were also, by definition, a more heterogeneous collection of white-collar
socialists who customarily earned their living by journalism, lecturing,
politicking, or any one of a large number of other verbalist activities.
Although most of them were respectable participants in the life of the

---

1. See chap. xi.

community, they were rarely the holders of organizational responsibility, either in government, business corporations, or trade-unions. The Labour Left represented the British polemical tradition that had been regarded (in differing language) as "rootless" by its opponents, from Edmund Burke to Ernest Bevin.

Distinguishing the body of left-wing socialist criticism from that of the Communists and their apparent allies is necessary but difficult. Before trying to draw the line, it is well to insert, parenthetically, a few words about the Communist party of Great Britain. Its political status was roughly similar to that of its American counterpart and thus entirely different from the mass French or Italian Communist parties. The British party did have two members in the first postwar Parliament, but in the elections of 1950 and 1951 they were defeated in the general debacle of Communist candidates.[2] The party's London newspaper, the Daily Worker, while it had to be taken seriously as a propaganda instrument, hardly enjoyed large or flourishing circulation, and its direct influence (like that of other openly Communist publications such as the Labour Monthly) was limited to a narrowing circle of adherents.[3] The Communist line was pointed, as it was elsewhere in Europe, to attacks on American "domination," spiced with sensationalized accounts of altercations between American servicemen and British civilians. Party propaganda also made obvious use of a few important Communist-led unions, including the relatively large Electrical Trades Union as well as a number of smaller organizations. In addition, Communist influence, without control, was present in a few other unions, some of them large, despite increased efforts on the part of top national officials to crush infiltration tactics.[4]

Virtually all the Communist propaganda carried on by such plainly party media can usually be separated from pronouncements of the Labour

2. In 1950 one hundred Communists stood for Parliament and together polled only three-tenths of 1 per cent of the total vote; in 1951, with only ten candidates, the Communist percentage was down to one-tenth of 1 per cent (see H. G. Nicholas, The British General Election of 1950 [London: Macmillan & Co., 1951], p. 325; and David Butler, The British General Election of 1951 [London: Macmillan & Co., 1952], p. 251).

3. Officially listed Daily Worker circulation figures in 1951 and 1952 were around 120,000, but unofficial estimates were lower.

4. The Amalgamated Engineering Union, for example, was heavily permeated.

Left, although there were striking similarities in theme. What raises a problem is the suspicion of covert Communist activity within the left wing of the Labour party. This suspicion is not laid to rest by the fact that Communists and members of Communist-front organizations were technically banned from Labour's ranks.[5] Thwarted electorally in their own organization, the Communists were not likely to let rules stand in the way of their infiltration of the Labour party. This was even an openly declared objective.[6] It was facilitated both by the possibility of affiliating through Communist-controlled unions and by the opportunity of joining constituency Labour parties where quasi-intellectual vestiges of the popular-front spirit remained alive. It was immensely useful to the Communists that they were still regarded, by many middle-class socialists, merely as the representatives of a more extreme left-wing movement and not of a morally reprehensible totalitarian dictatorship. General British tolerance of fellow-traveling, though declining slowly under the impact of events in the Soviet world, also helped to blur the distinction between Communist and left-wing Labour activities. The Communists were not, even in 1952, nearly so thoroughly ostracized by non-Communists as they were in the United States.[7]

Early in the postwar period they were not ostracized at all, and there turned up in the Parliamentary Labour party, after the 1945 general election, several "crypto-Communists." The number of these members of Parliament, presumed to operate under Communist discipline without acknowledging membership, was estimated at three or four by one

---

5. A Communist attempt to secure affiliation within the more or less federal structure of the Labour party was turned down after the war as before. (45th Annual Report of the Labour Party [London, 1946], p. 174). A list of proscribed Communist and Communist-front organizations was maintained (and published in each annual report). The members of these organizations were ineligible to belong to the Labour party. Keeping the list up to date was a difficult problem in light of multiple Communist organizing habits.

6. Note the statement of Harry Pollitt, general secretary of the British Communist party, as reported in the London Times, November 17, 1952, p. 3.

7. In mid-1952 it was still possible for a Communist-managed public meeting, operating under very thin cover, to muster an assortment of academic, religious, and pacifist leaders, in addition to the notorious Dean of Canterbury. Causes relating to China seemed, at this period, to take in the largest numbers of apparent non-Communists.

source and at eight or nine by another.[8] The closest to an official estimate was four, since this was the number of members of Parliament
who were expelled by the Labour party in 1948 and 1949 on account of
persistent Communist-oriented opposition to Anglo-American foreign
policy. These four—Zilliacus, Hutchinson, Solley, and Platts-Mills—
joined D. N. Pritt (who, after his expulsion in 1940, operated without
party label in the House of Commons). Under the title of Labour Independents,[9] all five lost their seats in the 1950 general election.[10] Whether
this constituted the elimination of crypto-communism from the parliamentary Labour party was open to some doubt. One of the five, Zilliacus,
later appeared as a Titoist instead of a Stalinist, and he was subsequently
readmitted to the Labour party without any recantation of his left-wing
hostility to the American alliance. More troublesome, for present purposes, than the question of whether Labour had mistakenly purged non-
Stalinists was whether some of the crypto-communists had been overlooked.

Although assuming that the expellees, with the possible exception of
Zilliacus, should not be treated as part of the genuine Labour Left, it is
possible that a few other left-wing critics, even in the parliamentary
party, should also be struck from consideration on the grounds of dubious
loyalty. In addition to the chance of there being crypto-Communists, there
was the more confusing possibility that some Labour members of Parliament (and journalists), while not accepting Communist discipline, ha-
bitually followed the Stalinist line in the classic fellow-traveling pattern.
On this score there was reason to doubt two or three of the most regular
foreign-policy critics; certainly, so regular a purveyor of the germ-
warfare charges as S. O. Davies must be suspected.[11] Rarely, however,

8. Three or four was the estimate of a left-wing journalist (New
Statesman, XXXI [March 2, 1946], 153), and eight or nine was the
number indicated by an ex-Communist (Douglas Hyde, I Believed
[London: Heinemann, 1951], p. 212).

9. The line of the future "Labour Independents" at various stages of
the cold war may be discovered at 427 H.C. Deb, 1542-52 (October
22, 1946); ibid., cols. 1690-97 (October 23, 1946), 450 H.C. Deb.
1182-94 (May 4, 1948), 453 H.C. Deb. 104-17 (July 5, 1948); ibid.,
cols. 288-93 (July 6, 1948), and 468 H.C. Deb, 1450-54 (October
26, 1949).

10. Nicholas, op. cit., pp. 251-52.

11. E.g., S. O. Davies claimed that there was evidence "proving beyond
all shadow of doubt that germ warfare has been carried on in North
Korea and China" (505 H.C. Deb. 1436 [October 23, 1952]).

was similarity to the Communist party line so clearly discernible.[12]

Occasionally, too, there was cause to wonder whether apparent fellow-traveling was more the result of socialist naïveté than of conscious pro-Communist intention. For example, just before the Italian election of April, 1948, there were twenty-two Labour members of Parliament who admitted that they had signed an encouraging telegram which was sent, under crypto-Communist auspices, to the Nenni socialist collaborators of the Italian Communist party.[13] Only a few of the twenty-two were subsequently labeled as Communists. Accounting for the motivation of the others is typical of the difficulty in distinguishing Labour Left from fellow-traveling left. It strains one's credulity to accept naïveté as an all-sufficient explanation. The Nenni incident took place long past the wartime revival of the popular-front conception and notably after Communist purposes had been revealed by the Czech coup. Some older or less well-informed socialists might have misunderstood the significance of the telegram or of the Nenni socialists to whom it was addressed, but there were others whose backgrounds did not permit so charitable an interpretation.

Consequently, there can be no certainty that what seems Labour Left is only that and no more. A conscientious attempt has been made to omit, or to treat separately, the most suspicious cases and never to rely on their line as characteristic of left-wing socialist opposition.

12. Thus Tom Driberg's persistent objections, as at 507 H.C. Deb. 1836-37 (November 19, 1952), to United Nations policies in Korean prison camps might, against the background of his general left-wing criticism, raise questions about his relationship to the Communists, but such questions appeared to be answered by Driberg's prominence as a member of the Church of England and as a Bevanite representative on the national executive of the Labour party. He should be counted, to be safe, as at the left wing of the Labour Left.

13. How many Labour members of Parliament had actually signed the Nenni telegram was a minor mystery. Originally there were supposed to have been thirty-seven Labour signatures (plus D. N. Pritt), but fifteen of these were subsequently reported either not to have signed at all, to have signed by misunderstanding, or to have quickly retracted. Of the twenty-two remaining, one was the man who had secured the signatures, Platts-Mills, and he was expelled forthwith. The other twenty-one gave a collective undertaking that their future conduct would be in line with Labour policy as the price of continued membership in the party. Three of these—L. Hutchinson, L. J. Solley, and K. Zilliacus—gave sufficient further offense, as already noted, to be expelled in the following year. The account of the Nenni affair, with a list of the twenty-one signers, is found in the London Times, April 21, 29, and 30, 1948, p. 4 (in each instance).

Egregious confusion should thus be avoided, although strict accuracy is admittedly elusive. Imperfection is necessarily caused by the probable shift, during the postwar years, of some from a Communist to a Labour position or, less likely, by a change in the opposite direction. Difficulties of this sort may be granted, however, without discounting the existence, on a scale manifestly larger than British communism, of an independently critical socialist view of relations with the United States.

Socialist Attitudes toward the Soviet Union

Almost entirely apart from direct Communist influence, many British socialists had long cherished so favorable a view of the Soviet Union that adjustment to an anti-Russian foreign policy was made difficult for this as well as other reasons. Traditionally, a pro-Soviet orientation had been characteristic of most of the Labour movement, though it was less of a fixture in the trade-union leadership than in the more socialist-conscious political ranks. Wherever the socialist label was accepted and proclaimed, there had existed, practically as a matter of doctrine, a basic sympathy for the objectives, if not the methods, of the U.S.S.R. This feeling ante- dated the wartime alliance, and it merely reached its plainest political expression in Labour's 1945 electioneering claim that, because "Left understands Left," a British socialist government could manage postwar relations with the Soviet Union better than a Conservative administration. At the time, these words may well have expressed the real hopes of Ernest Bevin and other moderate Labour leaders, as well as the more confident aspirations of the left wing of the party.[14] Thus Hugh Dalton and Sir Stafford Cripps, both later identified with the Labour government's patent inability to secure an understanding with Russia, were among the party campaigners who, in 1945, declared that a socialist Britain would be especially qualified to achieve good relations with the Soviet Union.[15]

Under the impact of postwar Russian hostility, this optimism was dissipated fairly rapidly in the center and right of the Labour party (es- pecially at the leadership level), where pro-Soviet attitudes were probably much qualified at an earlier date. But residues of sympathy for the Soviet continued to exert an influence on the thinking of the left. Perhaps this

14. Francis Williams, Ernest Bevin (London: Hutchinson, 1952), p. 242.

15. Dalton's remarks are reported in 44th Annual Report of the Labour Party (London, 1945), p. 104, and those of Cripps by the London Times, June 26, 1945, p. 4.

was because its optimism was more firmly implanted, in the first place, as part of a very thoroughgoing commitment to socialism. Or perhaps the mental equipment of the left-wingers was simply less flexible in this as in many respects. At any rate, there is no doubt that the left's grossly sympathetic interpretations of Russian policy persisted in the first two or three postwar years and that well after that they reappeared in subtle but nonetheless meaningful form. Even though open socialist approbation of the Soviet Union was rare by the 1950's, it had already played an important role in determining the nature of left-wing criticism of American policy.

One of the apparently odd features of Labour's residual pro-Sovietism was that it was often combined with a sharp animosity to the activities of the British Communists. Socialists regarded their own democratic movement as a block to the growth of communism on the Russian model, and this was increasingly the case during Labour's postwar period of office-holding. True enough, Communists were seldom (except by trade-unionists) castigated prominently and publicly, but they were unquestionably considered political rivals. Thus, Communist infiltration of British Labour organizations was attacked by so durable an apologist for Russian intentions as Harold Laski.[16] British socialist leaders necessarily responded to Communist undermining with a determined enmity of their own. This was maximized during the postwar years, but it was no new phenomenon. Even Aneurin Bevan had earned a reputation as a Welsh anti-Communist.

Certainly, the attitude of the non-Communist British socialist toward the Soviet Union requires extended explanation. It was compounded of many factors, among which Marxist intellectual influence was important but not overwhelming. The persuasive reason for caution in attributing the bulk of socialist pro-Sovietism to a Marxist base is that Labour's intellectual influence stemmed directly from various British (and sometimes American) sources and not from Marx and Engels. It is widely

---

16. Laski wrote The Secret Battalion (London, 1946) while he was chairman of the Labour party. He stated the distinction between Russia and the British Communists which the left wing sought to maintain: "Socialists can understand a straightforward negotiation with the Russian Communist Party which seeks a genuine entente between the Russia of the great Revolution and the Socialist parties of the Western world. They are bound to feel differently about the Communist parties outside Russia" (p. 15).

accepted that British socialism owes more to the Bible, the Fabian Essays, and a large assortment of other humanitarian and equalitarian works than to the Communist Manifesto or Das Kapital.

Acknowledging the meager Marxist contribution to the original development of the British Labour movement does not, however, exclude its subsequent imprint on socialist thinking. This was never so great as to make Marxism anywhere near pervasive or official, but, especially in the interwar years, economic determinist doctrines had seized the fancy of many academic and political intellectuals. Marxism-Leninism, when adopted, seemed to rule out the possibility of aggression or similarly offensive international action by a noncapitalist nation. In this view of the world the Soviet Union could not be visualized as an imperialist menace. A priori, the Marxist assumed that a state without profit-seekers had no incentive for expansion at the expense of other nations and that therefore the Soviet Union was inherently pacific, save when threatened. This general notion had, as will be seen, a largely nonintellectual base as well, but to some extent it was bolstered by specifically Marxist blinkers.

The Labour Left's postwar economic determinism was a looser affair, but it did have a relationship to the customarily sympathetic approach to the Soviet Union. Its intellectual domicile was chiefly in the pages of the New Statesman, which was the widely read journal of the high-brow left.[17] Although the New Statesman, after 1945, took slight comfort from Russian policies, its Marxist conceptions remained influential if not decisive. Kingsley Martin, the editor of the New Statesman, made this plain in describing his own ideological moorings. He admitted the totalitarian character of the Soviet system and expressed his own approval of democratic socialism for Britain and Western Europe.

---

17. No doubt the New Statesman deserved all the contempt with which Labour's political leadership regarded its wishful thinking and implausible left-wing theorizing, but nevertheless its intellectual influence cannot be brushed aside. Its circulation was about 75,000, which was remarkable for a plainly high-brow weekly, and it reached many relatively nonpolitical readers because of its literary and aesthetic criticism. Editorially, it was invariably left on foreign policy, but with several shades of opinion, from socialist to fellow-traveler. Much of the New Statesman's audience may have been politically naïve, as often charged, but it did consist of school-teachers, journalists, and other opinion-makers, as well as of future opinion-makers among the numerous students who read the journal in libraries or college common rooms.

Still Martin persisted in believing in the inevitability of collectivism, in one shape or another:

> To me the result of re-viewing Marxism is clear enough. Marx was right in thinking that technical changes force mankind into some form of collectivism and world organization. In countries where there is no democratic tradition of liberty, the result is likely to be totalitarian socialism. In the West, if civil liberty is to be maintained, the necessary change must be carried out, but the process must conform with national traditions and civilized values. In this sense the end is determined by the logic of history. But the future happiness of mankind depends on the means we employ, and they are largely of our own choosing.[18]

This brand of economic determinism was flexible enough to allow different means for achieving collectivism, but, despite Martin's words about "choosing" the means, it was evident that he recognized the likelihood of totalitarian methods in countries like Russia. Consequently, there was an amorality in his approach to the Soviet Union. Russian communism usually appeared, in the New Statesman, as though it were no worse than an unfortunate aberration from a generally desirable socialist development.

The quasi-Marxist intellectual considered collectivism, as such, to be valuable as well as inevitable. Therefore, in spite of the unpalatability of Soviet political dictatorship, Russia was considered "progressive" in a supposedly fundamental economic sense. It was in this light that the New Statesman commented on one of the earliest conflicts between Russia and the West over German policy:

> When the Russians say "democracy," they do not mean by the word what the Americans mean or what Mr. Churchill means. It is, for them, not a merely parliamentary word; it means a far-reaching change in the economic basis of society. This change has largely been accomplished in the Soviet Zone; it has not been even begun in the other three Zones. Naturally not; for the American-Churchill view of democracy rules it out. According to the latter view, political change comes first, and then the new political bodies are free to make economic changes if they will. But according to the Soviet view, no democratic political government is possible until the economic changes have been made.[19]

It was by no means clear, even in the first postwar years, that comment of this kind indicated a preference for Russian "democracy" over the American or Churchill pattern. But at the very least there was a degree

---

18. Political Quarterly, XVIII (July-September, 1947), 248-49.

19. XXXII (July 27, 1946), 59.

of uncertainty. Communist expansion pleased the intellectual Marxist by destroying capitalism, and this feature was not always overwhelmed (for the New Statesman) by the repressive political aspects of the Soviet regime.

Although in time, because of flagrantly repulsive Russian policies, favorable references to the Soviet economy did largely fade away, that was less significant than the fact that intellectually the journal was so oriented as to have conceived Russian collectivism as a desideratum. That point was never specifically abandoned, even if it was no longer thought to compensate for the political harshness of Communist rule. For the Marxist, the harshness was never the necessary or even the likely concomitant of extreme collectivism. Instead the Russian economy served the New Statesman as a potentially redeeming feature of the Soviet system. If this became less fully articulated, it nevertheless operated as a brake on the journal's condemnation of communism, which was hardly wholesale or thoroughgoing.

Yet, even among intellectual socialists, Marxism was not the only cause for persistently favorable views of the Soviet Union. And in the Labour party generally there were other, more direct influences. Many British socialists, regardless of doctrinal origins, thought of their "movement" (itself a significant word) as diametrically opposed to capitalist society and all its works. Historically, there were ties to a semirevolutionary past in which all the enemies of capitalism were comrades in a fight against oppression. To be sure, this was remote from the Britain of the 1950's—from the permanency of the welfare state and of intrenched trade-unions. But the past had not died easily in the British Labour movement. To older but still contemporary socialists, it seemed only a rather recent past when they had doubted whether parliamentary democracy, rather than direct industrial action or political revolution, was really the best method for meeting the demands of the working class. After all, there had been in Britain (much more than in America, though less than on the Continent) a sense of unbearable economic exploitation, relatively unmitigated by a ladder of opportunity after the American manner. It was hardly likely that British Labour should have been untouched by the atmosphere of class war, especially in mining and other areas where the record of economic suffering was most prolonged and most acute.

This provided the background for the affinity of British working-class activists with foreign movements directed against capitalism or, for that matter, against "landlordism" and old regimes generally. In this context the upper-class enemies of the Russian Revolution looked much the same as, or worse than, the domestic opponents of British socialism. Especially was this the case with respect to czarist despotism, which was traditionally abhorred by British liberals as well as socialists. The Russian Revolution, beginning (in what was really the first of two 1917 revolutions) with the overthrow of the czar, thus evoked a general identification, which was strengthened, in the minds of socialists, by the objectives of the second or Bolshevik revolution. The character of this socialist feeling was peculiar from the start, since it emphasized sympathy for the Russian cause but no widespread emulation of Communist method in Britain. The common cause was not communism; it was opposition to reaction and, as such, was another example of the historical devotion of British radicals to revolutions elsewhere (in America, France, or Hungary, for instance) without any corresponding desire for revolution at home.

The meaning of the Russian Revolution was more intense and more durable than any previous external event. Not only was the first news of the revolution greeted with "exhilaration,"[20] but soon afterward the British Labour party had occasion to declare its sympathy in definite fashion. The occasion, in 1919 and 1920, was the Allied, and especially the British, intervention in the Russian civil war and in the war between Poland and Russia. In opposing this intervention, Labour was taking a stand against the policies of the predominantly right-wing anti-Bolshevik British government. Consequently, the Communists were allies not entirely on their own account but at least as much because of a common enemy. In this way, it is possible to account for the role of Ernest Bevin as the leading opponent of British intervention. He was already a rising union official, and while he then appeared more of a radical figure than he did subsequently, nevertheless he was always well removed from the ranks of those who had gone overboard for the supposed virtues of the Russian Revolution.

The Labour protest was prolonged and strenuous enough to leave a lasting impression on the movement. In 1919 the Labour party adopted a resolution demanding that Allied intervention in Russia should be re-

---

20. Labour reactions to the Russian Revolution were described by Francis Williams, Fifty Years' March (London: Odhams, n.d.), p. 264.

sisted with the full power of the trade-unions. There was formed a "Hands-Off Russia" committee, and in May, 1920, twelve representatives of the party and of the Trades Union Congress went to Russia to study the effects of the intervention and blockade. Following a report by the twelve observers, one group of dockers refused to load munitions on a ship bound from Britain to Poland, and this refusal was backed by Bevin, who then ordered the rest of his dockers' union to pursue a similar policy. In the summer of 1920 Bevin organized a full-fledged campaign. His was the active force in the Council of Action which served to co-ordinate the efforts of the Labour party and the TUC in what amounted to the threat of a general strike. Whether it was this threat of the Council of Action or other factors which brought British and Allied intervention to an end was not entirely clear, but there was no doubt that Bevin and the Labour movement thought the major cause was their own firm stand.[21] Thus British Labour's protection of the Russian Revolution against its earliest outside enemies became a party legend. It mattered not why the movement had rallied to protect the Communists—it may have been mostly because of a desire to be done with war. The significant fact was that Labour had committed itself to a degree of support for the Russian Revolution.

This did not end in 1920 or soon afterward. Doubtless the feeling was kept alive in part by real British Communists who had an interest in doing so. But there was also something to the working-class tradition upon which Communists traded. It was especially easy to play on this theme in the 1920's and 1930's, which were neither prosperous years for British workers nor politically satisfying years for the British Labour party. There was a sense in which the chronically unemployed as well as the largely powerless socialists looked on Russia as a kind of promised land—where the opponents of capitalism were in control. This feeling was strengthened by the experiences of the 1930's and of the later years of World War II, when many British socialists gloried first in the popular front against fascism and then in the alliance of the war itself. Those experiences fortified the left-wing kinship of the older generation and also attracted a new generation to the deceptive comradeship of British socialist with Russian Communist.

Altogether there had been enough to establish a sense of solidarity

---

21. An illuminating history of the Council of Action is contained in Williams, Ernest Bevin, pp. 82-89.

that could be surrendered in the postwar years only very slowly and grudgingly. And it had a way of reasserting itself whenever the ancient capitalist enemy attacked the Soviet Union.[22] This was what R. H. S. Crossman, himself an intellectual socialist, called "The 'Russia' Complex" of the British Labour movement. He found, as late as 1948, "not only intellectuals but countless working-class socialists [who] want to think well of the Soviet Union and will give it the benefit of the doubt whenever they can."[23]

Apparently in deference to these socialist sensibilities, criticism of Russia remained heavily muted in the Labour movement. For example, at a party conference in mid-1947 a spokesman for the Labour executive took pains to point out that the policy of excluding members of the Communist-dominated British Soviet Society was not directed against friendship with the Soviet Union. "Friendship with Russia," he said, "is to be found in this movement, and the roots are too deep to be disturbed."[24] It was only against British Communists, not Russian ones, that the party ban was aimed. Rank-and-file sympathy for the Soviet Union was still potent, and even at the next Labour conference, in 1948, two cabinet ministers found it useful, in defense of the government policy with which they were now identified, to recall their own earlier records in behalf of Russia.[25] This, however, was obviously to be understood as a method of conciliating a left-wing following and not as a reflection of continued top-level optimism about the Soviet Union.

It was only on the left that these hopes remained significant enough to exercise a real influence on attitudes toward foreign-policy problems in the postwar period itself. Instead of reacting adversely to the evidence of Soviet hostility, there was a left-wing tendency to rationalize Russian conduct in charitable terms. The favorite device was that the Soviet's apparent aggressiveness was merely in response to fear of capitalist

---

22. The American sociologist, Edward A. Shils, wrote with keen insight in 1945 that the fear of offending Russia was "the residue of a long period during which the Labour Movement felt that it was called upon to protect the Soviet Union from the reactionaries of every country" (Review of Politics, VII [October, 1945], 514).

23. New Statesman, XXXV (January 24, 1948), 65.

24. 46th Annual Report of the Labour Party (London, 1947), p. 102.

25. 47th Annual Report of the Labour Party (London, 1948), p. 109 (Shinwell) and p. 195 (Bevin).

encirclement. Immediately after the war this old saw was applied rather tortuously, since Russia had responded to the installation of the Labour government by concentrating its hostility against nominally socialist Britain instead of capitalist America. How was this to be explained in terms of Russian suspicions of right-wing enemies? Easily, said a member of Parliament of the Labour Left, writing in mid-1946: "We are convinced that Russia's chief fear is of American dollar Imperialism. In attacking us diplomatically, she considers she is 'going for' the weaker of the two Anglo-Saxon Imperialisms. Unfortunately Bevin's words and deeds give her some justification for her false assumption that we are in the American camp."[26]

Something like this became a left-wing alternative to accepting the realities of Russian intransigence. The failure of "Left understanding Left" was blamed on Bevin and British policy, not on the Soviet. And the particular trouble was supposed to be, first, the appearance and then the actual fact of Britain's alliance with America. Harold Laski's criticism, for example, was in that vein, with heavy emphasis on fear as the prime motivation of Russian policy.[27] In 1950 (the last year of his life), while admitting that Russia had placed obstacles in the way of friendly relations, Laski was still complaining that Bevin had been "so ready to shape his policy to fit the effort of the United States to drive Russia into a position where its natural desire for security against an einkreisung sponsored by American diplomacy should lead the world to the brink of a third World War."[28]

Laski, it should be added, was not the most extreme of the socialist apologists for Russian conduct,[29] but he was fairly representative of the

26. John Baird, Left, July, 1946, pp. 149-50; see also J. M. Taylor, Left, March, 1946, p. 51; and New Statesman, XXXII (August 17, 1946), 109.

27. Glasgow Forward, October 4, 1947, p. 5.

28. Reflections on the Constitution (Manchester: Manchester University Press, 1951), p. 86. Other examples of Laski's views may be found in his address as chairman of the Labour party (45th Annual Report of the Labour Party, p. 106) and in the Left News, March, 1946, pp. 3448-51.

29. K. Zilliacus was the most extreme of the non-Stalinists, and, despite his temporary loss of Labour party status, he maintained a reputation among socialist semi-intellectuals for expertness in international affairs. His prolific output may be sampled in the 47th Annual Report of the Labour Party, pp. 185-86; at 427 H.C. Deb. 1711-26 (October 23, 1946), 464 H.C. Deb. 2073-83 (May 12, 1949), 467 H.C. Deb. 1029-42 (July 18, 1949)—to select only a few of many parliamentary remarks;

subtle transformation of left-wing attitudes from the old willingness to believe the best to a postwar unwillingness to believe the worst of the Soviet Union. Russia might seem different from the promised land it had once been for the British left, but there was enough of the old faith to preclude a frank recognition of Soviet aggressive intentions. Particularly was this evident in 1946 and 1947, when the New Statesman seemed incapable of imputing anything worse than error to Russian policy-making. Early in this period the hope was expressed that "the realists in the Kremlin" would again offer "the confused capitalist world an example of peaceful and successful Communism."[30] When the New Statesman did grant that Russia was unfriendly and unco-operative, the journal considered this less a sign of enmity than of a desire for "complete intellectual and physical isolation from the West."[31] Or it was argued that the Soviet did not constitute a military threat to the West, either because of a presumed Russian weakness or because of the assumption that Communist rulers, unlike Hitler, aimed at conquest mainly by pacific means.[32]

Although these rationalizations concerning Soviet policy had their American parallels (certainly in the Wallace campaign of 1947-48), what was different about the optimism of the British left was that it was usually independent of direct Communist manipulation. Therefore, in Britain, despite the fact that right-wing socialists, in the postwar period, increasingly expressed a definite anticommunism,[33] the left's relatively favorable views of the Soviet Union continued to maintain both an intellectual and a political home within the Labour party. To be fair, however, even the New Statesman did not carry into the 1950's its long-

and in Political Quarterly, XXII (January-March, 1951), 85-94; Manchester Guardian Weekly, May 3, 1951, p. 7. The expulsion of Zilliacus was debated by the Labour conference (48th Annual Report of the Labour Party [London, 1949], pp. 119-27). His re-entry was accomplished more quietly.

30. XXXI (March 23, 1946), 204.

31. XXXI (April 13, 1946), 257.

32. XXXIII (April 26, 1947), 287-88, and XXXVII (April 2, 1949), 316.

33. E.g., Socialist Union, a Labour party group formed in 1951 for the purpose of stating anew the principles of socialism (from a right-of-Bevanite point of view), granted that the socialist movement had for long been "blind to the true nature of the Russian regime and burdened with a feeling that it was necessary in some way to justify it" (Socialism: A New Statement of Principles [London: Lincolns-Prager, 1952], p. 20).

standing assurance that Russia would refrain from using military force. While the chance of a major war provoked by the Communists was always minimized, the need for some Western military preparation against Russian aggression was granted. The left-wing editors, especially R. H. S. Crossman,[34] were at least spasmodically aware of the exigencies of world politics. Hard as it was to treat the Soviet Union as a potential enemy, the Labour Left generally, as well as its principal intellectual organ, finally did so—but within limits of socialist choosing.

One of the special ways in which the left viewed the Soviet military threat, in the early 1950's, was to estimate its potency at a much lower level than was common. This minimizing tendency cannot be entirely attributed to the hangover of old beliefs in Soviet good intentions, since there was also the habitual left-wing reluctance to face up to any military problems. But when Aneurin Bevan, for example, spoke of the United States overrating Communist armed strength,[35] he was, in fact, appealing to the socialists who had formerly refused to believe altogether in Russian preparation for aggression. The low estimate of the Communist threat was peculiarly congenial in light of the reluctance with which that threat had been recognized in the first place.

Significantly, there was more than this shadowy remnant of socialist optimism in Aneurin Bevan's latter-day views of the Soviet Union. He seemed to suggest that, in the long run, Communist totalitarianism would so develop that it could be peacefully dealt with by the West.[36] The fact that it had not yet developed in that way Bevan considered no mark against basic Soviet conceptions. On the contrary, he peddled, in 1951, the old left-wing theory of why Russia had originally gone off the peaceful track:

> Let us also remember that the Soviet revolution would not have been distorted, would not have ended in a tyranny, would not have resulted in a dictatorship, would not now be threatening the peace of mankind, had it not been for the behaviour of Churchill and the Tories at that time. Do not forget that in the early days when that great mass of backward people were trying to find their way to the light, were

---

34. Crossman was probably the principal champion of the Labour Left's approach to foreign policy, in the New Statesman and in Parliament, but he did not share all the ideological background of his socialist supporters. He was more sophisticated on every count—attitude toward the Soviet Union, capitalism, and power politics. Yet, despite frequent deviations along highly personal intellectual lines, Crossman generally verbalized the international aspirations typical of the left.

35. In Place of Fear (New York: Simon & Schuster, 1952), pp. 130-35.

36. Ibid., p. 146.

trying to lift themselves from age-long penury and oppression, they were diverted from their objectives and thrown back into the darkness, not by the malignancy of Stalin at first, but by the action and malignancy of Churchill, the City of London, New York and all the rest of the capitalist world.[37]

Equipped with this strange view of recent world history, it was no wonder that the Labour Left shrunk from the prospect of using force to check Russian force and even more so from a strong policy against more recently founded Communist states (like China). It was assumed that a left-wing revolution was essentially good and only led astray by hostile outside reactions.

Antipathy to Power Politics

Dislike for the exercise of power in international affairs was not the exclusive property of socialists in the modern world. The outlook was much more widespread than that. In Britain and in America it was for long the international counterpart of liberal and humanitarian domestic programs. The Marxist had not been alone in thinking imperialism wicked and lumping it with such contemptibles as large military establishments, conscription, and balance-of-power diplomacy. Especially in the 1920's and early 1930's the aversion to the use of force as an instrument of policy, even as means of keeping the peace, was a fixture of Anglo-American opinion. Disarmament was the badge of liberal respectability. Most English liberals as well as socialists, and some Americans of similar persuasions, accepted the League of Nations as signaling the end of power politics and only very late in the interwar period appreciated the League's impotence without the use of force to back its decisions. Many of the old delusions never died, and after World War II they were revived in the shape of exaggerated claims for the efficacy of the United Nations. However, among nonsocialists in Britain and also in America (where there were, of course, very few socialists) the old antipathy to power politics did not fully reassert its hold. Its principal postwar location was in socialist quarters. There it received intellectual nourishment, and there it still flourished.[38]

---

37. Fiftieth Annual Report of the Labour Party (London, 1951), p. 121.

38. Note the comment on the "ethical repugnance to the use of power" by M. A. Fitzsimons, "British Labour in Search of a Socialist Foreign Policy," Review of Politics, XII (April, 1950), 203.

One reason for the special tenacity of socialist antipathy was that it had been so definite an article of Labour faith in the interwar period. Then, whether Britain should be armed was a question of political moment. The Labour party had stood essentially for disarmament until after the mid-thirties, only changing its official position when the Fascist menace loomed ominously large. Prior to the painful conversion, even Clement Attlee (who, as an advocate of collective security, replaced the pacifist George Lansbury as party leader) had maintained, in 1935: "It is impossible for us to get any kind of security through rearmament. The only way we can have it is by trusting each other, and armaments breed distrust."[39] In the same year Hugh Dalton, who shortly afterward was a prime factor in shifting the party from pacifism and disarmament, was also writing in the older, customary vein and urging a disarmament treaty with Hitler instead of engaging in an arms race by building up the Royal Air Force.[40] The commitment to disarmament, as late as the mid-1930's, by such responsible spokesmen shows how deeply the bias against power politics was intrenched in the Labour party. Neither Attlee nor Dalton operated at the margins of the party, and, while their language might have represented a play to a pacifist-minded gallery, that too was significant.

The Labour party did not, as a whole, shift readily from disarmament to armed security. The record of its change was slow and reluctant, especially in the section of the party which, in its personnel and ideas, had much in common with the present-day Labour Left. There was a good deal to be converted from. In the twenties Labour had opposed the power politics represented by the French postwar system of alliances and in the early thirties had opposed what inklings there were of a Tory policy of rearmanent.[41] It was not that Labour generally admitted any disbelief in collective security. It simply did not believe, at the time, in building up the necessary system of power. On the contrary, many Labour beliefs came close to suggesting that only through universal disarmanent would international order be possible. Mixed with this general attitude was the

---

39. Daily Herald, April 4, 1935, p. 17

40. Political Quarterly, VI (July-September, 1935), 327.

41. Interwar views were described with objectivity by William R. Tucker, The Attitude of the British Labour Party towards European and Collective Security Problems, 1920-39 (Geneva: University of Geneva, 1950), pp. 71-76, 96-97.

particularly strong feeling against military conscription, which Labour fought officially as late as April, 1939.[42]

However, despite its continued prewar stand against compulsory military service, the Labour party had, in 1937, taken the crucial decision to support British rearmanent. Although this was voted overwhelmingly by the Labour conference, there was a significant opposition to the change of policy. The veteran George Lansbury presented the straight pacifist argument,[43] and a rising young politician named Aneurin Bevan advanced a special left-wing case. Bevan would have been prepared, he indicated, to supply arms to carry out a Labour foreign policy, but he was unwilling to trust the Conservative government with any additional military strength.[44] This seemed to carry hostility to his political opponents to a startling length. Since there was no prospect of a change in British governments in time to affect Hitler's plans, the upshot of Bevan's position was to maintain the tradition of Labour hostility to the exercise of power. But, in founding his argument on opposition to a Conservative government having the arms to create British strength, Bevan articulated the distinctive aspect of the socialist abhorrence of power politics. It was power as an instrument of the *Tory view* the national interest that the Left did not recognize as valid. As Bevan said, arms for a socialist cause, for world peace, or against fascism would have been acceptable. Since in Bevan's mind the building of British national power was unrelated to those objectives, rearmament would have to wait.

In a modified form this tradition was carried into the postwar period. However, absolute pacifism also retained its adherents in the Labour party and occasionally in prominent places. Within the parliamentary ranks there were vigorous pacifist spokesmen, among whom Rhys Davies and Emrys Hughes were conspicuous. They consistently opposed military measures of all sorts and strongly criticized the American policies which stressed rearmament. In these respects, their position resembled the main bias of the Labour Left, although Hughes identified himself as a Quaker,[45] and Davies declared: "I will do or

---

42. Ibid., p. 212.

43. 37th Annual Report of the Labour Party (London, 1937), pp. 199-201.

44. Ibid., pp. 208-9.

45. 463 H.C. Deb. 508 (March 23, 1949).

say nothing which would induce the use of force between one man and another for any purpose whatsoever."[46] Evidently this absolute pacifism was on the wane in the Labour party, but Hughes especially was always assured of a hearing.[47] He occupied a unique position as the son-in-law of Keir Hardie, the venerated founder of the Labour party. Also Hughes had been, from 1931 to 1946, the editor of Forward, the principal socialist paper in Scotland, for which he continued to write regularly after 1946.

In practice, the strictly pacifist wing, with aid from less clearly defined sources, opposed the Labour party's postwar commitment to peacetime conscription.[48] Parliamentary spokesmen like Hughes and Davies were joined at Labour conferences by an occasional fellow-pacifist, and the ranks of unsuccessful parliamentary candidates did not lack for a pacifist example.[49] How much pacifism remained among the rank and file is difficult to estimate, but it would be surprising, in a movement whose attractions were so broadly humanitarian, not to find a fair assortment of pacifists along with foes of liquor and capital punishment. This was most likely in the areas of religious nonconformity, especially in Wales, where Christian principles often provided the basis for socialism. The route to pacifism as well as to equalitarianism had often started with a nonconformist interpretation of the Gospel.

Nevertheless, absolute pacifism was not the prime influence in fixing the general hostility to power politics. It was not, for instance, from so extreme a religious or ethical basis that the Labour Left reacted to the first and rather tentative proclamation of postwar Anglo-American policy—the famous Fulton address of Winston Churchill in March, 1946.[50]

46. 456 H.C. Deb. 944 (September 22, 1948).

47. Samples of the Hughes-Davies pacifist advocacy: 457 H.C. Deb. 1312-17 (November 8, 1948), 464 H.C. Deb. 2064-70 (May 12, 1949), 472 H.C. Deb. 1377-79 (March 16, 1950), 477 H.C. Deb. 552-58 (July 5, 1950), and 49th Annual Report of the Labour Party (London, 1950), p. 144.

48. 46th Annual Report of the Labour Party, pp. 108-13.

49. Early in 1951 Clement Attlee, then prime minister, and other Labour leaders were embarrassed by the nomination in a parliamentary by-election of an out-and-out pacifist (New York Times, February 11, 1951, Sec. 1, p. 26). It was usual for there to be a pacifist, among others, in every rearmament debate at a party conference; e.g., see the 51st Annual Report of the Labour Party (London, 1952), p. 146.

50. Text of the Fulton address in the New York Times, March 6, 1946, p. 4.

The adverse socialist reactions to this speech, while they were not at the time peculiar to one political position, did display the intensity of the Labour Left's allergic sensitivity to the calling-up of power to check opposing power. Churchill's "fraternal association of English-speaking peoples" represented, to the Labour Left, an old-fashioned military alliance to "frighten Soviet Russia into submission"[51] and "the shortest way to create the gulf across which the next war will be fought."[52] Underlying these remarks, to be sure, was the still widely prevalent hope that the U.S.S.R. really would be peacefully co-operative in the brave new world of the United Nations. But equally striking was the Labour Left's evident belief that the mere suggestion of an Anglo-American combination would work to destroy the possibilities of co-operation. To an extraordinary extent, Churchill was subsequently blamed for the rallying of American "reactionaries," which, it was claimed, had started a cycle of power politics leading to the complete East-West impasse of 1948 and after. Even in 1950 a frequent foreign-policy critic, while placing much of the blame for the cold war on Russia, insisted that Churchill had fired "the first shots" at Fulton.[53] The very essence of checking power with power, epitomized by Churchill in the modern world, was morally offensive to the Labour Left. Perhaps the method was considered especially offensive because it was directed at communism, but it was disliked for its own sake as well.

This state of mind made for hostility to much of the policy associated with the United States. The Truman Doctrine of aid to Greece and Turkey was anathema. American possession of atomic bombs and American capacity to deliver such bombs (from British bases, among others) constituted a threat of force that the left found unacceptable in the conduct of international relations. More and more the Churchillian Anglo-American power bloc seemed to become an American bloc from which, it was often urged, Britain should dissociate itself in a military sense. Logically this repugnance to postwar power politics should have led its left-wing champions to the full-blown neutralism of many Continental intellectuals. This was seldom the case.[54] Perhaps the explanation lay in the reputed

---

51. Tribune, March 8, 1946, p. 1.

52. Michael Foot (423 H.C. Deb. 1931 [June 4, 1946]).

53. Sydney Silverman (often charged with fellow-traveling) (476 H.C. Deb. 2139 [June 27, 1950]).

54. One close approach was that of Leonard Woolf, Foreign Policy ("Fabian Research Series," No. 121 [London, 1947]).

unwillingness of the British mind to push a narrowly and rigorously
logical line to the exclusion of all the realities.

Anticapitalism

More than by any other underlying factor, the Labour Left's response to American foreign policy was determined by the traditional
socialist suspicion of capitalism. This was specifically reflected in the
left-wing attitudes toward anti-Soviet moves, but it was also more directly related to whatever the United States did in world affairs. To the full-
blooded socialist, America as the nation of big business was bound to
have the international motivations, manifest or incipient, supposedly
characteristic of a highly developed capitalism. In applying this ideology
to postwar foreign policy, the Labour Left was only carrying on what had
formerly been the doctrine of most of the Labour party. With some justification, the left felt that the party leadership (especially when in government offices) had departed from the customary outlook of the movement.
To have a socialist foreign policy, distinct from the Conservatives at
home and from capitalist governments abroad, had been a **first principle**
of opposition. Clement Attlee had expressed its essence in 1937:

> There is a deep difference of opinion between the Labour Party
> and the Capitalist parties in foreign as well as home policy, because
> the two cannot be separated. The foreign policy of a Government
> is the reflection of its internal policy. Imperialism is the form
> which Capitalism takes in relation to other nations.[55]

Attlee granted that it was not for Labour to oppose everything a British
capitalist government did in international affairs, but, he said, "such
particular instances of action which can be approved by Socialists do
not affect the truth of the general proposition that there is no agreement
on foreign policy between a Labour Opposition and a **Capitalist Government**."[56] These were not random remarks from the political hustings
but the evidently studied thoughts in Attlee's book on the Labour party.
He thought enough of the book to have it republished in 1949,[57] although
by that time the foreign policies of his government belied, for many
socialists, what he had written.

---

55. The Labour Party in Perspective (London: Gollancz, 1937), p. 226.

56. Ibid., p. 227.

57. The book was unchanged (also the publisher), but there was added
     a short foreword by Attlee and a longer introduction by Francis
     Williams.

If, however, Attlee's government did not, or could not, act on the basis of a uniquely socialist international line, many in his party had long continued to profess that oft-repeated principle of their movement. The thought was a prominent feature of international discussion by the left on the eve of Labour's electoral victory in 1945,[58] and it never completely vanished. Significantly, its postwar inspiration was similar to that which called for a more thoroughgoing socialist domestic policy. The source was the same class-angled, emotional tradition that almost always preferred more radical change than that presented by official Labour policy. If not simply more Marxist than the party leadership, the postwar Labour Left was at least more likely to champion both public ownership and the leveling of classes than it was to rest its case on the efficacy of fiscal measures and social security. Theirs was not so much the socialism of a generation of government officials as it was the pure milk of the lamb. The Labour Left had in its ranks the old spirit of rebellion that had animated the pioneers of what was only recently a decided minority movement against all the powers that were. Now, to rebel against the rich and strong meant simply to be dead set against American capitalism.

The indeterminate Marxist component, hovering more than ruling over British socialist thought, was of some moment in fixing the image of America as well as of Russia. The two were really opposite sides of the same intellectual coin: what the New Statesman called "one of the most deeply rooted traditions of British Socialism."[59] Thus, in trying to refute the case for Ernest Bevin's policy of co-operation with the United States, the New Statesman insisted that Bevin's proponents disregarded, "as Liberal theory always has done, the Socialist analysis of the causes of both war and revolution. . . ."[60] "Socialist analysis" meant, among other things, that capitalism and capitalist nations pursued imperialist policies that caused wars. Specifically, in the postwar period, it led to a wariness of the United States. Leftist intellectuals, at many levels, were so instructed by their most energetic mentor, Harold Laski. In his version of Marxism-Leninism, American big business,

---

58. Not untypical, at the time, was Leonard Woolf, The International Post-war Settlement ("Fabian Research Series," No. 85 [London, 1944])

59. XXXII (December 7, 1946), 411.

60. Ibid., p. 412. What the New Statesman called "Liberal theory" really included most of the international thinking of right-wing socialists.

in caricature, was responsible alike for reactionary domestic policies and, in partnership with career militarists, for imperialist foreign policies.[61] Laski was significant not only because of his acknowledged influence as a teacher and writer. His attitude presented an interesting and revealing example of how even a large number of personally pleasant relationships with America and Americans did not alter the stereotype of capitalist wickedness.

What, from the outside, seemed a stereotype, and a rather worn one at that, remained part of the socialist's living faith. It was reiterated with special emphasis by Barbara Castle, speaking for the left in its Bevanite phase: "We are not anti-American. We are anti-capitalist—or used to be. Let us stick at least to those fundamental principles which alone can guide us through this chaotic world, and insist that the measuring rod of Socialism shall be applied to our international activities."[62] The meaning of this socialist measuring rod Aneurin Bevan intended to explain in his political summation, In Place of Fear. It differed little from the familiar lines of economic determinism, especially in the doctrinaire disbelief in the stable existence of a capitalist democracy. In that kind of society, he said, "either poverty will use democracy to win the struggle against property, or property, in fear of poverty, will destroy democracy."[63] Capitalism, Bevan was sure, could not secure willing consent in any country where it had achieved complete victory. The United States he refused to accept as a rebuttal of this contention, since its history, he said, was yet too short for any claims of permanence.[64]

For Bevan to accept American capitalism as different in kind from the British and European capitalism he rejected would have been most unsocialist.

---

61. Laski's postwar views of American foreign policy are to be found in many writings, but mainly in The American Democracy (New York: Viking Press, 1948), chap. xi, especially pp. 542-43. His audience was unquestionably very broad, both through his many books and pamphlets but also through his heavily attended lectures at the London School of Economics. Among British left-wing academics, Laski was almost a special case: he did not combine criticism of American capitalism with an upper-class snobism concerning American culture.

62. London Times, March 10, 1952, p. 3.

63. In Place of Fear, p. 3.

64. Ibid., pp. 58-59.

Capitalism was assumed to be fundamentally the same phenomenon everywhere. This not only was according to Marx, from whose doctrines Bevan claimed to have had his political training, but was derived from other sources as well. In fact, rather than being capable of making any kind of favorable exception for American capitalism, Bevan was more likely to think it unusually evil. For one thing, it was bigger and stronger than the home-grown product. And, besides, Aneurin Bevan had been schooled, before imbibing Marxism, on Jack London's lurid fictional account of the last Fascist-type stand of American capitalism against socialist revolutionaries.[65] The impact of such a picture of the United States, especially when absorbed in formative years, should not be underestimated. However, even without it, [there is every reason to think that the Labour Left regarded America, because it was capitalism incarnate, as the likeliest villain in world affairs.]

The Labour Left's immediate postwar reactions were in this vein. No doubt the unpopularity of the termination of lend-lease and the conditions of the Anglo-American Loan Agreement, previously described, contributed to bad feeling. But the fact that the left responded so much more vigorously than most of the rest of the British community indicated a predisposition to ascribe unfavorable motives to the United States. While the war was still on, in early 1945, Michael Foot, journalist and subsequently a member of Parliament, had already been convinced that American capitalism was "in one of its most arrogant moods."[66] This had some unpleasant connotations for those socialists who possessed the idée fixe that American bankers had deliberately produced Britain's economic crisis of 1931 and so forced the last prewar Labour government from office. Consequently, they were psychologically prepared to expect enmity for their postwar government.

The Truman Administration, in its first years, appeared to the British left to be as bent on destroying socialism as was almost every other force in the United States.[67] The American offensive, Tribune

65. See In Place of Fear, p. 19, for Bevan's account of the influence of Jack London, The Iron Heel (New York: Macmillan Co, 1908). One of the most learned and lucid British political scientists, D. W. Brogan, has written that "it is not being unreasonable to attribute Mr. Bevan's permanent suspicion of American policy to this literary cause as well as to his general social doctrine" (New York Times Book Review, May 4, 1952, p. 1).

66. Left News, January, 1945, p. 3044.

67. New Statesman, XXXI (June 1, 1946), 385.

editorialized, came from "the most merciless champions of competitive capitalism left on the face of this planet."[68] It was common enough to believe that to link up with America was to "destroy a chance of Socialism at home or abroad."[69] Just what the United States was going to do to destroy British socialism was never very clear and can properly be compared with American imaginings of a British imperial plot against the United States. Britain, it was insisted, was being "dragged at the heels of American big business and their representatives."[70] In 1947 one socialist newspaper was more explicit when it said that "the men who rule America are determined to go to any length to stop the development of Socialism and to open up the world as a vast colonial area for American capitalism."[71]

In relation to prevailing dogma, a special reason may be advanced for this temper of the Labour Left between 1945 and 1947. This was a time, shortly after Labour's advent to power, when socialism seemed most optimistically opposed to capitalism as such. In the full flush of enthusiasm over the nationalization that was to transform British society, it was easy to focus on American capitalism as a clear-cut opponent of the new way of life. Perhaps this helps explain why at the 1946 conference of the Trades Union Congress there was a very large minority supporting a resolution which objected to the "tying of the economy of Britain with that of capitalist America."[72] The unions had not generally been friendly to such ideological strictures. But late 1946 and early 1947 represented a high point in left-wing suspicion of American capitalism. It was then that the "Keep Left" group flourished in Parliament and published in a widely circulated pamphlet its complaints against the British alliance with a right-wing American government and a free-enterprise system.[73]

---

68. October 5, 1945, p. 2.

69. W. G. Cove, M.P., Left, October, 1945, p. 513.

70. Ellis Smith (430 H.C. Deb. 222 [November 13, 1946]).

71. Reynolds News, March 16, 1947, p. 4.

72. 78th Annual Report of the Trades Union Congress (London, 1946), p. 469. The vote for the resolution was 2,444,000, with 3,557,000 registered against.

73. R. H. S. Crossman, Michael Foot, and Ian Mikardo, Keep Left (New Statesman pamphlet [London, 1947]). In addition to the authors, twelve other Labour members of Parliament were committed to this pamphlet.

Tied to the socialist belief that capitalism meant war was the wide-spread assumption that the American economy was headed for a severe depression or, in British terminology, "slump." This not only made an American economic partnership seem dangerous for Britain; it also served to confirm the Labour Left in its vision of capitalism, beset by contractions in the domestic market, turning to armament, to imperialism, and to war. The inevitability of an American slump was, through all the postwar period, a set piece of the left-wing socialist thought which was still largely unmoved by Keynesian ideas. For the real socialists the palliatives of Lord Keynes were not enough to avert a slump or the con-sequences of a slump. On principle, only "socialism" could do that. Since America had not and apparently would not adopt socialist remedies, then the worst was to be expected. Indeed, this was forecast over and over, and with the certainty typical of prophets of doom.[74]

The many who believed in the uniqueness of the Labour government's promised solution of economic problems found it unthinkable that any benighted capitalist country could escape its fate. "Relative stability" in Britain was contrasted with "economic chaos in the U.S."[75] And out of that chaos of uncontrolled capitalism, how could any honest-to-goodness socialist think an economic slump was not to come—unless he were to turn his back on all his doctrinal upbringing and perform the nearly impossible task of shifting the ideological orientations with which he had always faced the world. British socialism, be it remembered, was now more than the passing intellectual fancy of one generation. It was a religion which had provided sustenance in the dark era before the dawn of 1945.

Consequently, the really firm prophets were not severely shaken as the postwar years of American prosperity rolled by. Only a few doubts had to be taken into account. In 1949 the New Statesman paid intellectual notice to the continued American boom that was gnawing at the vitals of socialist orthodoxy. Editorially, there was now an inclination to think that the United States might escape "the dilemma of over-production

74. To cite only a few of many examples, there were the remarks of the not-so-far left P. C. Gordon-Walker, 415 H.C. Deb. 1310 (November 7, 1945), and 437 H.C. Deb. 1825 (May 15, 1947); or, to take a mis-cellany of sources, Alaric Jacobs, "The Big Two and Ourselves," Political Quarterly, XVII (April-June, 1946), 114; New Statesman, XXXII (November 9, 1946), 330; and Mrs. Leah Manning, 443 H.C. Deb. 189 (October 22, 1947).

75. T. Driberg (430 H.C. Deb. 361 [November 14, 1946]).

without recourse to solutions of aggressive imperialism."[76] Even then, at the low point in the fulfilment of socialist predictions, the New Statesman was hedging its bet. It allowed that "the refusal of the ruling class in the United States to tolerate greater equality of incomes may ultimately bring to a head the classical contradiction of capitalism."[77] About a year later an Oxford economic seer, Thomas Balogh, was more confident of the fundamental socialist prophecy. There was, he granted, a recovery from the recession of mid-1949, but it might only be a transient recovery. "The probability," he said, "is that the American slump will be aggravated."[78]

How widely the socialist confidence in American economic depression continued to be shared in the Labour movement is difficult to estimate. The impact of hearing the prediction over and over, from press, Parliament, and platform, was bound to make some mark. Besides, a part of the working class was prepared to accept the likelihood of an American slump by something more meaningful than doctrine alone. The prolonged character of British unemployment before the war, and the advent of a Labour government, was one factor. Another was the story of the American depression in the 1930's. This had not been merely a large news item for many British workers. Some, notably from the Glasgow area, had themselves suffered American breadlines and soup kitchens, after leaving the already depressed Britain of the 1920's. They barely tasted the promise of American prosperity before the crash. It was not surprising that many returned with stories of the acute hardships of unemployment in pre-New Deal America, without social security or public works' spending. Even after twenty intervening years there were to be found working-class tales, first, second, or even third hand, of the hardness of American life in the great depression. It was easy to believe in the reality of its second coming.

At the intellectual level, explaining away the continued American prosperity became easier for socialists after 1950. It was simply said that good times were sustained by the rearmament program and implied that the acceleration of this program was made necessary because America was unwilling to adopt socialist remedies. This point was put in the language of the professional socialist

76. XXXVII (February 26, 1949), 196.

77. Ibid.

78. The Dollar Crisis (London: Blackwell, 1950), p. xvii.

economist[79] and also in the rhetoric of Aneurin Bevan:

> The United States of America is a very powerful and very rich country, and if great wealth, if great productive capacity, can rid a country of fear, then America ought to be the most self-satisfied and the most tranquil country in the world. But on the contrary America is hag-ridden by two fears, fear of war and fear of unemployment which is fear of peace. Read the publicists and read the commentators and you are told that the United States of America is a living monument to the success of competitive capitalism. The fact is that at the present moment American industry is being kept in full spate by the biggest piece of public enterprise she has ever undertaken—a big arms programme. . . . Economists in America, bankers, industrialists, all of them are frightened of the industrial consequences of a let-up in this vast rearmament programme. Why? Because there is no socialist planning in America to dispose of the surpluses when they arise.[80]

This passage, delivered to the 1952 Labour conference, was interrupted by "loud cheers," to employ the ever moderate language of the Times.[81] Actually Bevan's pronouncements on American prosperity were greeted with all the pent-up enthusiasm of the faithful. Here was a leader offering dramatic reassurance: capitalist prosperity could not be real. No socialist need think it was.

In addition to this doctrinal certainty, there was also a much wider British feeling that American prosperity was somehow temporary and that it depended on a fortuitous combination of pent-up wartime demand, extraordinary overseas aid, and, finally, an armaments boom. The consequences of substantial American governmental retrenchment of public expenditures were feared by economists of many persuasions. Indeed, it was known that numerous Americans shared this same fear and lacked full confidence either in the economy's ability to maintain its postwar levels or in the American Administration's capacity to apply adequate Keynesian remedies. But to have doubts about America's economic future was very different from the left wing's positive assurance that capitalism was bound to fail.

79. "Unless very revolutionary intellectual progress is made in the United States in the direction of the Fourth Point & c., it is difficult to see how they can afford not to increase armaments at an accelerating rate" (Thomas Balogh, letter to the London Times, January 16, 1952, p. 5).

80. 51st Annual Report of the Labour Party, pp. 82-83.

81. September 30, 1952, p. 2. "Loud cheers" were distinguished from what were called "Cheers" at another point; the former was typical British understatement for what an American would call "almost tearing down the house."

Perhaps the Bevanite prophecy served to fortify the socialist élan in relation to American economic success. However, as part of a larger anticapitalist outlook the left-wing critique of the American economy was chiefly significant because it indicted war against communism in terms of capitalist imperialism. It summoned the leftist flock to believe once again that armaments were in proportion to the exigencies of capitalist society, that overseas strong points against Russian advance were bastions of colonial exploitation, and that wars were Wall Street adventures in quest of markets.

Marginal Character of the Labour Left

There is an obvious sense in which the Labour Left was marginal. It represented opinion near (though not quite at) one extremity of the Labour party. But most of the Labour Left was also marginal by virtue of the fluctuations in its attitudes toward the United States. Socialist suspicion was a postwar constant, but hostility was operative during the first postwar years and the early 1950's in a way that it was not during the era of Anglo-American good feeling—roughly from late 1947 to late 1950. Among some of the Labour Left there was little discernible shift; among others good feeling was perhaps a little grudging; but there was an articulate majority genuinely hopeful about the United States in the late 1940's. What caused British left-wing socialists, without forsaking their socialism, to see America in a favorable light? The answer helps to explain a state of mind which is at once different from that of the Communist and fellow-traveler, and from that of the liberal democrat.

Evidently the Marshall Plan was the principal impetus for the favorable image of the United States. It was liked so much that the Labour Left could not ascribe its motivation to capitalists. Tribune, warmly praising Secretary Marshall's proposals, claimed that, instead of acting on the advice of business groups, "his counsels came from other quarters, progressive and relatively powerful."[82] The editorial went on to speak of New Dealers, trade-unions, and liberals. These were the elements which the Labour Left, especially in the pages of Tribune, began to consider the dominant forces in the Truman Administration and in American politics generally. No longer did big business appear in the saddle, oppressing the weak at home and abroad. Now the picture of American government was

---

82. June 13, 1947, p. 2.

transformed into something with which a socialist could identify, not precisely but generally at any rate. Or most socialists could manage it.

There were some exceptions. Harold Laski remained dubious; he thought American aid might be used to rebuild the old class order.[83] Geoffrey Bing, M.P., was still declaring in mid-1948 that the European Recovery Program was bound to founder if "coupled with a cold war with the Soviet Union";[84] he wanted Britain to get ready to dispense with American aid. And another Labour member of Parliament, Ian Mikardo, was wary enough of American military policies to maintain a separate position of his own.[85] But these were unusual cases. Most of the left-wing criticism of American policies had been temporarily sapped by the external circumstances nearly coincident with the beginning of the Marshall Plan: the Communist coup in Czechoslovakia and the Berlin blockade.

In 1948 the left's infatuation with the potentialities of the Truman Administration was almost unsullied. It was observed that the United States was, after all, a democracy, and therefore its instincts were those of peace.[86] No one actually said that America had ceased to be capitalist, but the unfavorable image just faded away in favor of the stress on common political principles. Truman himself became a minor hero.[87] The New Statesman proclaimed that on domestic issues his recent record had been "sensible economically and shrewd politically."[88] (This was amusingly at variance with the journal's previous omniscient judgments that President Truman was a "simple farmer from the Deep South" or

---

83. Glasgow Forward, July 26, 1947, p. 1.

84. 453 H.C. Deb. 310 (July 6, 1948).

85. See chap. vi for a discussion of Mikardo's objections to the Atlantic Pact.

86. Tribune, April 2, 1948, pp. 1-2.

87. The change in attitude toward the Truman Administration may be observed to have begun in Tribune early in 1947. The editorial opinion of American politics shifted drastically, so that what had been regularly denounced as a hopelessly conservative Administration now became the hope for the free world.

88. This judgment was rendered simultaneously with the New Statesman's disavowal of its old hero, Henry Wallace (XXXV [January 3, 1948], 2).

possessed of "Babbitt-like incompetence.")[89]

The Truman victory of 1948 was greeted happily by the Labour Left, and it opened the way to an almost boundless optimism concerning the leftward future of American politics. More and more, the Democratic party began to look like an American version of the Labour party, and the Fair Deal as the beginning of socialism.[90] Consequently the sources of pro-American sentiments were remarkable. For instance, there was Jennie Lee, M.P., an editor of Tribune, and wife of Aneurin Bevan. The organized workers had "their candidate in the White House." The American people, she deduced from the 1948 election, "were catching up with our ideas of the welfare state."[91] The New Statesman went further in linking the campaign of British socialists with that of American progressives: "Mr Truman's political future is bound up with that of Mr Attlee and Mr Churchill's with Senator Taft's."[92] The announcement of President Truman's Point Four proposals only added to the enthusiasm for the incipient socialist who had hid so long in the snug double-breasted uniform of American business.[93] Clearly this overidentification was too good to last.

While it held, however, there was a large degree of acceptance of America's policy in the cold war. This was, it is true, at a time when the cold war meant relatively few armaments and apparently no large-scale military engagements. On that basis, R. H. S. Crossman, the spokesman of the old "Keep Left" criticism of Anglo-American policy, became a full-throated supporter of the cold war. As a case study, Crossman (despite his obvious erratic deviations) serves the limited purpose of showing how far from a strict anticapitalist foreign-policy basis one of the Labour Left could travel. (Crossman's critics, of course,

---

89. Ibid., XXIX (April 21, 1945), 252, and XXXII (September 28, 1946), 217.

90. E.g., in Tribune, November 5, 1948, pp. 1-2, and January 14, 1949, pp. 1-2; and in Margaret Cole's Foreword to Mark Starr, Labour Politics in U.S.A. ("Fabian Research Series," No. 133 [London, 1949]), pp. 3-4.

91. 460 H.C. Deb. 1195 (January 27, 1949) and 467 H.C. Deb. 723 (July 14, 1949).

92. XXXVIII (October 8, 1949), 373.

93. By all odds, the Point Four program was the favorite of the Labour Left. Witness the New Statesman, XXXVII (January 29, 1949), 95-96; XXXVIII (September 10 and December 24, 1949), 263-64 and 747.

would say that even his anticapitalism was erratic.) The beginning of his foreign-policy conversion from "Keep Left" to "Keep in Step with America" was, typically, the Marshall Plan. This, he pronounced at the start of 1948, was an advance from the military containment of the Fulton speech and the Truman Doctrine. "I will be frank," Crossman told the House of Commons. "My own views about America have changed a great deal in the last six months. Many Members have had a similar experience. I could not have believed six months ago that a plan of this sort would have been worked out in this detail with as few political conditions."[94]

For one of the Labour Left to have supported the Marshall Plan was not in itself news. What was striking was the wholehearted fashion with which Crossman defended the American Administration's policies in other respects. From the old days of imputing the worst motives to the Truman Administration, Crossman had temporarily moved to the point of expecting the best developments from Washington. As late as September, 1950, when the unpopularity of American Far Eastern policy had cast its shadow over some of the Labour Left enthusiasm, Crossman applauded the appointment of Marshall as secretary of defense and continued to bank on "President Truman, and Mr Acheson and the Fair Dealers" as collaborators of the British Labour government.[95] The American Administration, he declared, shared the same ideals and wanted the same sort of world desired by British socialists. And more on this tack was yet to come. In an article published at the very beginning of 1951, Crossman's allegiance to the cold war reached its high-water mark, from which its recession was afterward very rapid. The likelihood of that recession seems, in retrospect, to have been clear from Crossman's concept of the cold war to which he was giving such unstinted allegiance. It was not, he insisted, a straight American anticommunism based principally on military strength. Rather, it was an American policy largely of Crossman's own invention: a world-wide extrapolation of the Marshall Plan along socialist lines. In this sense, Crossman thought the cold war a "creative force" making for international economic planning and a Fair Dealer's manipulation of the United States "back from free enterprise to a controlled economy." Finally the dream took on a grandiose quality: "Accept the Cold War as the challenge of this century and the Fair Deal as a potential ally, and you have the beginnings of a socialist foreign policy which

94. 446 H.C. Deb. 566 (January 23, 1948).

95. 478 H.C. Deb. 1269 (September 14, 1950).

can achieve that 'agreement to disagree' between East and West which is the only alternative to war."[96]

The essence of the Labour Left conception was that the United States and its government had socialist promise and direction. In the matrix of left-wing ideology this was the prerequisite for the Anglo-American alliance. The socialist blinders were never removed so that the realities of international power could be seen as the compelling force. Instead, the blinders were only tilted slightly, and, in the transient circumstances of 1948-50, American foreign policy was somehow related to socialist objectives.

This could be accomplished by the Labour Left only during the American emphasis on economic aid. [When, after 1950, military preparedness became the outstanding aim of the United States, the switch-hitters of the left began to bat from the other side of the plate. In returning, at that time, to their earlier postwar attitudes, socialists were also impelled by a variety of other events, mainly connected with the Far East, which shattered illusions about a left-wing orientation of the United States. The reactions to American policies of the 1950's hardened rapidly into the Bevanite political movement, in which context particular foreign-policy attitudes can best be described.] However, these were not, in fact, divorced from the growingly unfavorable socialist view of American domestic events. For example, the congressional election of 1950, which destroyed lingering hopes for the success of supposed progressive allies in the United States,[97] involved Far Eastern affairs as well as Fair Deal issues. And in such a matter as the growing American desire for a military agreement with Franco Spain (the left's prized enemy), socialists saw a victory for domestic right-wingers as much as a triumph of power politics over ideological sentiment.[98]

---

96. Political Quarterly, XXII (January-March, 1951), 14-15.

97. At this time the New Statesman discarded its remaining hopes for the leftward future of the United States ("America Veers Right," XL [November 11, 1950], 413-14, and a special article by a staff member just returned from the United States, Norman MacKenzie, "The Broken Spectrum," ibid., December 9, 1950, pp. 576-77).

98. Objections to dealings with Franco were frequent, as in Tribune, January 27, 1950, p. 4; March 31, 1950, pp. 5-6; January 12, 1951, pp. 4-5; July 27, 1951, pp. 1-2. Also critical questions were raised in Parliament (491 H.C. Deb. 439-43 [July 25, 1951]).

The fact that the Labour Left had withdrawn its accolade from the American government in 1950 must be borne in mind when considering attitudes toward the American presidential election of 1952. At most the Republican victory added ammunition to a tiresomely familiar campaign against the United States and made for a more lurid portrayal of the economic and political dangers of right-wing policy.[99] It was true that the left, like much of the British political community, had preferred Stevenson but, it would seem, as a lesser evil. Since a Stevenson victory would almost certainly have meant a continuity of America's 1950-52 domestic and foreign policies, it was hard to see how such a result could have caused a cessation of the left-wing hostility which had already been established in relation to those policies. A few progressive straws in the wind might temporarily have diminished the attack, but any repetition of the 1947-50 honeymoon was ruled out by the military emphasis which the United States had adopted in the face of Communist power. American foreign policy was now, by definition, "unsocialist."

---

99. Some immediate postelection examples: Crossman's recollection of "Hooverism" (Sunday Pictorial, November 9, 1952, p. 2); Tribune's black headline, "U.S. Election Brings Peril of a Slump," November 7, 1952, p. 1; and the Reynolds News play on "3 Dangerous Men, Taft, Dulles, and McCarthy," who were headlined as pulling "the strings behind 'Ike'" (November 9, 1952, p. 4).

VI / THE VISION OF THE THIRD FORCE

Sustained dissatisfaction with American leadership was related to the Labour Left's search for an alternative foreign policy. The most obvious choice, and probably the only real one, was to move from the American to the Russian orbit; but, at least after the first few postwar months, this was almost unthinkable and wholly unmentionable among non-Communists. Nor was the Labour Left really so trustful of Russian intentions as to rely on the neutralism toward which the pacifist and semipacifist abhorrence of power politics seemed to lead. Perhaps in time neutralism would have a future in Britain. Its blandishments could become attractive to a new generation reared entirely in the consciousness of the nation's secondary power status.

But in the postwar years Britain still seemed of crucial importance in world affairs, at least as much to the Labour Left as to the rest of the community. Therefore, an alternative foreign policy was ordinarily based on an assumption of British strength—sufficient, at any rate, to build a separate power bloc. This was the doctrine of the Third Force. It combined the neutralist's dislike for both the American and the Russian camps with additional attractions. The essence of the Third Force objective was to achieve ideological independence of both communism and capitalism, as well as international independence of Russian and American power. Democratic socialism was to be the faith, and Britain the focal point of the power bloc. Furthermore, the Third Force had in its heyday of 1945-47 a vague appeal to nonsocialists, who occasionally shared some of the underlying intellectual assumptions of the doctrine.

Bases of Support

In the particular case of its arguments for the Third Force, as in its general antipathies to power politics and capitalist intentions, the Labour Left was the heir to established traditions. The Third Force represented the internationalism that a Labour government was supposed to practice in harmony with social democratic administrations in other countries. The existence of common international objectives among socialists had always been assumed, and this had even included for a

113

time the "socialists" of the Soviet Union. After the Russians had ruled themselves out, the social democrats of the West remained as proper collaborators for a Labour Britain. There was thus maintained a good deal of the pre-1914 fancy that working-class solidarity transcended national boundaries in the form of socialist parties. This had been expressed in the 1920's in a Labour party hope for a combination of British, French, and German socialists, in order to accomplish a European peace that was just and lasting.[1] Since, in those days, Labour had not held the power necessary for such an effort, the idea was still untried in 1945. Thereby lay much of its appeal. It was one of many left-wing conceptions which, it was said, "only needed to be tried" to make for a better world.

At the beginning of Labour's office-holding in 1945, the left wing evidently expected an effort to develop a socialist international grouping. Ernest Bevin, the new foreign secretary, had been known to speak of Britain as in between the United States with its private-enterprise system and Russia with its socialized economy.[2] That he did not put the ideological conception into practice hardly indicates that he did not think of doing so. On the contrary, his biographer has stated that he was urged to seek a Third Force of Western European powers and that he "considered this possibility seriously." The biographer, Francis Williams, added that for a time Bevin "was inclined to favour it. It was an idea which appealed to all his democratic socialist emotions."[3] And it appealed to the "democratic socialist emotions" of the rest of the Labour party as well; so much so that many were less ready than Bevin to accept the dictates of postwar international power. The Labour Left was least ready, of course, but that segment had in the beginning a great deal of company.

A surprisingly large section of the party clung to the old faith long after Bevin had accepted the Anglo-American alliance.[4] What's more,

1. William R. Tucker, The Attitude of the British Labour Party Towards European and Collective Security Problems (Geneva: University of Geneva, 1950), pp. 17, 242.

2. 44th Annual Report of the Labour Party (London, 1945), p. 115.

3. Francis Williams, Ernest Bevin (London: Hutchinson, 1952), p. 262.

4. A year after the end of the war, R. R. Stokes, M.P., later a Labour minister, and not representative of the left so much as of his own Catholic social philosophy, spoke of the possibility of British Labour establishing "a Christian Socialist order in Western Europe" and of

Bevin's acceptance was not always recognized by his own defenders. At the Trades Union Congress of 1947, for example, in replying to a left-wing attack on Britain's ties with "dollar diplomacy," one union leader declared that Bevin and the Labour government were really pursuing a foreign policy that was "socialist" in the sense of being "between American capitalism and Russian Communism."[5] Quite probably this was so much the language of the Labour movement that any defense of foreign policy had to be couched in the old terms. It could not bluntly be admitted, only two years after the promises of 1945, that the Third Force was but a mirage.

The Labour Left pressed the doctrine more fervently as the likelihood of its adoption faded into the background. In part, this was because its conviction about the special mission of democratic socialism had been so definite in the first place. At the beginning of the 1945 Parliament, Michael Foot had declared: "Britain stands today at the summit of her power and glory, and we hold that position because today, following the Election, we have something unique to offer."[6] The Anglo-American alliance was a Churchillian legacy from which a socialist government had to make its ideological departure.[7] Foreign Minister Bevin should seek a policy that lay between "the sharp alternatives of a world ruled by America and a world ruled by Russia," as the Labour government at home was seeking "a middle way between capitalism and Communist planning."[8]

For Bevin not to pursue this middle way in foreign affairs (it was pretty clear by mid-1946 that he had gone in another direction) was to doom democratic socialism itself to failure. Somehow, it was figured, socialism would fail at home unless it was strengthened and spread abroad. In the words of the "Keep Left" members of Parliament, the

---

the desirability of a "Socialist planned economy" in Germany (427 H.C. Deb. 1729, 1732 [October 23, 1946]).

5. 79th Annual Report of the Trades Union Congress (London, 1947), p. 487.

6. 413 H.C. Deb. 340 (August 20, 1945).

7. William Warbey, M.P., "Britain and U.S.A.," Left News, December, 1946, pp. 3724-27.

8. New Statesman, XXXII (September 21, 1946), 199.

world should be offered more than "anti-Communism and Communism."[9]
Instead of the anticommunism of capitalist America, Labour Britain
was to represent the noncommunism of the socialist state. Political democracy, it was admitted, was shared with the United States; but, as part
of the left's residuum of pro-Sovietism, something called "economic democracy" was shared with the Soviet Union. British socialists thought
that they had a fortunate combination of the two.

The conceptions at the base of the "middle-way" formula were never
made any plainer. In this connection, as in the approach to Russia generally, the Labour Left did not trouble to explain in what sense the Soviet was
an "economic democracy." The term was just accepted, although its two
obvious meanings, either of relative equality of incomes or of freedom
of opportunity, were manifestly absurd as descriptions of economic life
in the Soviet Union. But, as a myth, Russian economic democracy was
of value to the British left. After it ceased to be primarily useful as
the basis for urging a British understanding with the Soviet Union, the
idea served as the intellectual underpinning for the apostles of the Third
Force. Only by attributing to Russia one of the socialist virtues could
Labour Britain be said to represent a middle way between Russia and the
United States. It was as necessary to the mental creation of the Third
Force to describe Russia as an economic democracy as it was to play
down the importance of political democracy as a factor in Anglo-American unity.[10] If the idea of the Third Force was to be cherished, Labour
Britain could neither appear entirely dissimilar to the Soviet system
nor almost completely similar to the American. With respect to the
United States, this required just the opposite ideological gymnastics to
those employed between 1948 and 1950 to establish a social democratic
bond with the Truman Administration. But, given the intellectual quasi-
Marxist moorings of the Labour Left, the rationale of the Third Force
was the more congenial.

Among those for whom the Third Force had an irresistible fascina-
tion were the remnants of the Independent Labour party. Not only had its
interwar revolutionary spirit contributed in general to the Labour party,

---

9. R. H. S. Crossman, Michael Foot, and Ian Mikardo, Keep Left (New
Statesman pamphlet [London, 1947]), p. 34.

10. Socialist Commentary (December, 1946, p. 503) suggested that
ideological affinity with the United States was overstressed "especially when considering what the present rulers of America actually stand
for in the world."

where the absorbed ILP members were prominent in the Labour Left,[11] but what remained of the ILP itself was especially intransigent in its refusal to accept an alignment with either Russia or America. The spirit of the ILP was anti-Stalinist as well as anticapitalist, and on both counts it was so rigid as to have insisted on the desirability of a Third Force at times when the main body of the Labour Left was not specifically committed. This was the case in mid-1945 when most other socialists figured on co-operation with Russia, and more evidently in 1950 when the journal of the ILP was almost alone in urging a strict separation from the United States.[12] In its continued juxtaposition of social revolution to power politics, the ILP presented a caricature of the socialist position. But, like so many caricatures, the very distortion revealed the quirks of left-wing utopianism in international affairs.

A great variety of less thoroughly ideological arguments were made in behalf of a Third Force. For instance, the leading Labour proponent of a United States of Europe mixed his federalist case with the socialist idea of creating a unit strong enough to resist both America and Russia.[13] And even in the Third Force advocacy of G. D. H. Cole, a genuine leftist, there was an argument that was not exclusively socialist at its base. For Cole, ideological contradistinction to America was reinforced by a sense of separateness of Old World civilization from that of the United States. He believed that the peoples of Western Europe had their own standards:

> Our differences from the Americans in values and way of life are based mainly on this—we in Western Europe are old, settled peoples, with long, continuous national traditions, living thick on the ground, and long accustomed to the husbanding of scarce resources. The Americans are a new people, of very mixed racial composition, still imperfectly fused into an American nation, and living scattered over a vast continent, whose resources they have been accustomed, until quite recently, to regard as boundless.[14]

11. Their views were reflected in <u>Left</u>: see C. A. Smith, "Britain's Position in the Post-war World," December, 1945, pp. 566-73; Fenner Brockway, "The Socialist Alternative," April, 1946, pp. 83-88; and (unsigned), "The United Socialist States of Europe," July, 1947, pp. 153-67.

12. <u>Socialist Leader</u>, the organ of the Independent Labour party, was conspicuous for its Third Force advocacy throughout 1950, when the left within the Labour party was only rarely propagating the faith (see Vol. XLII).

13. R. W. G. Mackay, <u>You Can't Turn the Clock Back</u> (Chicago: Ziff-Davis, 1948).

14. <u>Labour's Foreign Policy</u> (New Statesman pamphlet [London, 1946]), p. 44. Cole argued similarly in "Living Together in Europe," <u>Fortnightly</u>, CLXIX (February, 1948), 102-11.

This sense of a European, or a British, way of life was a part of the general climate of British opinion in the first few postwar years. If the Third Force idea itself was not widely embraced in the community, nevertheless there were various symptoms of the state of mind which lay behind the policy.[15] The relatively confined English circle of intellectuals and publicists, of which the Labour Left was a fringe, had some approaches in common. Except for most of the self-consciously Tory thought, articulate Englishmen in 1945 and 1946 seemed to assume, along with the left, that Britain and probably Western Europe were evolving a social democracy distinct in kind from American capitalism. The Economist is a good case in point. In the summer of 1945 it raised the question, which always plagued the Labour Left, whether the American and the Russian conceptions of the good society and the means of achieving it could be reconciled. In answer, the Economist said: "There was never more need for an intermediary to break down the absolute opposition, and at first sight it would seem that no power was so well equipped as Great Britain to fulfil this role." The journal wanted "an assertion of a third possibility"[16] between the two extremes. More specifically, after Labour's electoral victory, the Economist urged the new government to give a lead to Europe as "in between" the United States and Russia.[17] This, it was plain enough, rested not only on geography but on a general though loose ideological assumption of a middle ground. The idea was "in the air" of public discussion.

It found an echo almost everywhere in the House of Commons in the first year or so after the war. To take one example, there was R. A. Butler, Conservative front-bencher and future chancellor of the exchequer, who referred to the American and the Russian systems and then said:

---

15. Superficially, but only superficially, the Third Force school had company on the extreme right. For example, the paper Truth (CXL [December 27, 1946], 651), wanted Bevin "to build up between Russia and America the independent might of Britain." This disposition was patriotic, in the most unadulterated sense, and it could not be joined to socialist or even semisocialist aims.

16. Economist, CXLIX (July 21, 1945), 73.

17. Ibid., August 4, 1945, pp. 148-49. This note, while uncharacteristic of the Economist in later postwar years, did not die away immediately. Over a year later, this comment appeared: "A Western European bloc would be in many ways a buffer and a factor of balance, while from its very nature, not being formed around a single overwhelmingly strong power, as any America-centered combination must be, it would be less of a potential threat to Russian security" (CLI [December 19, 1946], 612).

"In our view the Government are not taking positive enough steps to make
the camp to which we belong exist, and to do more than exist—to live to
the full an economic, political, cultural, and spiritual life, the traditions
of which go back so far in the history of our Western civilization."[18]
In such hands this was hardly the full-blown doctrine of the Third Force
as the Labour Left understood it. Nonsocialists were clearly unwilling
to detach Britain from American power. Their hankering for a separate
path was necessarily imprecise.

At the intellectual level, Arnold Toynbee illustrated this mode of
thought. He did, in fact, reject the creation of what he called the "Third
Great Power," which he regarded as impractical. Instead he wanted
Britain and Western Europe to fill the role of mitigating Russo-American
tensions but without functioning as a power bloc. This role, Toynbee thought,
could be played by virtue of Europe's in-between social and economic system.
Europe was to reduce the tensions caused by the mutual attractiveness of
communism to those in capitalist areas, and of capitalism to those in communist areas. Ideological rivalry, as a disturbing factor, would be diminished by the very existence of a less sharply defined system.[19]

As international policy, the prescription was vague. In not representing it as a substitute for Anglo-American co-operation, Toynbee was
characteristic of the nonsocialists who valued British, and European, developments as a prospective middle way. The facts of postwar international relations bore so hard against the conception that only the confirmed ideologists of the Labour Left could really advocate the Third
Force as an alternative foreign policy.

The Force of 1945-47

For a few years the Third Force had a tangible meaning for its real
believers. In 1945-47 the Labour Left thought conditions did permit, and
even require, Britain to form a separate bloc in world affairs. The principal favorable circumstance was the existence of a nominally socialist

18. 423 H.C. Deb. 1860 (June 4, 1946). Worth observing also are the
    comments of Robert Boothby, something of a maverick Conservative
    member of Parliament (419 H.C. Deb. 1252 [February 20, 1946]).

19. Arnold J. Toynbee, "The International Outlook," International Affairs,
    XXIII (October, 1947), 475-76.] Another rather similar point of view
    was expressed by Edgar Stern-Rubarth, "The Ultimate Choice,"
    Contemporary Review, CLXXII (November, 1947), 295-300.

government in Britain and of governments of similar profession elsewhere. [At its broadest, the force might consist of Britain, Western
Europe, and the nations of the Commonwealth.] About this last component
there was some vagueness. Presumably Britain could not join any bloc
without the commitment of the whole of the Commonwealth. The strictly
dependent parts of the Empire evidently were qualified ideologically by
virtue of Britain's socialism; also Australia and New Zealand both had
Labour governments at the time, and so they would have met the test.
But what of the rest of the Commonwealth? Canada and the Union of
South Africa, for instance, had neither socialist governments nor any
prospects of getting them. In so far as this was taken into account—and
it never played much part in the discussion—it was simply assumed, in
a left-wing version of imperial conceit, that the British dominions as
well as the colonial possessions were "united by a common philosophy—
that of social democracy."[20] If the nations were "British," either they
were socialist or else their deviations were apparently minor enough so
as not to mar the general Commonwealth picture.

[However, the Labour Left was not highly conscious of the Commonwealth's role in the Third Force. Attention was focused almost entirely on Western Europe.] It was there that socialism was to muster
its strength. Accept Britain's new status as an "integral part of Europe,"
said the editorial spokesman of the Third Force, "and, together with
our neighbours," exploit the balance of power between East and West.[21]
But which nations were the socialist neighbors? As late as May, 1947,
France was the main hope. The Anglo-French alliance, it was said,
should be developed "into a European regional security system under
Uno."[22]

Naturally it was necessary that the France with which Britain was
going to build the European Third Force should be socialist. This, the
Labour Left was prepared to believe, was the case for almost two postwar years, although during that time the French socialist party was only
one of three components in a tripartite cabinet, consisting also of the
Catholic republican party (Mouvement Républicain Populaire) and of the

---

20. R. H. S. Crossman, "Britain and Western Europe," Political Quarterly,
XVII (January-March, 1946), 12.

21. New Statesman, XXXIV (November 1, 1947), 341.

22. Ibid., XXXIII (May 3, 1947), 305.

Communists. The MRP was not counted as socialist, and it was really on a combination of French socialists and Communists that the New Statesman, for example, rested its belief in the emergence of France as an agency of the Third Force. Only by such a combination, it was urged, could there be achieved in France and generally on the Continent "the retention and acquisition of power by the working-class."[23] This was nothing more nor less than the resurrected popular front—not for Britain, however, but for the Continent. To its dubious cause some British socialists remained faithful after their French (and Italian) counterparts had already seen the not-so-hidden hand of Communist manipulation and eventual domination.

Thus the New Statesman was critical of the French socialists (as it had also been of the right-wing Italian socialists) for their attempt, beginning in May, 1947, to function in a government without the participation of the Communist party.[24] In the case of France, in particular, the New Statesman was prepared to see the same game played which Eastern European socialists had already lost to their Communist colleagues. Unless it were to be assumed that the chief intellectual protagonist of the British Labour Left was simply following the Communist party line in urging the French socialists to sell out their cause, then it must be said that the New Statesman was trading on a complete fantasy. It had to be imagined that a joint Communist-socialist government, in a situation in which the Communists were the larger party, would not turn out to be another adherent of the Russian bloc. And how could such an optimistic notion be envisioned? Probably the Labour Left was refusing to accept French Communists as the real Kremlin-dominated article, but why that blindness should have existed is a great mystery. It might be that some British socialists wished so much for the ideological partnership of a French socialist government that the most ridiculous dreams could be entertained. Certainly the reality of French (or Italian) socialist political strength, taken alone, never held the slightest promise of securing power in the postwar environment. But to have also ruled out its accomplishment on a popular-front basis would have meant the almost complete abandonment from the very beginning of the hopes for a socialist Third Force.

---

23. Ibid., January 18, 1947, p. 42.

24. Ibid., p. 41, and May 10, 1947, pp. 325-26.

One of the fruits of a flourishing Franco-British force was expected to be "a European policy towards Germany"[25] as opposed to the non-socialist American occupation. So, when the Labour Left was convinced that the United States was trying to set back the cause of German socialism, the rallying of Western European resistance seemed all the more desirable. It was customary to speak loosely of the need to socialize the industries of the Ruhr. In this Britain was to take the lead regardless of the presumed ideological objections of capitalist America. Whether the Germans would freely have chosen the blessings of coal and steel nationalization was not a prime consideration, if it was a consideration at all. Socialization of the Ruhr was one of those apparently concrete applications of a socialist foreign policy, and therefore it was to be pursued. The fact that it was not successfully pressed by the British government constituted, for the Labour Left, a tragic monument to the absence of a Third Force strong enough to contend with American influence in Europe.

The expectancy with regard to German policy was in its way typical of the significance attached to the Third Force. It was envisioned as a positive and dynamic element in world affairs, and notably in European affairs. No doubt, like the neutralists, the advocates of the Third Force wanted to avoid taking sides in what was called "the Russian-American struggle for power."[26] But it was not from weakness that Western Europe was advised to take a middle road. Quietude was not to be the policy. The European bloc was to be strong enough to wield an influence both for socialism and for peace. Its power was to be in some way commensurate with that of Russia and America. Rather than trying merely to be neutral in the event of war, the Third Force was to deter, by virtue of being neither in one camp nor in the other, the outbreak of a Russo-American conflict.[27]

This was not so very far from Toynbee's desire for a European middle ground to lessen East-West tension, but the Labour Left was much more insistent on the separate restraining role. Britain must actively conduct, it was argued, "a policy of mediation,"[28] and for success this

---

25. Ibid., XXXII (September 14, 1946), 181; ibid., XXXIII (March 8, 1947), 147-48.

26. Ibid., XXXII (September 7, 1946), 163.

27. Socialist Commentary, XII (February and June, 1948), 97-99 and 193-95.

28. William Warbey, "Foreign Policy," Fabian Quarterly, winter, 1947, p. 20.

required a mediating group of powers. The proposers of the Third Force were, by this emphasis, clearly and consciously distinguishing themselves from the advocates of retirement from great-power affairs. Really it was a kind of power politics that was wanted. The new combined socialist (that is, the good and the unaggressive) power was to be set alongside the threatening American and Russian blocs. Its peaceful intentions would be recognized, especially by Russia, which was assumed to be fearful of an American-dominated Europe. The very creation of the Third Force would, on the prevailing left-wing interpretation of Russia's defensive-aggression, have been an act making for peaceful relations. The notion lingered that Russia would be more friendly in its reception of a socialist than of a capitalist European neighbor.[29]

That kind of illusion was no more strikingly evident in the case for the Third Force than was the fiction at the root of the whole conception: that the Europe of 1945-47 had the economic and military strength to stand independently of America as well as of Russia. So illusory was this very foundation of the doctrine that its grip on the Labour Left constituted a most remarkable instance of fancy defying facts. This having been done for two years, however, what then caused the Third Force to fade from the forefront of socialist consciousness? In large part the dissipating factor was the readier identification with the United States which came with the popularity of the Marshall Plan. However, this coincided, in 1947 and 1948, with an unmistakable right-wing domination of French and Italian cabinets. The vision of socialist allies on the Continent had vanished. Now the French government was a coalition "dominated by bankers and men of affairs." The policy of 1946 and 1947 had been "ruled out by events."[30] What should have been the "Anglo-French Socialist policy" in 1946 was by 1948 only a lost opportunity. After all, a still Labour Britain could not very well join the Continental abjurers of socialism. The retreat from the Third Force may not have been headlong, and perhaps it was only a temporary, tactical withdrawal, but the old group of "Keep Left" members of Parliament made it almost official with the simple pronouncement that their foreign policy of April, 1947, "had to be scrapped."[31]

---

29. E.g., Cole, Labour's Foreign Policy, p. 11.

30. New Statesman, XXXV (February 14, 1948), 127, and February 21, 1948, p. 147.

31. Keeping Left (London, 1950), p. 19.

By 1949 and 1950 some of the erstwhile friends of a European bloc found themselves using the old ideological arguments to resist American pressure for economic integration. For that policy the Labour Left had even less desire than most of the British community. Tribune did not at all want a "plunge into European 'integration' which would compel us to fall in with methods of ruthless deflation, and laissez-faire now prevalent on the Continent. . . ."[32] The same principles were used as had earlier been turned, and would be turned in the future, against economic ties with capitalist United States. For the moment, however, if going it alone was impossible, then America was the lesser evil for a socialist Britain. So the Labour Left, for the most part, was willing and often anxious to go along with the Labour party's open rejection, in 1950, of anything smacking of the Third Force. It could even accept, in the Labour national executive's brutally frank pamphlet attacking proposals for European unity, the statement that "in its social and economic policy Western Europe as a whole would stand to the Right of the U.S.A., not between America and Russia."[33] For some former voices of the Third Force in the Labour party, this marked an apparently permanent conversion to the American alliance.[34] For others, the assent, in chorus, to the Labour party's position may have been less a surrender of the Third Force preference than a recognition, in context, that what was being rejected was a "capitalist-inspired" European integration.

Residues

Because of the suspicion that the Labour Left's abandonment of the Third Force doctrine was performed only under the duress of peculiarly coincident circumstances, there is more to this chapter's exploration of the once-popular ideological commitment than beating a dead horse. The preference for a Third Force alternative to an Anglo-American alliance never really disappeared; its topical appeal simply fell away when Continental socialist partners were in short supply, both actually and potentially,

32. Tribune, November 25, 1949, p. 7.

33. Labour Party, European Unity (London, 1950), p. 9.

34. E.g., Socialist Commentary, which had shifted its editorial position relatively early in the postwar years, retained after 1950 the commitment to the American alliance which it expressed at that time, (XIV [July, 1950]), 156-57). Consequently, during the foreign-policy disputes of the later Bevanite period Socialist Commentary was pro-Attlee in orientation.

and when, worse yet, Britain itself ceased to be socialist, technically after the 1951 election but virtually in 1950.

Nevertheless, even between 1947 and 1950, there were a few signs of the Labour Left brooding over the old desire. It was suggested that through the Marshall Plan Western Europe might become a sufficient power to do what it had not done in 1945 and 1946: act independently of the United States and in that role perform the typically Third Force task of preventing a Russo-American war.[35] There was a similar note in the occasional protest against the existence of Anglo-American military commitments—despite their inconspicuousness—during the Marshall Plan period. The signing of the Atlantic Pact in 1949, which generally had so little immediate effect on the Labour Left's honeymoon with American foreign policy, did cause the rather rare socialist objector to revive his attachment to the preferred alternative. This was the case with Ian Mikardo, who was almost alone among prominent figures of the Labour Left in explicitly denouncing the new military ties with the United States. Mikardo objected because he thought the Atlantic Pact meant a conclusive turning-away from a purely European bloc, in a sense that Britain's acceptance of the Marshall Plan had not, in itself, indicated. He still believed, he insisted, in making Western Europe a balancing Third Force, after the 1945-47 manner.[36] But, in being so definitely committed to the old doctrine, Mikardo was at least temporarily out of step with his former colleagues of the "Keep Left" group. When others now talked about the Third Force, it was usually in vaguer and more subtle forms.[37]

After 1948 there were traces of the Third Force spirit in the infatuation with Titoism which seized a number of left-wing British intellectuals. Starting with the ubiquitous Zilliacus, rushing in ahead of his brethren, socialists began a doctrinal pilgrimage to Yugoslavia. The road to Belgrade was eventually taken by Crossman and Bevan, among many others. In time, the tour also became popular in wider circles of the Labour party and among other groups; in 1952 Foreign Minister Eden made the trip too. But "national Communism" was the special favorite of the Labour Left. Now, quite without the taint of Stalinism, British socialists could intellectually luxuriate in the company of a left-wing Continental

35. Tribune, September 26, 1947, pp. 1-2; see also New Statesman, XXXV (January 10, 1948), 23.

36. Ian Mikardo, "Why I Disagree," Tribune, May 20, 1949, p. 6.

37. As in the editorial in the New Statesman, XXXIX (June 17, 1950), 673.

power. It was true that Yugoslavia was not much of a power; but its weakness and economic dependence were overlooked in the excitement of a new-found ideological partner. Neither did the accidental origin of Titoism detract from its charm. What mattered to British socialists was that Tito was not returning to Western democracy and free enterprise but was evolving what Crossman called "a unique phenomenon." This meant, of course, that it was different from English socialism, but, if it were not the right recipe for Great Britain, it was just what Crossman prescribed for the Continent. "National Communism—in revolt against centralised bureaucracy and privilege at home, and against Russian dictatorship abroad—is what other peoples besides the Yugoslavs are looking for." If only the same thing had happened elsewhere (Italy, for instance), Crossman added yearningly, then in 1951 "Europe would not be faced with the bleak choice between the American and Russian facades. . . ."[38]

Titoism might seem a remote and strange depository for the memories of the Third Force. That it served in this way mainly signifies the durability of the desire for an independent socialist bloc. The fact that it was in 1951 that Titoism stirred Crossman's old hopes is worth noting. By that time the desire for independence from America, which had so largely been relinquished under the Marshall Plan, was reasserted in response to the stimuli of rearmament and a not-so-cold war. Now, far from admitting an ideological abandonment of the Third Force, Crossman was one of many who thought back to 1945 and 1946 as the years of the lost opportunity. The Labour Leftists came to think that perhaps they had been right all along in their fight with Foreign Minister Ernest Bevin. Titoism reminded them of the possibilities in times past, without necessarily bringing to mind the entirely ludicrous suggestion that Britain, when once again socialist, should form a bloc with Yugoslavia.

Mostly the 1950-52 revival of the Third Force doctrine was much less definite than it had been in its earlier phase. Certainly there was not then any talk of likely Continental partners. Europe generally was at least as far right, and probably farther, than it had been in 1948. Whatever the chances of the Communists taking over in one country or another, it was evident enough there would be no socialist victories of major consequence (outside Scandinavia). Even in Australia and New

---

38. "Between Two Facades," New Statesman, XLII (September 22, 1951), 301.

Zealand, Labour was temporarily out of power. Was there then nothing for the Labour Left to advocate by way of an alternative foreign policy, in face of the evident dissatisfaction with the American alliance? Could socialists only discuss among themselves, as they were doing aimlessly in 1952, how and when postwar Labour Britain had made the supposedly fatal decision against forming an independent bloc? Some claimed the great mistake was to have wed Britain to American capitalism by accepting the loan agreement in 1945. Others said it was the tacit extension of permission for American atomic bombers to use British bases. Or the Atlantic Pact. Or the failure to get tough with America over the socialization of the Ruhr. Or any one of many steps which the Labour Left was never willing to grant as necessary and therefore outside the free choice of any British government.

However, the Third Force was alive as more than a memory of what might have been. In 1952, when the dislike for American policy was intensified, the old idea began to re-emerge as an aspiration concerning future policy. Even without any prospective bloc of nations, there was a revival of the vaguer concern with achieving "British independence" so as to be able, perhaps with India, to present a third alternative to the rest of the world. This sentiment actuated a large number of the foreign-policy advocacies at the 1952 Labour party conference. As one speaker said: "The oppressed peoples of the world are looking to us to give them that lead. When we get back to power we can have a say in international affairs. The democratic countries look to us and we must not fail them."[39] Something very like this view was expressed in a resolution, moved from the floor and adopted by the conference, in which it was declared that "we can best serve the cause of peace by sticking to our distinctive Socialist principles and refusing to subordinate them to American, Russian or any other pressures."[40] The Labour party, and certainly its left wing, had not been nurtured on the special virtues of socialist policies, abroad as well as at home, in order to forsake them at a time when a Conservative government was in alliance with the greater capitalism of America. If there were no apparent alternative to the alliance, one was still going to be desired. The significance of this socialist desire, without an overt declaration of a Third Force policy, may be discerned in the subsequent discussion of the ambiguities of Bevanism.

39. 51st Annual Report of the Labour Party (London, 1952), p. 118.

40. Ibid., p. 116. The resolution was carried in the conference by a voice vote (p. 142).

[Despite the undeniable attraction exerted by left-wing ideology, the Labour party's postwar foreign policy was determined by very different considerations. At the very time the Third Force was advocated within the party, the Labour government committed Britain to the American alliance and to the cold war against the Soviet Union. Eventually, also in opposition to the left wing, the government undertook a large-scale rearmament program. While these policies originated from above, that is, from the cabinet and not from the party ranks, and for adoption required the acquiescence only of the Parliamentary Labour party, nevertheless the policies had to have substantial supporters within the movement in order to be maintained against repeated attacks from the left— in 1945-47 and particularly after Labour lost office in 1951.]

Support was derived from a loosely defined right or center position within the Labour party. Two partially overlapping groups were of principal importance. First, there was the political leadership, plus a number of intellectual supporters in and out of Parliament. Second, there was the leadership of the trade-unions. Basically, the foreign-policy views of these two groups were in agreement, and it was from the ranks of the unions' leadership that Ernest Bevin emerged to become the crucial figure in the determination of foreign policy at the political level. However, there remained a sufficient distinction between the orientations of the political side and the union side to warrant separation in analyzing responses to American foreign policy. Even with that separation, the classification is very rough. Each of the two groups, especially the political one, contained within itself meaningful differences of conviction on matters of doctrine as well as of policy.

The Political Leadership

Here one still deals with professed socialists. When divorced from its trade-union backing, the political leadership of the Labour party often looks similar to the left in ideological orientations. While distinctions are significant enough to help explain the way in which the party's foreign commitments broke so drastically from the preferences of the left, nevertheless the common faith in socialism should not be overlooked. Attlee, Morrison, Cripps, and company did not forsake their socialist convictions in order to accept American leadership, nor had they previously surrendered their socialist aspirations during membership in the wartime coalition. Rather, it is plain that those who justified Labour's postwar American connection did so in spite of their socialism.

Displacing capitalism, in one way or another, was the fabric of the party faith, and to it the political leaders adhered no matter what their foreign policy had to be. Their anticapitalism was less adamant and less vividly expressed than that of the left, but their officially adopted domestic programs reflected a general predilection for public ownership. Nor was confidence in the superiority of socialism entirely out of mind in international discussion. For example, while still prime minister in 1950, Clement Attlee reminded his followers that the "policy of democratic socialism" was the only dynamic alternative to totalitarian communism. "Capitalism, you know, has lost faith in itself," he added. "It certainly cannot give the enthusiasm that is needed if you are to conquer the very dangerous fanaticism that seeks to overturn the whole of the basis of our Western civilisation."[1]

Unlike the left-wingers, the party leaders abstained from attacks on postwar American capitalism as such. But they did not refrain from polite reference to the ideological distinction between themselves and the Americans. "Of course," Herbert Morrison said, "the ideas of the United States are very different from ours. Their whole conception of politics and economics is very different. They are nearer to the Leader of the Opposition and, therefore, they are likely to be critical of our outlook sometimes."[2] These, it might be said, were essential political admissions, since anything less would have opened the Labour leaders to left-wing charges of socialist faithlessness. At the same time it was necessary to offer reassurances, doubtless to themselves as well as to their followers, that American capitalism was not imposing its domestic economic policies on Britain as a price of the alliance. Attlee made this point when he insisted in 1952 that socialists must be willing to join in international efforts with other countries despite disagreements: "The United States of America has not got the same economic conceptions as

1.   49th Annual Report of the Labour Party (London, 1950), p. 99.

2.   443 H.C. Deb. 726 (October 28, 1947).

ours. We work together, and we work with them very cordially, and I never found on the side of America that they would not work with us because we were a Socialist Government nationalising things."[3]

Not only was the assertion of independence in home affairs a necessity for Labour leaders, but, in the party generally, those who supported the American alliance had to explain that their own doctrinal purity was unimpaired by foreign-policy commitments. For instance, in 1948, one not very sophisticated member of Parliament felt obliged to answer the charge that, because he was on the same side as capitalist America, he was against working-class interests. He remained, he said, an "unrepentant Socialist,"[4] and he had "no defence to make for capitalist America at all."[5] Other facets of American life, he argued, were both favorable and significant enough to allow socialists to accept the alliance.

Only in a loose way was this agreement to differ over economic systems the equivalent of the willingness of American capitalists to swallow their own ideological objections in order to extend both military support and economic aid to a socialist Britain. Besides the possibility that ideological scruples were usually more important to socialists than to capitalists, there was also the point that no American capitalist had to face the likelihood of his country being outweighed in the affairs of the alliance by its partner. Even if Labour did not fear American interference in domestic affairs, it was certainly aware that American predominance in international relations meant that Britain's chances of pressing for socialism abroad were correspondingly reduced. Apart from anything specific, merely being a lesser partner of a capitalist nation was a peculiarly difficult psychological burden for British socialists of all sorts.

However, the burden was borne. The major party leaders apparently squared the American alliance with their socialist consciences. To some extent this was accomplished because the socialism of the leadership, while no less wholehearted in its way, was different in emphasis from that of the left. Its intellectual inspiration was often derived from the moral and humanitarian equalitarianism of R. H. Tawney, from managerial-minded Fabians, or from Radical reformism. Marxism was a minor source, and the development of Russian and American policies was not viewed

---

3. 51st Annual Report of the Labour Party (London, 1952), p. 89.

4. G. Lang (446 H.C. Deb. 414 [January 22, 1948]).

5. Ibid., col. 417.

through the narrow lens of economic determinism. The fading postwar
hopes for Soviet friendship were unsupported by any Marxist emphasis
on the virtues of economic collectivism. And, on the other side, American capitalism might be disliked, but its existence was assumed to be
compatible with the validity and stability of democratic political institutions. Present-day American capitalism, it was said, "however deep
our misgivings about it, at least leaves room for free institutions to
flower and survive."[6]

This soft-shelled socialist doctrine allowed for the sharing of a political way of life regardless of differences in economic system and did
not cast America into ideological darkness because of its capitalism.
⌐For the decisive forces in the Labour party, political democracy was an
even more highly cherished principle than social ownership, in which
ᵛ case their disapproval of the American economic system did not loom
ᴸso large.⌐ Nor, without the focus of strict economic determinism, would
American foreign policies appear primarily as manifestations of capitalist motives.

In economic doctrine the Labour leadership had positive leanings
that set off its brand of socialism from that of the left. Its addiction to
public ownership was often inclined, as in the case of Herbert Morrison,
to be pragmatic rather than doctrinaire. And there were a few distinct
right-wingers whose definition of socialism sometimes wavered in the
direction of stressing the virtues of a mixed economy, marked chiefly
by fiscal controls and welfare measures. There was a vogue for this
kind of thinking during the latter years of Labour's office-holding, when
some responsible ministers, pleased with the establishment of full employment and social security, seemed almost thoroughly Keynesian.
Significantly, Hugh Gaitskell, who as chancellor of the exchequer was
considered a representative of the Keynesian school, was also one of the
firmest and most outspoken advocates of the American alliance.[7] Undoubtedly, the milder the socialist outlook, the less alien a capitalist
economy and therefore the less difficult the adjustment to American
leadership.

Whatever role may have been played by right-wing socialist ideology
in justifying the American alliance, its acceptance in the first place was

6. Socialist Commentary, XIV (August, 1950), 181.

7. See, e.g., Gaitskell's speech at the party conference (51st Annual
    Report of the Labour Party, p. 149).

not related only to a predominance of moderate sentiment in the postwar
Labour leadership. More significant was the fact that the leadership, including a few whose socialism had not previously been considered at all
moderate,[8] was responsible for the conduct of Britain's foreign affairs
from 1945 to 1951. It was as heads of the nation, as well as of the party,
that Labour's political leadership met the challenges of the postwar world.
Not only did this circumstance necessarily condition governmental policy,
but while in opposition after 1951 the prospects of having again to assume
responsibility could not be forgotten in the framing of international programs. Attlee himself indicated the chastening effects of governmental
experience when, in 1952, he defended the party's previous commitment
to large-scale rearmament: "It would have been quite easy to have taken
the line: 'We do not believe in the reality of the danger,' but we were not
people without responsibility. We were the responsible Government of
this country, responsible for the lives of our people and responsible, a
very heavy responsibility, for taking the lead in defending the social
democracies."[9] The same point was aimed more directly at the Labour
conference's foreign-policy traditions by Christopher Mayhew, a former
undersecretary of foreign affairs. He posed the question whether Labour,
returned to an opposition role, was to continue to face the "reality of
world politics," as it had while in power, or whether the party was to
"pretend that all-out opposition to capitalism" was once again an adequate
basis for foreign policy.[10]

While in office Labour had had to accept the fact of Britain's dependence on American strength. The point was driven home partly by
economic experience, but also by the Soviet military threat. This was
evidenced by the Labour government's negotiation of the Atlantic Pact,
which Foreign Minister Bevin hailed as a "historic occasion" because
it marked the first peacetime pledge of American power to the defense
of Europe.[11] Bevin subsequently declared: "The situation which we had
in 1914 and 1939 and particularly 1940 and 1941, when we had to hold the

8. The most conspicuous example of a prewar Marxist extremist in the
   Labour government ranks was John Strachey, whose The Theory
   and Practice of Socialism (London: Gollancz, 1936) had been a bible
   for fellow-travelers in the 1930's.

9. 51st Annual Report of the Labour Party, pp. 152-53.

10. Ibid., p. 123.

11. 462 H.C. Deb. 2533 (March 18, 1949).

fort waiting and wondering when other nations would realize the gravity of the aggressive menace, while at the same time we were using up and exhausting our resources—that situation should not be allowed to occur again."[12] The same general statement of Britain's dependence was made by other Labour spokesmen while the pact itself was still in its formative stages.[13]

The party found itself doing what would have been in the interest of any British government to do: act so as to secure the promise of adequate American military pledges.[14] Mayhew, in reviewing five years of Labour's foreign policy, put it this way: "It always seemed of the utmost importance from many points of view that Europe and the United States should go ahead together, and that no encouragement should be given to isolationist elements in the United States by any appearance of cold-shouldering from Europe."[15] Obviously socialism vis-à-vis American capitalism had, in matters of foreign policy, become irrelevant under the pressing demands of national security.[16] [The sources of policy were not Labour manifestoes but Churchillian texts and Foreign Office knowledge.]

Although having thus received a policy from outside, as it were, the Labour leadership was not entirely without intellectual arguments with which to defend it. There was one fairly young but serviceable party doctrine: the gospel of collective security. Associated originally with Labour's commitment to the internationalism of the League of Nations, collective security was the rallying slogan which had finally routed the completely pacifist forces in the prewar Labour party. As such it had some claim to be a Labour, or at least a liberal, doctrine, as opposed to the nationalism and imperialism associated with the Conservatives. In

12. 464 H.C. Deb. 2016 (May 12, 1949).

13. References to the facts of dependence were not yet frequent in the early postwar period, but there were a few (see Denis Healey, "The Political Aspect," Fabian Quarterly, summer, 1948, pp. 7-8; and Aidan Crawley, 462 H.C. Deb. 613 [March 3, 1949]).

14. Only a handful of fellow-traveling and pacifist Labour members of Parliament openly opposed the Atlantic Pact in the House of Commons (464 H.C. Deb. 2127-30 [May 12, 1949]).

15. International Affairs, XXVI (October, 1950), 483.

16. In time it was frankly said that Britain could not maintain a Commonwealth policy, among other things, without working with the United States (P. C. Gordon-Walker, 51st Annual Report of the Labour Party, p. 128).

prewar days not only Attlee but Philip Noel-Baker, Hugh Dalton, and others subsequently prominent in Labour leadership were associated with the advocacy of collective security. Its appeal to the party was somewhat less than complete when the emphasis was on the use of military force, but even the employment of power was not so antithetical to socialists when it was invoked in the name of an international organization. The heavy stress which Labour leaders placed on the United Nations authority in justification of Britain's participation in the Korean campaign testifies to the store the party set by the doctrine of collective security.[17]

Military preparedness and the Anglo-American alliance were also, despite the inconvenient absence of a straight United Nations argument, favorably represented in terms of the practice of the universal principle of security against aggression. Thus a link was established to the position which Labour was fond of saying it advocated in the late 1930's: collective security against Hitler.[18] The popularity of the earlier stand was drawn upon for the support of a postwar international policy which was not, on its own, capable of arousing socialist fervor as had antifascism.[19] Attlee persisted in reminding his party that Labour's postwar foreign policy was only an application of such long-standing general principles. "That policy," he told Labour in 1952, "has been held over a number of years now. It has been based on a belief in collective security. It is not a policy of absolute pacifism but a recognition of the fact that if you want peace there must be forces behind you."[20] And, as usual, this was closely coupled with a reiteration of faith in the United Nations. By implication, Attlee was telling his left-wing opponents that any break from rearmament would constitute a desertion of collective security. More specifically it was urged, from the same position, that America was virtuous by reason of its support of the security doctrine.

17. See Attlee's remarks on Britain's relation to the Korean campaign (478 H.C. Deb. 979 [September 12, 1950]).

18. The Labour party believed that collective security failed before the war only because others were unwilling to support it. This was alluded to from time to time, as by Mrs. Freda Corbet, M.P., 51st Annual Report of the Labour Party, p. 129.

19. Bevin himself, partly because of his own association with the advocacy of collective security in the 1930's, drew upon the earlier experience to justify his postwar course (49th Annual Report of the Labour Party, p. 149).

20. 51st Annual Report of the Labour Party, p. 153.

There was hardly any higher Labour praise for American postwar foreign policy than that offered by Herbert Morrison: "In my judgment the United States has been a genuine and loyal member of the United Nations."[21] This was a more attractive justification of Labour co-operation with the United States than an appeal purely to the British interests which bound the nation to American leadership.

Yet implicit in any meaningful acceptance of collective security was a recognition of the validity of the use of power in international relations. Chary as the Labour party was about having this frankly said, it did come to play a part in the intellectual defense of the party's foreign policy. It was really the only way to meet head-on the attacks from the left. As early as 1947, W. N. Ewer, obviously writing in behalf of the then seldom articulated official position, argued forthrightly that a close British association with the United States was sufficiently justified by the need to stand firm against Soviet threats. Any weakening of the combination, he declared as plainly as Churchill, would only encourage Russian expansion.[22] These arguments were not, of course, unusual in the British community at large, but within the Labour party it had not been customary to state baldly, as did Ewer, "the thesis of the two camps."[23] That this was in fact the basis for the foreign policy of the government, and consequently of the party, only very slowly became apparent. In time, however, as part of a more thorough counteroffensive against the left, which was launched from the international bureau of the party headquarters, the difficult task of educating socialists in the realities of power politics was undertaken.[24] The media were not lacking. There was the more or less official newspaper, the mass-circulation Daily Herald, and there were various party publications in addition to public speeches by party leaders. At an intellectual level the monthly Socialist Commentary became, in the 1950's, a

---

21. London Times, October 25, 1952, p. 3.

22. "A Critical Comment," attached to Leonard Woolf, Foreign Policy ("Fabian Research Series," No. 121 [London, 1947]), pp. 27-34. Ewer was the diplomatic correspondent of the Daily Herald, and his views, like those of his paper, may be assumed to reflect more definitely those of the Trades Union Congress than of the political wing of the party.

23. "The Labour Government's Record on Foreign Policy," Political Quarterly, XX (April-June, 1949), 117.

24. One such effort was the Labour party's discussion pamphlet, Problems of Foreign Policy (London, April, 1952).

significant participant in the mission of reorienting the traditions of Labour thinking on foreign policy.[25]

Among the political activists in the party, the task remained complicated by the expectancy that foreign policy should have a specifically socialist content. Consequently, even while rejecting the possibility of a "distinctively socialist" foreign policy, a proponent of the official party position had to claim that he was at least "trying to apply to international affairs the same broad principles of justice that inspire socialist policy at home."[26] But socialists, who might well have been impressed with this claim in reference to programs for underdeveloped areas, for example, would not be so likely to square the most prominent feature of British policy—military ties to the world's leading capitalist nation—with their "broad principles of justice." Socialist principles were not usually interpreted so generously in party ranks as among the more sophisticated leadership.[27] But if, in this important respect, party leaders might get out of step with many of their most active workers, they may well have been closer to the millions who, while voting Labour, were only vaguely interested in socialism. Squaring doctrine with international necessities was strictly an internal party problem.

The Trade-Unions

Fortunately for the maintenance of Labour's foreign-policy commitments, the leadership's position did not depend primarily on the tenuous support of the socialist-minded political side of the party. At times, in 1946-47 or again in 1952, it was more than doubtful whether the constituency political organizations, as such, were loyal to the principles and terms of the American alliance. [The fact that the Labour party, as a whole, pledged and repledged its support was due to the predominance

---

25. Primarily in relation to Labour ideas about America, the journal sought to minimize the party's apprehensiveness (see especially "America—Fact and Prejudice," XIV [November, 1950], 13-14, and "Too Pro-American?" ibid., December, 1950, p. 65). "Let us get rid of the idea," the latter editorial declared, "that everything American, which has any business support behind it, must of necessity be opposed, even though it is supported by Labour as well."

26. Socialist Commentary, XVI (October, 1952), 219.

27. On "sophistication" of Labour members of Parliament in relation to approval and disapproval of American policy see Marjorie Bremner, "An Analysis of British Parliamentary Attitudes concerning the United States in the Post-war Period" (unpublished Ph.D. dissertation, University of London, 1950), pp. 83-84.

of trade-unionists in the process of party decision-making. Not only did
the unions, meeting in their own congresses, generally stand firm for
Anglo-American co-operation, but it was their votes in party conferences
which decided that there was to be no turning in the direction of the Third
Force, either in the earlier or in the later postwar controversies over
foreign policy.

Most important in determining conference results was the combined
strength of the two massive general unions, the Transport and General
Workers (Bevin's own creation) and the General and Municipal Workers.
These two, usually joined by the National Union of Mineworkers, required
the help of relatively few additional organizations in order to overwhelm
left-wing opposition. This was simplified by the fact that each set of
delegates cast the votes of its union en bloc. In the process, the influence
of union officers concerned with policy formulation was naturally very
great. Organizational structures, most obviously in the general unions,
were hierarchical, after the manner of large-scale creations of all sorts.
There was considerable authority in the hands of union officers, and the
question of whether the authority was exercised in accordance with the
will of union members was as difficult to answer in this case as in most
others where policy-formulating officials were responsible to politically
passive followers.

At any rate, the hard-pressed political leadership of the Labour party
had reason to be thankful for what the left wing disparaged as the "block
vote" cast by the unions. The former defense minister, Emanuel Shinwell,
even went so far, at the 1952 conference, to "thank Heaven for the Trade
Union Movement at this time" and to offer similar praise to the deity for
the existence of union voting en bloc.[28] This kind of massive support was
something to count on, at least so long as the principal union leaders were
roughly of one mind and were able to retain the confidence of their own
organizations. The predominance of the unions in the Labour party was
not only assured by the fact that their membership bulked larger than that
of the purely political components; the unions were the financial backbone
of the party, and their heads were not above reminding dissidents of
that cardinal point.[29] Furthermore, the unions had a highly developed and

---

28. 51st Annual Report of the Labour Party, p. 106.

29. "You know you would listen if you wanted to get money from the
    trade unions," Arthur Deakin, secretary of the Transport and
    General Workers, told some Labour party hecklers (ibid., p. 78).

influential organization outside the formal confines of the Labour party. The Trades Union Congress was itself a potent center within the movement, having its own bureaus concerned with the formulation of policy, international and domestic.

There are several bases for difference between what may be called the TUC approach to foreign policy and that more typical of the political section of the Labour party. To start with, the British union movement was not socialist by definition, although many of its members were no doubt so by conviction. The unions did not exist primarily to build a socialist society, even if they were sometimes pledged to proposals for nationalization of industry. Rather the main organizational aims were to advance immediate interests of the working class. Consequently, while the language of the unions stressed class solidarity, it was really not ideological in tone.[30] Foreign policy, like domestic policy, did not have to be specifically "socialist." Of course, this is to speak generally. There were unions with left-wing traditions where the American alliance was as hard to justify as it was to socialist political groups. In such instances, the trade-unionists who supported the Labour government's foreign policy were almost as vulnerable as were the party leaders to the charge of desertion of established precepts. But usually attitudes were sufficiently pragmatic so that doctrinal preferences could be openly challenged.[31]

So far as the TUC was concerned—and there can be no question of the leadership's importance on this score—orientations were meaningfully influenced by the appreciation of power which came with experience in labor-management relations. Heads of important trade-unions inevitably knew something about the importance of strength in dealing with opponents and also about the disasters that might accompany weakness. What was understood by way of the need for power in behalf of one's union organization seems to have been readily transferred to the acceptance of strength as an instrument of foreign policy. This line of emphasis was never absent from the trade-union defense of rearmament and the Anglo-American alliance. "We will negotiate, but we will rearm until we are in a

30. A good example of the language of class rather than of general doctrine was provided by the defense of rearmament made before the TUC by an official of the National Union of Mineworkers (84th Annual Report of the Trades Union Congress [London, 1952], p. 375).

31. The left opposition within the TUC necessarily brought doctrinal differences into the discussion, as, e. g., in 82d Annual Report of the Trades Union Congress (London, 1950), pp. 411-25.

position to be able to negotiate with some degree of equality,"[32] one official told the TUC. The language, it is clear, was not so different from
that which a unionist would apply to the need for marshaling his own
organization's strength before trying to bargain collectively with a strong,
well-intrenched employer. The need to build armed strength looked like
the international counterpart of a well-stocked union treasury. Calling
attention to the Soviet's already highly prepared state was analogous to
pointing out the wealth and resources of an employer's industrial empire.

Union heads could well understand the term "negotiation from strength."[33]
It was the key to the reiteration of the TUC's support for rearmament and to
the General Council's argument, in 1952, that weakness meant defeat.[34] The
"immediate necessity of rearmament" was proclaimed in definitive terms.[35]
Thus the TUC's general secretary told the left opposition: "What do you do
when you negotiate? Do you go with your coffers entirely empty and with
a bold front? It is the same with international affairs. We say quite
frankly, 'Yes, we want to negotiate, but from a standpoint of equality.'"[36]
None of this would have escaped responsible union officials who had ever
faced the possibility of a strike.

In the TUC leadership there was no tendency to assume that the Soviet
Union, in particular, could be dealt with from a position of weakness.[37]
Russian intentions were thoroughly suspect, certainly by the 1950's, and
the TUC believed that the West had to be well armed as a prerequisite to
any negotiations. This suspicion of Russia, much plainer than in the rest
of the Labour movement, coincided with a vigorous anticommunism. In
fact, the top officials of the largest unions were more outspokenly hostile
to Communists than almost any other important element in British public
life.[38] This was, in part, because the TUC leaders had to expend so much

32. D. Currie (Clerical and Administrative Workers' Union), 84th Annual
     Report of the Trades Union Congress, p. 377.

33. See the speech of the TUC president, Alfred Roberts (83d Annual Re-
     port of the Trades Union Congress [London, 1951], p. 76).

34. 84th Annual Report of the Trades Union Congress, p. 188.

35. Ibid.

36. Ibid., p. 381.

37. E.g., the remarks of T. Williamson (National Union of General and
     Municipal Workers), ibid., p. 375.

38. Representative of the TUC attitude was Arthur Deakin (Transport and
     General Workers' Union), "British Trade Unions and the Communist
     Conspiracy," National and English Review, CXXXIX (December, 1952),
     337-39.

effort defending their own organizations from Communist infiltration.

This defense, incidentally, became increasingly tough and aggressive as the postwar period went on, and the leaders moved at least as fast as their movement would allow in banning Communists from positions of control.[39] In this respect, the working class (however it compared to its American counterpart) was generally considered to contain a more drastic anticommunism than existed among middle-class members of the Labour party. The only available detailed study bears out this popular impression.[40] It was a distinct possibility that the working class, except where penetrated by the Communists themselves or by some sections of the Labour Left, shared the TUC leadership's hostility to the Communists to a greater extent than did many of the more articulate intellectuals.

In addition to having a grasp of international politics that was unclouded by wishful thinking about Communist intentions, the TUC organization was impelled, by its economic responsibilities, to appreciate the facts of Britain's postwar dependence on the United States. American economic aid was recognized as essential to the very livelihood of union members. The TUC leaders were not likely to sacrifice the living standards of British workers to the ideological blandishments of the Third Force. Nor were they impressed with the chances of defending, without American power, the overseas economic stake on which Britain so largely depended.

By setting its foreign-policy course on a hard factual basis, the TUC was acting with the same determination that it displayed in the 1930's, when it had accepted rearmament before the Labour party itself had moved decisively in that direction. Ernest Bevin figured in the settlement of both the prewar and the postwar policies of the TUC and so prominently that his personal role must be taken into account. In sensing the importance of power, Bevin was the epitome of the TUC point of view;

---

39. The TUC terminated, in 1952, the registration of the London Trades Council because of its Communist domination (84th Annual Report of the Trades Union Congress, pp. 113-14, 331-35), but no similar action was taken against Communist-controlled unions as such. A trades council could be disciplined in a way an affiliated union could not.

40. The Manchester Fabian Society studied nine local party organizations (at the ward level) and found, among other things, that working-class members "were more willing to ban the Communist Party than those in other classes" (Fabian Journal, February, 1952, p. 29).

but, because of the strength of his own convictions and because of his tremendous influence, he was a cause as well as a product of the foreign-policy orientations of the unions. His ascendancy among trade-unionists, established through his position as head of the Transport and General Workers before the war, meant that he was a dominant figure in the Labour party as well. On matters of foreign policy, this dominance was fully displayed during the years of his foreign secretaryship, covering most of the Labour party's postwar tenure of power. It was primarily Bevan who defended the Anglo-American alliance before Labour conferences, and his personal force was in large degree responsible for securing the party's reluctant approval.

Often Bevin's limited educational background was said to have made him merely a puppet of the Foreign Office, but this seems well wide of the mark. No doubt, Bevin was in many matters more dependent than some other foreign secretaries on the expert advice of his career staff; without Foreign Office briefs, his expositions were often obscure. But there is everything in his record, particularly in the 1930's, to indicate that he himself appreciated the importance of strength in international relations.[41] And that would necessarily have led him, with or without a Foreign Office, to seek working economic and military relations with the United States if Britain and Europe were not to fall before the Soviet power.

Although no foreign secretary could have made Labour's postwar foreign policy acceptable to the full-blooded socialists, it is reasonably certain that Bevin's association with it tended to minimize the inevitable opposition in the movement generally, especially among active unionists. Partly this was because Bevin himself was so deeply rooted in the British working class. He could always call on his movement and his class for its traditional loyalties. Fellow-unionists were not likely to think that their forthright leader had sold out to America. He had proved himself as a union leader. All the ethos of the working class was on his side when he said that he "was stabbed in the back" by a left-wing rebellion at a time when he was negotiating with the United States.[42] The full measure

---

41. Bevin's role in Labour's foreign-policy travail of the 1930's is described by Francis Williams, Ernest Bevin (London: Hutchinson, 1952), chap. 18.

42. Bevin used this famous phrase during a dramatic speech that crushed his left-wing opponents at the 1947 conference (46th Annual Report of the Labour Party [London, 1947], p. 179).
   Loyalty was evidently also a factor in the support Bevin obtained from back-bench trade-unionist members of Parliament, who, as a

of his personal importance was reflected in the number of times his name was invoked, after his death, in behalf of foreign policies which other Labour leaders found difficult to defend. For instance, in 1952 the Trades Union Congress was reminded that Bevin had set much store by the North Atlantic Treaty Organization and that the unions were only being asked to support what Bevin had begun.[43] Also, in the same year, it was pointed out to the Labour party that Russian non-co-operation was something of which Ernest Bevin had spoken, so that it could not be regarded as a piece of capitalist propaganda.[44]

The name of Bevin was less useful, however, than his personal force and magnetism. The TUC's difficulties in holding the line on foreign policy admittedly increased after the Foreign Secretary's death in 1951. At the same time, of course, Anglo-American relations were subjected to new strains that complicated the task of working-class leaders. Yet that task, it should be emphasized, was not in general so difficult among unionists as it was among political activists. Most workers had no clear ideological bias against American capitalism, and they were un-touched by the blight of cultural anti-Americanism that afflicted many intellectuals and quasi-intellectuals. In fact, it was chiefly the working class which appeared to like American goods and American entertainment. When unaffected by Communist propaganda or a general socialist outlook—and usually political apathy stood in the way of either effect—the British working class was far from hostile to the United States.

The absence of anti-American orientations did not automatically make for an acceptance of Anglo-American foreign policy. To that end, the TUC carried on a fairly active campaign, through various publica-tions and other means of communication from central headquarters to local branches.[45] The importance of retaining trade-union support for

---

group, were found in the late 1940's to be more hostile than Labour intellectuals to American foreign policy (of course, Bevin himself displayed some of this hostility, notably in the Palestine affair) (Bremner, op. cit., pp. 124-25).

43. Sir Vincent Tewson, 84th Annual Report of the Trades Union Congress, p. 360.

44. Ernest Jones (National Union of Mineworkers), 51st Annual Report of the Labour Party, pp. 146-47.

45. E.g., the TUC's official magazine, Labour, in its issue of August, 1952, sought to immunize workers from the Communist charges of American germ warfare. Generally, through this magazine, the leadership gave its views on rearmament and foreign policy, in the hope of reaching unionists at a serious but nonintellectual level.

Labour's foreign-policy commitments was something which was well understood. It became the key to Labour's struggle with Bevanism.

Concern with American Politics

The moderate political leadership and the dominant heads of the TUC had many similar problems in defending the American alliance within their own ranks. Despite the differences in climate of opinion between the political and the union side, in both cases it seemed necessary, in the process of defending the alliance, to emphasize the role of American political forces that were relatively attractive to British Labour. This sometimes meant, as it usually did for the left, the discovery of illusory socialist developments. But for the Labour right and center, American foreign policy did not have to shift, or appear to shift, decisively away from the build-up of military strength. Instead, it was that very policy which the leadership sought to justify, and to do so by stressing that the Americans who framed and supported the policy were of essentially similar political stuff as were those who made up the British Labour movement.

This affinity, it might be assumed, not only was important as a means of recruiting rank-and-file support for the party's foreign policy but was also useful in strengthening the conviction of the leaders themselves that they were, after all, on the right side. Reassurances became more important when there were aspects of American foreign policy which went against the political grain of the Labour party, as did, for example, America's military arrangements with Spain. These were protested by Labour moderates, not just by the left wing;[46] the TUC, in 1951, was adamant enough in its hostility to Franco to pass a resolution against the arrival of a Spanish ambassador in Britain.[47] If deviations of this type were not to become the basis for a more general condemnation of American "Fascist" or "reactionary" tendencies, it was essential that general political developments in the United States be understood in a favorable light.

For this purpose, Labour spokesmen did more than call attention to America's political democracy. The potency of common political institutions in establishing Anglo-American kinship was evident in the Labour party, as elsewhere in the British community, but it was not the most

46. 491 H.C. Deb. 511-24 (July 25, 1951), to cite only one of many occasions of Labour restiveness on the Spanish question.

47. 83d Annual Report of the Trades Union Congress (London, 1951), pp. 421-22.

specific Labour means of seeking identification. What was looked for was a common interest in social and economic programs. Consequently, the achievements of the New Deal were considered the marks of American advance along the path marked out by the Labour party. America's pace might be different, "but slowly and inexorably," one moderate member of Parliament remarked in 1946, "the capitalist system there is being modified."[48] In the later days of satisfaction with the Marshall Plan, this became the standard approach of the Labour party, even (as has been noted) of a considerable portion of the left wing. However, it was mainly for the Labour right that New Dealism had long-run attractiveness. The American economic reforms were not so far from the aspirations of moderate socialists as they were from the more far-reaching schemes of the left. As Ernest Bevin said: "This so-called welfare state has developed everywhere. The United States is as much a welfare state as we are only in a different form."[49] And, he added, American unemployment insurance was actually higher than Britain's. Almost as meaningful as social security was the program of the Tennessee Valley Authority. Both Attlee and Morrison, for example, alluded to it in their catalogues of the "good side" of American political life.[50]

Just as it was possible for most of Labour to welcome what it regarded as American social advances of the past, so it was possible to approve wholeheartedly of the American political forces which were pressing for more of the same. While the left was only temporarily infatuated with American "progressives," the bulk of the Labour party was more permanently identified. Perhaps its American counterparts were fighting for different specific policies, but they were nonetheless recognized as constituting an analogous party of change. Even before the announcement of the Marshall Plan, a middle-of-the-road Labour member of Parliament had chosen Hubert Humphrey and Walter Reuther as true friends of Labour Britain.[51] The preference for the liberal wing of the Democratic party remained a constant,[52] as might have been expected,

---

48. Aidan Crawley (427 H.C. Deb. 1564-65 [October 22, 1946]).

49. 467 H.C. Deb. 1096 (July 18, 1949).

50. 446 H.C. Deb. 619 (January 23, 1948), and 51st Annual Report of the Labour Party, p. 108.

51. P. C. Gordon-Walker, Tribune, April 4, 1947, pp. 1-2.

52. There were many instances of this identification, especially after 1948 (see the remarks of J. E. Haire, 446 H.C. Deb. 600-602 [January 23, 1948]).

and Labour's enthusiasm for the results of the 1948 presidential election was, for the right as well as the left, predicated on the assumption that American progressivism had triumphed at the polls.[53] The principal Labour newspaper hailed Truman's election as a "defeat for reaction" and as "a shock not only to the American Republicans but to the British Tories."[54] The Tories, of course, had only been defeated figuratively, since it was by no means clear that they had linked their cause with that of the Republicans or had even been hoping for a Republican victory. The bracketing of Republicans and Tories was a sign of Labour's general attachment, at that stage, to the fortunes of the Fair Deal.

Carrying matters so far had its disadvantages. In addition to the subsequent disillusionment of the left-wing commentators themselves, about which the party leadership could do little one way or the other, there was an obvious danger that much of the Labour following was being persuaded to rest its favorable views of the United States on the thin ice of Fair Deal political victory. However, this was not entirely the case in the trade-unions, where there existed a sturdier bond than a transitory political one. The Trades Union Congress had links with American unions as such, and not only to the political causes they supported. The party favored by American union leaders did not have to be in office for British unionists to appreciate that labor remained a strong and independent force in American affairs. Free trade-unionism was, in the eyes of the TUC, the sine qua non of democracy. Support of American foreign policy by American unions was enough to indicate that transatlantic representatives of the working class saw, as well as did the TUC, the validity of military strength and solidarity against Russia. It was satisfying proof that American policy represented more than the will of capitalists. "Read the declarations of the American trade union Movement," one TUC leader told his conference, "and you will find them in line with the declarations of the British Trades Union Congress." That was "what our own people in America say, or people who are in a comparable position to ourselves."[55]

This sense of American unionists being the same kind of people was

53. Socialist Commentary was one of several Labour publications which greeted the 1948 election with enthusiastic attention. See XII (December, 1948), 340-46.

54. Daily Herald, November 4, 1948, p. 2.

55. Lincoln Evans (Iron and Steel Trades Confederation), 84th Annual Report of the Trades Union Congress, p. 374.

not an empty phrase, nor did it rest only on the general sense of per-
forming similar social and economic roles. Besides the obvious community of interest, an actual discussion of mutual problems was facilitated by the common language and by the pragmatic approach which TUC
officials felt they shared more fully with their American opposite numbers than they did with Continental union leaders. Since the war, communication between British and American unions had increased, partly
as a result of official sponsorship of productivity teams and of other
informational exchanges and visits. But there was a long history to the
relationship between the Trades Union Congress and the American
Federation of Labor. Since 1894 the two organizations had sent fraternal delegates to each other's annual meetings, and the occasions had
been suitably graced by speeches, exchanges of gifts, and other hearty
accouterments of the convention atmosphere. Personal relationships
thereby established are not easy to calculate in their political effects,
but they are certainly worth mentioning. It might also be noted that
among the TUC's fraternal delegates to the AF of L's San Francisco
convention of 1915 was Ernest Bevin, then a rising, militant organizer
of British dockers.[56]

Although these transatlantic ties rested fundamentally on the nonpolitical aspects of union activities, nevertheless the TUC did join in the
general Labour hopes for election victories by American progressive
forces.[57] Especially after 1950, it became the regular practice of the
defenders of the American alliance, against renewed left-wing attacks,
to emphasize the potency of their American "friends" relative to their
capitalist "enemies." One Labour conference was told: "I say to those
people who too often easily say we are dominated by Wall Street: there
is a good America, there is a growing democratic movement in America
now, a growing consciousness amongst American trade unionists of the
need to follow the path of social democracy."[58] President Truman was
hailed as labor's champion in the fight against reaction, and there was
optimism concerning the fortunes of his party. "So let us not discourage—

---

56. Ibid., p. 6.

57. Even the general secretary of the TUC, in replying to left-wing
    attempts to cite General Eisenhower's campaign speeches as
    evidence of American aggressive intentions, said it would have
    been more helpful to the union conference to have quoted Governor
    Stevenson (ibid., p. 381).

58. 49th Annual Report of the Labour Party, p. 144.

because we could discourage," said Herbert Morrison in October, 1952, "the progressive forces in America. . . ."[59] Don't think, he said, that America is Senator McCarthy. Morrison thought that would be as unfair as thinking that Britain was really represented by one Sir Waldron Smithers, a Conservative member of Parliament whose antediluvian politics were almost a British music-hall joke. Minimizing, in this way, the importance of those Americans whom Labour disliked was precisely the opposite of the left's habit of emphasizing the influence exercised by a variety of disapproved American Republicans.

In any event, the moderates as well as the left wing of the Labour party tended to present American political issues in oversimplified terms. For example, in 1952 Denis Healey, M.P., a leading young proponent of the official party foreign policy, was so concerned to prove that it was not American capitalism with which Labour was aligned that he said flatly: "America is not run by Wall Street. Wall Street has lost every American Election for the last 20 years and it will lose this one. It is not Wall Street that has run America's foreign policy since the war. It has been backed by the 15 million organized workers in the American Labour movement, and they are our blood brothers."[60] This line may have had propaganda value at the time, portraying as it did a political battle of good versus evil, in which good was sure to win. The trouble, now so obvious, was that if the party of "the 15 million organized workers," that is, the Democrats, ever lost an election, it would seem to follow (in Healey's language) that Wall Street would have won control over America's foreign policy. How, then, would the American alliance be justified to a Labour audience?

This problem did nòt appear to cause qualms until after November 4, 1952. During the presidential election campaign, Labour seemed so sure of Democratic victory that its identification with Stevenson was virtually complete. The same could be said of much of the British community, but in the case of the Labour center and right the identification was a good deal more serious. It was almost as though its defense of the American alliance rested on another Democratic victory. Stevenson's views, as well as the general position of his party, were regularly invoked

59. 51st Annual Report of the Labour Party, p. 108.

60. Ibid., p. 123. Healey himself could rest his case for Anglo-American co-operation on a much less ideological basis, as in "Power Politics and the Labour Party," in New Fabian Essays, ed. R. H. S. Crossman (London: Turnstile Press, 1952), pp. 161-79.

in arguments directed at left-wing critics. Consequently, the American election news was a shock. One former Labour minister, who had been among those most confident of Stevenson's victory,[61] said the results constituted a "black day for free mankind."[62] Depression and unemployment were to follow in the wake of Republican, or, as was said, of "Tory big business-men when they get political power." The Daily Herald, the official voice of Labour, was somewhat more careful, and more typical, in its conclusions, but it did not fail to mention that "the Party which comes to power has in its ranks, high in authority and strong in influence, men who are, in their attitude to all social progress and to organized labour, starkly and unashamedly reactionary."[63]

This open discouragement, so vividly manifest, should not be confused with the more violent reactions of the Labour Left (and of the British Communists) to the presidential election of 1952. Those at the Labour center and right did not want to believe the worst of the new Republican Administration. As defenders of the American alliance they had nothing to gain and everything to lose, within their own party, by any really unattractive turn in American policies. Both the leadership of the party's political section and that of the Trades Union Congress were too deeply committed to rearmament and Anglo-American co-operation to move readily in any other direction, and there is no reason to assume that they would have been so foolish as to think there was a realistic alternative foreign policy for Great Britain. Therefore, they were almost bound to begin looking for relatively "progressive" signs in the new Republican Administration, so that they could restore their tactical, argumentative position in the Labour party. If unable, however, to find any aspect of the new Administration with which to sympathize, Labour leaders would have greater difficulty defending Anglo-American co-operation. The defense was unlikely to be abandoned entirely, but it could become less wholehearted and less effective in response to Republican policies that looked increasingly unfriendly to Labour ideology.

---

61. This was Maurice Webb, who had visited the United States during the 1952 campaign and flatly predicted a Stevenson victory (Reynolds News, September 14, 1952, p. 4).

62. Ibid., November 9, 1952, p. 4.

63. November 6, 1952, p. 4.

VIII / LIBERAL AND INDEPENDENT OPINION

Except perhaps in the very early days of the Labour government,
socialist preferences were not characteristic of nominally independent
British commentary. Neither, in the postwar period, was Conservative
traditionalism the major note. Instead, the most influential of the
quality newspapers and weekly journals were usually committed to an
outlook that, for want of a better term, can best be described as "liberalism." This was not identical with the doctrines of the waning Liberal
party, although there were important links between that party and the
postwar independent press.

The moderate papers that were unpledged to either of the two
major parties probably did have a special appeal to the remaining
Liberal voters (9.1 per cent of the electorate in 1950, and 2.5 per cent
in 1951, when there were fewer than one-quarter as many party candidates). Liberal-minded editorials also appealed to those who had formerly voted Liberal and to new electors who might have preferred the Liberal
party if it had had a chance. Despite the apparently rigid division of the
postwar British electorate between Labour and Conservative, there were
obviously many whose opinions, if not their votes, favored predominantly
moderate policies. Each of the two major parties had such a following
and possessed, in addition, a number of politicians whose attitudes and
personalities were recognized as attractive to middle-of-the-road thinking. Anthony Eden and, in a different way, R. A. Butler were pre-eminent,
in this respect, among Conservatives, and Attlee, Morrison, and Gaitskell
in the Labour party. The Labour right and the Conservative left had a
good many things in common, and their views were often very close to
those of the independent press. However, the exigencies of party politics,
and of accompanying convictions, make it impossible to isolate liberal
orientations, as such, within either of the major parties.

Nor is it reasonable to consider the politicians of the Liberal party
as significant spokesmen for the in-between point of view. The independent portion of the quality press constitutes a much more important and
responsible source. It regularly reached most educated and politically
conscious Englishmen, who, regardless of fixed political convictions, cannot be assumed to have been uninfluenced by reading learned editorials

149

(or "leaders") in their favorite newspapers. The audience was mainly middle class and, judging by the election returns, more likely to vote Conservative than Labour. Indeed, the serious papers themselves were, with some justice, charged with leaning politically to the right more than to the left. That, at any rate, was the situation during the general elections of 1950 and 1951.[1] The "independent" press was usually either neutral or opposed to Labour. But this was still some distance from a consistent championship of Conservatives.

Defining "independent" in this way, so as to exclude party organs, leaves the bulk of the serious papers to be accounted for. First among them is the Times, whose semiofficial reputation makes it difficult to identify with a particular political orientation. While the Times, in postwar years, did reflect many middle-of-the road attitudes, its comments cannot be considered typical of liberal thought, except in the most general sense of the term.

The Manchester Guardian was the liberal paper, historically and otherwise. Its influence as such was recognized nationally as well as in Lancashire and the Midlands. Among dailies, it was the principal alternative to the Times, and often preferred by those in any degree left of political center. (The same brand of liberalism was, of course, reflected in the Manchester Guardian Weekly, which serves as a source for this work.) The other prominent Liberal organ was the News Chronicle, published in London and still supporting the Liberal party. But, as a more popular paper, it did not operate at the same level of editorial influence as did the Guardian. If separate Sunday papers are included, the Observer has to be added as a medium for the expression of a variety of liberal and independent opinion.[2]

In the category of serious weeklies, the Economist was by far the most important conveyor of nonparty views on international affairs and political issues generally. Although a large portion of its contents was directed to the business community, its commentary on public policy,

---

1. Analyses of the role of British newspapers in postwar political campaigns are contained in H. G. Nicholas, The British General Election of 1950 (London: Macmillan & Co., 1951), pp. 143-210, and D. E. Butler, The British General Election of 1951 (London: Macmillan & Co., 1952), pp. 129-36.

2. Despite the acknowledged importance of the Observer, it is not used as a source for this chapter because its views, when definable in terms of a given position, may also be derived from the dailies and weeklies whose attitudes are analyzed here.

domestic or foreign, had a broad and respectful audience.] In the context
of Britain's domestic economic policies, the journal's recommendations
had, particularly in later postwar years, a decided right-wing quality.
On this score as on general political matters the Economist was really
adhering to traditional British liberalism. In effect, much of this had
become conservative doctrine, but the intellectual orientations of the
Economist, despite many variations, were still broadly liberal.

Another independent weekly, the Spectator, was also somewhere between a liberal and moderately conservative position in the postwar years.
Its public was not so much distinguished by a party label as by a taste for
the mixture of political and aesthetic discussion, like that presented by
the New Statesman, but without the latter's left-wing slant. Time and
Tide, less well known, was also independent and vigorously "middle of
the road."

This catalogue of the serious independent press almost exhausts
the list of quality papers of national circulation. The outstanding omis-
sions have been the ordinarily Conservative Sunday Times (entirely
distinct from the Times) and the avowedly Conservative Daily Telegraph.[3]
In Scotland and in some provincial centers, the few local papers of serious
import, usually Conservative in politics, did not bulk very large in comparison with the nationally circulated English papers. The independent
and liberal papers, already noted, played the dominant role in furnishing
serious news and views.

General Attachments

Of primary significance in considering the large body of middle
opinion is its attachment to the principles of political liberty. This is
now, of course, a nearly universal attitude of the British community,
but both in historical background and in present emphasis the liberal
has been most concerned with the establishment and the maintenance of
the fundamentals of political democracy. Both major parties have, in

---

3.   Also omitted are primarily nonpolitical papers reaching special
     (though often substantial) audiences. Notably this means the omis-
     sion of publications representing Roman Catholic opinion, which, it
     should at least be noted, has appeared more aggressively anti-
     Communist than the liberal and independent press in Britain. In
     a different category, though omitted as well, is the very widely cir-
     culated weekly published by the British Broadcasting Corporation,
     the Listener. It has published many political talks, but the maga-
     zine has of course no settled political point of view.

this sense, been "liberalized," or have become heavily permeated by the liberal outlook. Labour and Conservative statements of faith in political democracy are indistinguishable from those arbitrarily classified as liberal. It is the very universality of democratic convictions that was noted, in the beginning of this study, to be so important in establishing common ground between Britain and America. But among socialists this shared political faith has been complicated by deep divergencies with respect to economic philosophy; and among Conservatives the attachment has been affected, though less clearly and in a very different way, by traditional party beliefs. What may be abstracted here is the liberal faith in political democracy, relatively unencumbered by other considerations.

British liberals, so defined, have usually been favorably oriented toward the United States. Historically, there was every reason for this to be the case. From the time of the Revolution of 1776, British liberals sympathized with the aspirations of American democracy. In nineteenth-century struggles for the suffrage in Britain, the Radicals (who, as extreme liberals, were the prime exponents of the universal franchise) looked to the United States as a favorable example of the practice of their principles. Rallying as it did so many religious dissenters, the Liberal party was bound to admire American religious toleration and, often, the absence of an established state church.

These causes were by no means exclusively middle class or always of the Liberal party. Especially in the middle of the nineteenth century, the workingmen who flocked to the banners of Radical Democracy also saw the United States as the home of an experiment congenial to their interests and ideals. The virtues of the American Republic shone all the brighter when the Emancipation Proclamation put to rest the anti-slavery qualms of the liberal conscience. To Abraham Lincoln and the cause of the Union there was accorded a sympathy that the British government itself had refused. Most impressive was the well-known example of the Manchester cotton workers who remained faithful to the transatlantic democracy despite unemployment in Lancashire mills, caused by the North's blockade of southern cotton.

Although America's rise to wealth and primacy necessarily weakened this sympathy for the newcomer or the underdog,[4] the traditional

---

4. The change in European radical attitudes toward the United States was discussed by Bertrand Russell, "The Political and Cultural

attachment was kept alive by the re-emphasis on common political institutions during the two world wars and by both the Wilsonian and the
Rooseveltian symbolizations of democracy. There was, in 1917-19 and
again in 1941-45, a sense in which British faith in America's political
message was quickened. Those who remained liberals, rather than becoming socialists, could respond without the inhibitions imposed by a
dislike for private capitalism.

Of greater importance for the nonsocialist than differences in economic preference were apparent American departures from democratic
political principles. Liberals were always in the vanguard of the widespread British disapproval of restrictive American legislation affecting
immigration or civil liberties. American anticommunism, even short
of the investigations of Senators McCarthy and McCarran, was assuredly
not shared by the British independent press. In this it seemed to reflect
the attitude of the general public, and especially of the middle class, whose
dislike of strenuous anti-Communist practices has already been noted.[5]
But liberals, while deploring American developments they disliked,
nevertheless showed no readiness to emulate socialists who, consistent
with one version of their doctrine, could throw up their hands and conclude that the American Republic had succumbed to machinations of
capitalists-turned-Fascists. The despair of the economic determinist
was, for liberals, even less congenial than it was for the right-wing of

Influence," in The Impact of America on European Culture (Boston:
Beacon Press, 1951). However, the shift in the British image of
the United States, from the home of equalitarian opportunity to that
of industrial capitalism, was already under way in the last decades
of the nineteenth century (see Richard H. Heindel, The American
Impact on Great Britain, 1898-1914 [Philadelphia: University of
Pennsylvania Press, 1940]).

5. In chap. ii. Unfortunately, it would be a large and difficult task to
explore the reasons for the pronounced difference between British
and American reactions to Communists. This difference has been
widely commented on, especially in Britain, where it has been popular to describe American anticommunism as a manifestation of a
basic "insecurity" afflicting the community. More serious as an
explanation than this fantasy of mass psychoanalysis has been the
effort to portray the stronger American consciousness of 'Communist
conspiracies as a reflection of the fact that the middle class in the
United States was not vitiated, in relative status and spirit, as was
the British middle class, by high taxation and other economic ad-
versities. This was one of the points advanced by Arnold Toynbee:
"I suppose one reasons that the American middle class still has
more to lose than the West European middle class, and they are
not yet broken in to the idea of losing what they have" ("The Study
of History in the Light of Current Developments," International
Affairs, XXIV [October, 1948], 558).

the Labour party. It was entirely out of line with the settled conviction that the Americans and the British had "a common approach to life."[6]

This accord was recognized with only slightly less thoroughness during the early postwar years when socialist conceptions were most pervasive. The Economist, though at that time not uncritical of American capitalism, was usually clear in its recognition of the common ground. If ideology must be brought into a discussion of foreign policy, it remarked, "there are much deeper divisions of faith between Soviet Russia and either Britain or America than any that separate these two."[7] Others stated the matter more positively in terms of "our liberal faith" and "the ideals and the methods of freedom."[8] Or, more bluntly, the United States and Great Britain, among the great powers, were described as the only "successful democracies."[9]

It was on this basis that liberals rejected the sometimes tempting notion that Britain was socialist middle ground and, as such, should try to be an ideological bridge between Russia and America. Naturally the case was bolstered by subsequent manifestations of Russian totalitarianism and by well-received turns in American policy. The Marshall Plan, in this way, was striking confirmation of the inherent goodness of the American democratic process. Liberals did not, like many socialists, have to justify their welcome of the initiation and congressional approval of the Marshall Plan by imagining that it was the product of a growing socialist or even Fair Dealish force in American politics. It was not required that democratic forces should be noncapitalist in character in order to support the British liberal's faith in the good intentions of the United States.

Undoubtedly, the liberal position is distinguished from the socialist approach by this absence of an anticapitalist bias (though not, in this respect, so very clearly marked off from the right wing of the Labour party). If, however, the British liberal was, in his preference for the common ground of democracy, ready to count capitalists as his ideological brethren, he was also settled in the conviction that socialists,

---

6. Stephen King-Hall, "Russia's Place in the Post-war World," Fortnightly, CLXIV (August, 1945), 77.

7. CLI (November 23, 1946), 818.

8. Wickham Steed, "Between East and West," Contemporary Review, CLXXI (May, 1947), 262.

9. Wilson Harris (437 H.C. Deb. 1913 [May 16, 1947]).

in general, were within the same political fold. Directly this had nothing to do with the liberal attitude toward the American leadership, unsuspected, as it was, of socialist affinities. But indirectly it meant that liberals were offended by any indication that the United States intended to treat social democrats, along with Communists, as ideological enemies.

For the most part, moderate British opinion did not accept the view, often advanced in the Labour party, that American foreign policy was really antisocialist. Only in 1946 was there any appreciable liberal fear of American intentions on this score. It was then that the Economist advised Americans to appreciate "not merely that Socialists can be democrats but also that the great majority of the world's democrats are now Socialists."[10] And this was at a time when that journal, which was ordinarily the apostle of competitive capitalism, had temporarily been impressed with the apparent fait accompli of socialism in Europe.[11] American preferences for the restoration of capitalist practices then seemed less plausible to the Economist than they did in the later postwar period. But, attractive as the American advocacy of business competition eventually became, British liberals were still bound to react adversely to any tendency to place British Labour outside the democratic pale. Labour's acceptance of parliamentary principles was ordinarily taken for granted (as indeed it had to be if Britain were considered a viable democracy); furthermore, this assumption by liberals was strengthened, despite growing opposition to socialism, by sharing the humanitarian impulse for social and economic reform which was one of the Labour party's conspicuous motivations.

That degree of affinity should not conceal the fact that the basic economic doctrines of liberalism were such as to make for an almost uniquely favorable reception of American postwar trade policies. Unlike the Conservatives, whose position was affected by their tradition of Imperial Preference, and unlike the Labour party, wedded to state planning and control of international trade, liberals were usually committed to free trade. Historically, this had been the outstanding principle of the Liberal party, for whose remnants it continued to be the uniting and distinguishing element. And among many nonaffiliated liberals, it was only the party which had been abandoned as a lost cause; the belief in free

---

10. CL (March 9, 1946), 362.

11. "Conditions of free capitalism" were not enough, the Economist proclaimed (CL [May 25, 1946], 826).

trade remained alive outside the narrowing political ranks, although not burning so fiercely as within. Consequently, when in 1946 most of the rest of the British community was hostile to American plans for removing international trade barriers, the <u>Manchester Guardian Weekly</u> welcomed the attempt to practice the principles of Adam Smith.[12] Always, as was emphasized in the previous discussion of trade policy, this favorable reception was coupled with admonitions, similar to those offered by Englishmen of all persuasions, to the effect that America must lower its tariffs.[13] But, while allowing for the especially strong liberal feeling that the United States should further reduce the barriers of its trade and customs regulations, there was no inclination, within this school of economic thought, to believe that favorable American policies could solve all of Britain's problems. On the contrary, the free-traders appreciated the need for British industries to become satisfactorily competitive in world markets. It was part of the doctrine that all restrictions on the free exchange of goods, whether imposed by American tariffs, Empire trading arrangements, or other forms of government intervention, tended to prevent the adjustments necessary to the most economic production of goods.

Postwar political exigencies often prevented the advocacy of the immediate removal of British trade restrictions, and liberals joined in criticism of the early American pressure in that direction. However, on general principles there was really an agreement with the view that British industries had to become efficient enough to meet the conditions of competitive capitalism. "Costs and prices in the insulated sterling area are too high for it to have any chance of balancing accounts with the dollar area" the <u>Manchester Guardian Weekly</u> declared in 1949.[14] Again a year later, repeating its regular economic theme, the principal liberal newspaper urged that Britain, as well as America, had its responsibility for overcoming the dollar gap: "There can be no working system for a healthy world trade unless British exports are competitive throughout the international markets and the efforts of British industry are bent to a large volume of trade."[15] To be sure, exhortation of this sort was

---

12. LV (October 18, 1946), 202-3.

13. See chap. iv.

14. July 14, 1949, p. 8.

15. Ibid., June 1, 1950, p. 9.

very general in Britain, especially after the Marshall Plan, but in the case of the liberals it was tied to a conscious and largely uninhibited preference for a competitive and capitalist world. It was entirely compatible with fundamental American economic precepts—in so far as these precepts were not flatly contradicted by the success of American business in establishing protective tariffs.

Acceptance of capitalist principles did not preclude doubts about the working of the American economy. Liberals shared the widespread British fear of a depression in the United States. However, unlike the socialist's misgivings, the liberal's were not based upon an absence of faith in private enterprise as such; it was only that liberals were not so sure, especially in the first postwar years, that the United States was settled, as was Britain, upon the use of governmental measures to control the ups and downs of business activity. Plainly, the liberals were Keynesians, whose faith in capitalism was bounded by a firm conviction that fiscal and budgetary tools were required to maintain economic stability. So, in 1946, the Economist turned a jaundiced eye to the "gradual unfolding of uncontrolled economic processes" in the United States.[16] The past record, it was remarked with reference to 1929, was not so encouraging. Nor did these warnings disappear in the next few years of continued American prosperity. How long, the Guardian asked in early 1948, can the boom last? "For the sake of Europe as well as of America's future," it was added, "one must hope that the economy will be brought under effective control before it is too late."[17]

Nevertheless, while pessimism was easily revived,[18] in time the tone of liberal commentary on American economic prospects became less discouraged, partly because of a growing assumption that the United States Administration was capable of exercising effective control if and when necessary. Instability, said one observer, remained characteristic, but it was subject to checks.[19] This view was consistent with the usual liberal position vis-à-vis business cycles. It had never been believed that drastic slumps were chronically and inevitably the product of non-

16. CLI (September 14, 1946), 402.

17. January 15, 1948, p. 2.

18 Typical misgivings were noted in the Economist, CLVI (January 29, 1949), 179-80.

19. Graham Hutton, "The Economic Basis of American Power," Nineteenth Century and After, CXLIII (February, 1948), 71-78.

socialist economies. Therefore, the favorable experiences of the post-war years greatly mollified the fears which had developed out of the circumstances of the prewar period. Liberal economic doctrine was flexible and pragmatic and most readily reconciled to the success of private enterprise.

This was demonstrated by the attitude of liberals toward Britain's economic crisis of 1949. Instead of following the popular Labour line of blaming the relatively slight American recession for the deterioration of Britain's dollar earnings, there was a tendency to minimize both the severity and the effects of anything that had happened in the United States. To some extent, this difference from Labour opinion reflected the fact that liberals, being unattached to the party in power, had no political reason to point toward a foreign scapegoat. But the emphasis which liberals now placed on the need for British industry to become properly competitive also showed that they had really edged much closer to the American outlook than to the doctrines of the Labour government. The Economist, in mid-1949, displayed a page of graphs which were designed to depict the error of "some Labour spokesmen" who had blamed "the chronic instability of American capitalism" for Britain's dollar shortage. The facts indicated, in summary, that the American economy was not in a slump but only in a "healthy pause for breath after a period of rapid expansion."[20]

Moderate British voices were now raised in what had largely been the American complaint: that Britain not only was producing less than it should but also was spending more than the nation could afford.[21] Finally, this became a steady refrain, especially in the Economist, which was the most prominent advocate of the capitalist virtues of hard work, saving, private investment, and lowered government expenditures. Given this point of view, it was clear that any liberal objections to America's economic policies were going to be offered in a drastically different context from socialist criticism.

After 1948 liberal misgivings of an ideological character, in so far as they existed at all, were ordinarily confined to political ground. Here objections arose not only on civil liberties issues but also at the point where political values touched foreign affairs. The conspicuous example

---

20. CLVII (September 10, 1949), 541.

21. E.g., Spectator, CLXXXIII (August 26, 1949), 255-56.

was the changing American policy toward Franco Spain. While the liberal press did not remain so adamantly critical, as did Labour, of closer relations with Spain, it displayed, at the very least, a considerable ambivalence. In the early stages of American hints of military and economic arrangements with Franco, there was an open hostility from both the Guardian and the Economist. There were reservations about anything that looked like outside economic help for Spain.[22] "A mood of shame and indignation," the Economist said, "comes over any European Liberal or Socialist who hears talk of coming to terms with the regime established 12 years ago."[23] But in 1951 the same journal granted that "it would be unrealistic in the future not to treat the Spaniards as possible allies. . . ."[24]

This did not yet mean that a full partnership with Franco was at all palatable to liberals, whose sensibilities were always likely to be offended by prospective American moves for closer co-operation of Spain with Western Europe.[25] But their sense of compatibility with American political democracy was not so shaky as to be decisively affected by the American desire to draw Spain into the task of defending Europe. It would take a much larger pattern of uncongenial American activity for the liberal commitment to be changed. Much more probable was that British liberals, like their American counterparts, would slowly and reluctantly move, as they had already done in the Spanish affair, to further acceptance of military necessities overriding political preferences in relatively minor matters. At worst, dealings such as those with Franco were considered mistaken. They were not regarded as prima facie evidence of the desertion of the democratic faith.

Hopes for American International Participation

The absence of basic doctrinal barriers in the liberal approach to the United States meant that this main body of middle opinion could reflect, without serious doubt, the original postwar British desire that

---

22. Manchester Guardian Weekly, October 14, 1948, p. 9.

23. CLV (October 16, 1948), 612.

24. CLX (January 13, 1951), 68.

25. Thus the Economist (CLXI [July 7, 1951], 5-6) hoped that the inclusion of Turkey in the North Atlantic Treaty Organization would set no precedent for Spain. Despite its air of certainty, the Economist did not always speak with the same voice. Some of its commentary contained a harder core of "military realism" than was typical of the liberal outlook reflected more regularly by the Guardian.

America play an increasingly important role in international affairs. This rested primarily on a realistic diplomatic and military appraisal of Britain's need for American economic assistance and military support. The adjustment to American leadership was no simple matter, for liberals or anyone else, but in the beginning it must have been eased considerably by a ready conviction that the United States stood for liberal ideals.

The problem of American participation in world affairs, in 1945 and 1946, appeared much as it had between the two wars and, most poignantly, between 1939 and 1941. It was for the United States to see that it had interests in common with Britain, not the other way around. The enemy was isolationism. Until the announcement of the Truman Doctrine in March, 1947, liberal commentary on American foreign policy was dominated by the fear that the United States would return to its prewar isolationism or, at any rate, fail to make clear that its resources were dedicated to the defense of Britain and Europe. There seemed to be nothing wanted so much as the American assumption of international responsibilities. Specifically, it was hoped that the United States would "help Britain in Greece" and so indicate that there were "limits beyond which the United States would not see Europe and the strategic points of the world brought under the domination of an aggressive Power."[26]

In light of this anticipation, the Truman Doctrine should, presumably, have been entirely welcome, and, in general, the American commitment which the Truman Doctrine contained was well received in the liberal press. However, President Truman's announcement itself was greeted with some reserve. The President's speech lacked, it was said, "the slightest trace of subtlety or diplomatic finesse."[27] The challenge to Russia was more direct than British liberals had bargained for, although the American assumption of the responsibility which Britain could no longer carry in the eastern Mediterranean was all to the good. What was disturbing, said the Manchester Guardian Weekly, was "the fear that in taking up our cause in Europe and the Mediterranean—the cause of democracy and freedom and independence—the United States may increase the tension with Soviet Russia to a point where peace itself is threatened."[28]

---

26. Manchester Guardian Weekly, March 13, 1947, p. 2.

27. News Chronicle, March 14, 1947, p. 2.

28. March 20, 1947, p. 2.

This dislike of a too openly anti-Russian tone in American policies did not originate entirely with the proclamation of the Truman Doctrine. The independent press had responded in a similar way, off and on, ever since the United States had formally adopted a "get-tough" line in 1946.[29] To some extent, this attitude, while not ideologically sympathetic to the Soviet Union, was representative of the lingering hopes for Anglo-Russian co-operation. These were not so different in kind from the American hopes of 1943-45, but they were slower to fade from public consciousness (in contrast, in all probability, to official British attitudes, which never seemed to have been so optimistic as those of the Roosevelt Administration). The tenacity of the hopes for getting along with Russia rested in part on an intense war-weariness, which led to a reluctance to challenge anyone, and more particularly on Britain's very large wartime fund of good will toward the Soviet Union. This was much less the creation of left-wing propagandists than of the recollection of the dark days of 1941 and 1942 (though not of 1940) when the Russians bore the brunt of a German attack that might otherwise have been hurled against Britain. Consequently, at least in liberal (as well as in socialist) circles, really anti-Russian sentiments remained bad form in the first year or two after the war.[30]

Nor was this the only consideration in misgivings about the admittedly desired and necessary exercise of American power. Prominent for the first time in response to the Truman Doctrine was the fear that American anticommunism would take command. The Times, though generally favorable to the Truman Doctrine, added: "The potency of the new policy will clearly depend upon the manner and the mood in which it is applied. The danger that it may yet be perverted into a barren and restrictive anti-Communist crusade cannot be ignored; a 'red scare' is already in full swing against Communists and 'fellow-travellers' in the American Administration and the labour movement."[31]

29. The Spectator was disturbed by "those unmeasured anti-Russian arguments which were advanced more and more frequently as reasons for granting a loan to Britain"(CLXXVII [July 19, 1946], 55-56).

30. In March, 1947, direct London interviews by one opinion survey organization "showed rather fewer people openly favorable to the U.S.A. than to Russia" (Tom Harrisson, "British Opinion Moves toward a New Synthesis," Public Opinion Quarterly, XI [fall, 1947], 327-41).

31. March 27, 1947, p. 5.

In a similar vein, the Economist reflected the two sides of the liberal attitude toward the Truman Doctrine. So long, it declared, as it could be regarded as "the starting point for an eventual understanding between the Russians and the Americans, it should have British support."[32] These words were more than typical of the anxious mood of early 1947; they were also precursory of what eventually became the characteristic tone of the commentary of the independent press on American policy. But, save briefly, this cautionary emphasis was not the dominant British theme until about three years after the Truman Doctrine. Partly, no doubt, the pacific tone of the Marshall Plan mollified incipient anxieties, as it had the deeper socialist dread of American military policies. But there was also a growing recognition, increased by the Berlin blockade, of the implacable nature of Russian hostility and of the danger that hung over Western Europe. Liberals had, after all, been relatively untinged with the socialist belief that Russia was incapable of contemplating aggressive expansion. Consequently, opinion generally reverted to the original postwar emphasis on American involvement as a desired means of maintaining Allied strength. Especially from 1948 to 1950, British liberals were specific in their wish for American military commitments in the defense of Europe. Again, the more obvious fear was that the United States would do too little, not too much; that a recurrent isolationism would prevent American recognition of the need for clearly displaying the nation's intention to stand against military aggression.

In the year or so before the acceptance of the Atlantic Pact, the desire that the United States should become involved in such an arrangement was evident enough, although there was an occasional reappearance of a note of caution. Thus it was suggested that in the process of appreciating the importance of defending Europe the United States might become either so thoroughly impressed with military factors as to neglect economic assitance for its own sake or generally so adamant in its dealings with the Soviet Union as to make impossible the dim but still cherished chance for a future East-West agreement. This ambivalence was not uniquely the property of the liberal mind, and the Times probably reflected a good deal of the general British attitude in its editorial prompted by the effects on American policy of the Communist coup in Czechoslovakia. The Times, consistent with its standing preference for the Marshall Plan over the Truman Doctrine,

---

32. CLII (April 12, 1947), 522.

now regretted that Czech events had complicated the congressional discussion of European-aid proposals with "other considerations," namely, with those of anti-Communist politics and strategy. However, it was admitted that American awareness of these other considerations. might have a good side too. Any exclusive emphasis on a military pledge was decried, "but an American pledge would clearly be a powerful, perhaps decisive, reinforcement."[33] During the remainder of 1948 this latter opinion came to be much more positively presented. There was high praise for the Vandenberg Resolution and its promise of peacetime military support. Its approval, it was said, would be a milestone, like that of the Marshall Plan, in the American route away from isolationism.[34] And, in favoring the Atlantic Pact, the Times indicated near the end of 1948 how fully it had come to accept the need for American power: "Only when the west has clearly marshalled its defensive, economic, and moral strength will a possible way be opened for practical arrangements with the east."[35]

Much of the independent commentary in the discussion preceding the Atlantic Pact stressed the uncertainty of American help. There was a realization that the organization of strictly European arms under the Brussels Treaty was inadequate to the task at hand. There was no certainty of its effectiveness, according to the Spectator, "unless the arms, men and guarantees with which the United States is prepared to back it are precisely known. We are still a long way from that knowledge and the Americans themselves hardly seem near to it."[36] Getting the American signature to the Atlantic Pact seemed, therefore, a real accomplishment. The very fact of American membership in the treaty organization provided the assurances which had been wanting in 1948. Now there was publicly stated what the Economist called the only known deterrent to war: "America's willingness to defend its European partners, if need be."[37] It was also noted that, under the Atlantic Pact, the United States could furnish its allies with arms, but this seemed, at the time, of much less significance than American involvement, by treaty, in the defense of

---

33. March 16, 1948, p. 5.

34. London Times, May 21, 1948, p. 5.

35. Ibid., November 10, 1948, p. 5.

36. CLXXX (April 30, 1948), 512.

37. CLVI (February 19, 1949), 314.

Europe.[38] "We can be sure," said the <u>Manchester Guardian Weekly,</u> "that the historic importance of the United States' decision will not be lost on the Russians."[39] There seemed, among liberals, no fear that the pact would be interpreted as an aggressive act. Its defensive intentions, it was assumed, were clear enough. One reason the pact seemed so pacific to British liberals was that they, like Ernest Bevin, regarded it as essentially a British or European achievement, into which the United States, though admittedly the really important element, had been brought.

Arrangements for the pooling of strength against potential aggression appealed also as a manifestation of the collective-security doctrine. To this, liberals had been pledged in the 1930's, although, like the prewar Labour party, only belatedly to the military force required to make the doctrine meaningful. Belief in the United Nations, as in the League of Nations, was cherished liberal internationalism. Although the language of collective security did not have to be invoked so often, as in Labour circles, to justify the use of Anglo-American power in world affairs, nevertheless the authority of the United Nations was important in the liberal support for the Korean campaign. And, in the face of subsequent criticism of American actions, the United States was defended because it had "shown itself a loyal member of the United Nations."[40] This was hardly the principal recommendation of the United States as an ally, but it played a part in sustaining the attachment.

Under whatever rationale, it remained overwhelmingly important that the United States should not lapse into a neo-isolationism with respect to Europe. That prospect never seemed completely absent from the liberal attitude, but it did diminish between the outbreak of the Korean war and the Chinese intervention in that war. This was a time when the United States, in the first response to Communist military aggression, began to press for increased European defenses and to take a very large lead in rearmament proposals. Observing this, in September, 1950, the <u>Economist</u> no longer saw any reason to fear "American half-heartedness"; it thought that perhaps the American pace might now be faster than Europe could bear.[41]

---

38. London <u>Times</u>, March 11, 1949, p. 5.

39. March 24, 1949, p. 8.

40. <u>Ibid.</u>, December 21, 1950, p. 8.

41. CLIX (September 16, 1950), 467.

But before American participation could really be taken for granted—and so objected to because it was too strenuous—the threat of withdrawal re-emerged. It was precipitated by the great American debate that followed former President Hoover's revival of the isolationist alternative in the winter of 1950-51. Pulling out of Europe, it was plain, was still seriously considered in the United States, and British policy had to be adjusted accordingly. This meant, it was carefully admitted, acting so as to increase American confidence in Europe's own efforts to defend itself. A larger rearmament program was thus required. It was the kind of thing which would enable the American Administration "to make the answer to Mr. Hoover fully effective. . . ."[42] British liberals retained their outward confidence that Hoover's viewpoint would not prevail, but they thought that evidence of greater European determination would cause American policy to move further "away from the isolationist extreme."[43]

This was widely held, not only by liberals, to provide a reason for Britain's undertaking, in 1951, the very large rearmament program, which was heavily criticized and eventually had to be "stretched out" for economic reasons. In fact, those who advanced the rearmament program, that is, the Labour government, were accused of doing so only because of a desire to please the United States and specifically to counter, as the liberal press seemed to think necessary, American neo-isolationist sentiment. In 1952, as the involvement of the United States in Europe took on aspects of permanency, the old but still prevailing British fear of American curtailment of military and economic assistance came to be sharply challenged. Liberals, as well as everyone who for similar reasons supported the British rearmament program, were told that they really imputed a kind of stupidity to American policy-making by thinking that the United States could contemplate the desertion of Europe. Perhaps, it was suggested, the fear of American withdrawal was only an illusion cherished by Englishmen who wished to perpetuate feelings of superiority to their not-so-wise allies.[44] This Bevanite debating trick—twisting the charge of anti-Americanism so that it applied to liberal opponents—may not have been intended

---

42. Ibid., December 30, 1950, p. 1182.

43. Spectator, CLXXXVI (January 12, 1951), 33.

44. Remarks to this effect, directed specifically at the right wing of the Labour party but applying to the liberal viewpoint as well, were by Thomas Balogh, Oxford don and Bevanite economist, in a lecture sponsored by the Fabian Society in London, November 18, 1952.

seriously, but it did touch upon a crucial point. Whether the possibility of American withdrawal was only an illusion, serving psychological purposes, was a moot point. But, realistically based or not, the desire to avoid even a partial American retirement had undoubtedly affected the foreign-policy responses of the independent press.

Lack of full confidence in America's participation was related to the tone of the criticism of American policies during 1951 and 1952. Of course, the liberals were much more inclined, even in the period of general British suspicion of the United States, to emphasize "the fundamental moderation and the peaceful objectives of American policy"[45] than were the left-wing opponents of the Anglo-American alliance. The independent press was by no means immune from the prevailing notion that the United States should be restrained in its military and diplomatic activity, especially, as will be observed, in the Far East; but the Manchester Guardian Weekly was typical in wanting restraining tactics that were inoffensive. What escaped the Bevanites, it said, was that hectoring was less effective than persuasion.[46] As the Times said early in 1952, "frank speech between Governments" was necessary in light of "rash and alarming statements" by influential Americans. "The British Government have a part still to play in urging prudence on the United States." This part, the Times urged, could only be played in the "climate of friendly association" which Prime Minister Churchill sought to foster.[47]

Getting tough with America was ruled out. But how much longer would a soft approach seem required by Britain's need for American protection? The protection itself was undoubtedly going to be needed almost indefinitely, but at the point where American participation in European defense could be assumed as a matter of course there might be a shift from the customary postwar attitude of having to court the United States. The suitor would have the American dowry and could start laying down the terms of the marriage. The places to watch for any such drastic change in British outlook were the opinion-making editorials of the nation's quality press. More than indicating a particular political perspective, papers like the Times or the Economist displayed the broad lines of thought that affected the determination of British policy.

45. Economist, CLXI (July 14, 1951), 67.

46. July 12, 1951, p. 8.

47. February 27, 1952, p. 5.

Political Reactions

Befitting a consciousness of their status and respectability, the quality newspapers were less frankly the champions of a given American political cause then were Labour sources. Liberal faith in the United States did not rise or fall so sharply with the success or failure of Fair Dealish social and economic programs. The independent press was mainly concerned with American political parties as they impinged on the development and conduct of foreign policy. Approving generally of the Truman Administration's policy, British liberals were therefore ranged against the Republican critics on issues relating to Europe as well as Asia.

Of this partiality, there is no more meaningful example than the rallying to the defense of Secretary of State Acheson. Not only was the Republican objection to Acheson linked to what liberals considered an attack on freedom of thought in the United States, but the Secretary symbolized the best-liked qualities and programs of American foreign policy. His appearance, his manner, and his subtlety of mind were what the British admired in a diplomat; he seemed a more determined-looking Anthony Eden. That the United States should produce Acheson as its secretary of state seemed almost too good to be true. The Times displayed the satisfaction felt for his appointment: "In this country there will be complete confidence in a Secretary of State who has proved himself a firm friend over so many years and who has played so large a part in the unfolding of American policy with all that it means to-day for freedom and democracy."[48] It was fondly recalled that an Acheson speech of May, 1947, had foreshadowed the development of the European Recovery Program and the broad assumption of American responsibility in world affairs.

British confidence in Acheson was raised by the record of American foreign policy in 1949, especially by the successful negotiation of the Atlantic Pact. In consequence, there was only dismay when the Republican attack was leveled at the Secretary in early 1950. What appeared to disturb Acheson's American opponents had not bothered British liberals at all. There was no inclination to blame the State Department for the conquest of China by the Communists, and there was no feeling that Acheson was unreliable because of his association

---

48. January 8, 1949, p. 5.

with Alger Hiss or because of insufficient vigilance in rooting out Communist subordinates. On the contrary, the tendency of independent British newspapers, stronger than that of their American counterparts, had been to place so much greater emphasis on the protection of freedom than on the finding of Communists as to preclude even a political understanding of the basis of the campaign against Acheson. Acheson represented the preferred line of American policy—stressing the defense of Europe, economically and militarily. His line was strong, without being too strong for British tastes. The Republican attack was "almost incredible," as one journal put it.[49] It was a "horrifying spectacle"[50] to a large section of the educated British public, for whom Acheson was something of a hero or champion. Often it was said that the Secretary was the victim of an American "atmosphere of fear and suspicion,"[51] which was then beginning to alarm defenders of civil liberties in Britain as well as the United States.

Alarm increased at the time of the 1950 congressional elections, which seemed, unlike 1948, to have involved foreign-policy issues. The results, from the British pro-Acheson view, were not encouraging. The Manchester Guardian Weekly interpreted the results as suggesting that "vociferous 'Red baiting'" was good politics,[52] and the Economist found the methods of attacking the State Department thoroughly objectionable.[53] In the remaining two years of the Truman Administration there was no doubt that moderate British opinion accepted the idea that the forces for and against Secretary Acheson were, respectively, those of good and evil. Praise was offered the Administration's policy, on the grounds of its sanity and courage, and scorn was heaped upon outright opponents. The absence of customary restraint was understandable. This was not viewed simply as a question of American party politics, in which Englishmen should not take sides. It was a defense of an Administration whose policies seemed very much closer to those of Britain than did the apparent advocacies of Acheson's opponents. And

---

49. Spectator, CLXXXIV (March 24, 1950), 357.

50. Robert Boothby (Conservative) (473 H.C. Deb. 261 [March 28, 1950]).

51. S. K. Ratcliffe, "America and the New Crisis," Contemporary Review, CLXXVIII (August, 1950), 67.

52. November 16, 1950, p. 9.

53. CLIX (November 18, 1950), 789.

also it was a defense of Administration officials with whom, by this time,
many influential Englishmen were personally acquainted.

The strength of the identification with Acheson (and Truman) owed
something to the fairly long-standing British preference for the Democratic party, and especially for Roosevelt Democrats. The most prominent factor was the general feeling that Administration Democrats had
always been more sympathetic to Britain than had their political foes.
Historically, this might be traced, in the minds of erudite liberal economists, to the fact that Democratic low tariff programs were more
congenial to nineteenth-century British principles of free trade. Much
more sharply defined, however, was the British attachment to both
Woodrow Wilson and Franklin Roosevelt in their struggles with Republican isolationists. In the second instance, from 1939 to 1941, the American political contest seemed of such life-and-death significance to the
future of Great Britain that the party of Roosevelt became a real national
choice. The Democrats were established as Britain's friends. Among
liberals, of course, the Roosevelt-Truman domestic doctrines were also
thoroughly acceptable. To the Manchester Guardian Weekly, occupying
a middle position in British politics, there was something especially
congenial about the Fair Deal program which President Truman presented at the beginning of his second term. It had the virtue of being
progressive without being socialist. It was conceived, the Manchester
Guardian Weekly revealingly remarked, "more in the spirit of Lloyd
George Liberalism."[54] Proposals to advance civil liberties and social
services fortified the existing sympathy for the Democratic party.[55]

Appreciation of the Fair Deal program did not mean that it played
so important a part, as it did for many Labourites, in disliking the
prospects of a Republican victory. The Republican party was disapproved not so much, if at all, for this reason, but rather because of
what it might want to do in the international field. The fear of the Republican party was mainly the fear of American isolationism. The first
Republican victory, in the 1946 congressional elections, reminded the
Economist of 1920, although it granted that this time the results were

54. January 13, 1949, p. 8.

55. The Truman program was ordinarily presented to the British public
    in an appealing way, as by D. W. Brogan, "Trends in American
    Policy," International Affairs, XXV (April, 1949), 125-36.

not really so bad.[56] American international participation seemed more
likely to continue than after the first war. But, the British public was
told by a regular and familiar commentator on American affairs, "the
older form of isolationism is still entrenched in the Republican Party;
this is made evident by the unimpaired prominence of Senator Taft and
his associates."[57]

When the influence of Taft appeared to diminish, as in the 1948
presidential campaign, there was less worry about the consequences
of Republican victory. Dewey's likely election was not provocative,
coming at a high point in American bipartisanship. Nevertheless, there
was satisfaction as well as surprise over Truman's victory; fewer iso-
lationist-minded pressures were expected,[58] and there was less chance
of reductions in European aid. The Republicans, it was remembered, if
no longer isolationist were not so firmly anti-isolationist.[59] That point
was driven home between 1948 and 1952 by what was regarded as the
rallying of isolationists to the banners of "Asia first." The conflict between President Truman and General MacArthur sharpened the issue,
from the British view, so that the Republicans looked almost as unfriendly as in 1940.[60]

It was against this background that the British interest, as reflected
by the independent press, focused on the 1952 political campaign in the
United States. Many readers must have echoed Arnold Toynbee's wish
to vote in the American elections,[61] so intimately did they feel that
Britain's fate was tied to the results. The public was prepared to believe
that the nomination of Senator Taft would have been a major calamity, and

---

56. CLI (November 9, 1946), 737. See also Spectator, CLXXVII
    (November 8, 1946), 472-73.

57. S. K. Ratcliffe, "President Truman's Defeat," Contemporary Re-
    view, CLXX (December, 1946), 329.

58. London Times, November 4, 1948, p. 5.

59. Economist, CLV (November 6, 1948), 731-32.

60. This was true in 1951 even in the case of a magazine like the
    Spectator, which, pursuing very moderate editorial policies, had
    not previously lined up with the Democrats as had more obviously
    liberal papers. See CLXXXVI (April 20, 1951), 509, for its re-
    actions to the removal of General MacArthur and to the subse-
    quent Republican furor.

61. Toynbee was so quoted in the New York Times, April 27, 1952,
    Sec. 1, p. 41.

there was considerable relief when General Eisenhower was chosen as
the Republican candidate. Eisenhower had been regarded as a friend
ever since the war and especially during his leadership of the North
Atlantic Treaty Organization. But, as foreign-policy issues figured in
the subsequent campaign, opinion reverted to a rather clear-cut Democratic preference. Eisenhower's campaign association with the Republican enemies of the Truman-Acheson foreign policy was the most
likely factor, and, in this context, his apparent advocacy of "liberation"
assumed considerable importance. It was contrasted to the measured
tones of Governor Stevenson's speeches, whose content as well as style
had an appealing similarity to the editorials of the British quality press.
There was sufficient difference in emphasis between the two candidates
to suggest to highly sensitized British minds that their customary faith
in Democrats instead of Republicans was entirely justified.[62] The tone
of the independent press betrayed this preference, and so did the cover-
age and the comment of most of the popular papers—including those not
specifically identified with Labour. "Stevenson would be best for us"
was the way in which the campaign was widely understood.

Despite their preference for Democratic victory, the liberals did
not have so much of their allegiance to the alliance staked on its outcome that adjustment to Eisenhower's election was patently difficult.
Unlike many Labour sources, moderates did not view the results as
disastrous. The Times, for instance, was now inclined to be charitable
about previously troubling lines in Eisenhower's campaign, since "an
American Presidential election is the most confusing of all roads to great
office."[63] There were hopes for the best, along with occasional questions
as to whether Eisenhower could be "master in his own house" and so
practice the internationalism toward which some fellow-Republicans were
hostile.[64] Although there were immediate fears for the future of Ameri-

---

62. E.g., the Economist reflected its basic inclinations in "Ike and
    Adlai," CLXV (October 18, 1952), 137-38. And the London Times,
    while even more cautious, editorialized critically on Eisenhower's
    campaign address to the American Legion, with its references to
    "captive peoples" in Eastern Europe and the Far East. "It is more
    than likely," the Times said, "that when General Eisenhower drafted
    his speech to the Legion he did not weigh all the awkward implica-
    tions which some passages might have for his Secretary of State
    should he be elected President" (August 27, 1952, p. 5).

63. November 6, 1952, p. 7.

64. Manchester Guardian, November 6, 1952, p. 4. Reference, in this
    instance only, is to the daily, not the weekly, edition.

can tariff policy, among other things, the general theme was uncertainty and not consternation. Feelings were well summarized by a cartoon of the Republican elephant, being led by Eisenhower amid recollections of "Taftism-McCarthyism-MacArthurism." The caption was "Will the elephant forget?"[65]

Even if the elephant did not forget and there were very considerable isolationist pressures, liberals were not at all likely to turn away from the American alliance. Nor would they, however much disapproval they voiced, be any less ready to link British interests with those of the United States. There was no alternative attraction in a Third Force or even in the purely domestic cultivation of socialism. [Nothing that the United States might do, short of abandoning Europe entirely, could cause liberals to feel that the American alliance did not have something worth while to offer.] The long-standing appreciation of the need for American power was not altered by the election results. Nor was the liberal identification with the United States seriously disturbed by a changed emphasis from Fair Deal to business-minded domestic programs. Ideologically the Eisenhower Administration looked almost as compatible as the Truman Administration. The difference was only of degree, and the apparently more rigid Republican devotion to private enterprise was not very disturbing to British middle-of-the-road opinion, which had, by 1952, largely recovered from its quasi-socialist distrust of capitalism in the immediate postwar period. On the other hand, the failure of the Eisenhower Administration to distinguish itself from anything that looked like "McCarthyism" was certain to shake the British liberal's confidence in the United States.

---

65. Cartoon by Vicky, News Chronicle, November 6, 1952, p. 2.

IX / THE CONSERVATIVE POSITION

There is a recognizable Conservative party approach to foreign
policy despite broad agreement with liberal and right-wing Labour
opinion on many international issues. The Tory holds some values toward which the rest of the community is either hostile, indifferent, or
lukewarm. From these, a distinctive foreign-policy emphasis emerged
in the postwar period. Naturally, the members of the vast Conservative
party cannot, any more than the activists in any other large British
movement, be expected to have identical international attitudes. If there
were not, from 1945 to 1952, such open divergencies as those in the
Labour party, differences in point of view certainly existed within Conservative ranks. However, these differences were neither so large nor
apparently so basic that they broke the virtually unanimous front of the
Conservative party on political and military relations with the United
States.

The fact that substantial agreement was achieved, in spite of well-
known Tory disputes over American trade policies, may be attributed
to the political habits of the Conservative party as well as to its
basic preferences in international matters. Although the party had had
notable rebels in the recent past and appeared to have some minor ones
again in 1953, the postwar years were characterized by a general inhi-
bition against public revolts in opposition to policies of the established
leadership. This was less the result of internal authoritarianism than of a
self-imposed discipline flowing from membership in a respectable club.
The restraining spirit, characteristic of upper-class life, was intensified
by the resistance of Conservatives, "with their backs against the wall,"
to the advance of postwar socialism.

Party loyalty was embodied in respect for the stand of the Conservative "Leader," as he was frankly called. It was more than simply a devotion to the person or opinions of Sir Winston Churchill himself. In the
structure of the Conservative party the Leader was acknowledged as the
formulator of policy, limited only by the party's advice and by its consent
to his occupancy of the key position. Of course, the Leader could not
dictate policies offensive to the bulk of his followers, particularly to those

173

in the parliamentary ranks. Nor could he forget that there were always likely to be some Conservatives waiting for an opportunity to displace him. Nevertheless, the Leader, once installed, was fortified by the power to appoint the chief officials of the party's central office and by the power to control expenditures for general propaganda and for direct campaign purposes.[1]

To question the Leader's policy pronouncements would have been extremely bad form. His pre-eminence, in this respect, may be understood by reference to two Conservative customs. One was that the Leader, not the party as a collectivity, issued the statement of principles upon which a general election campaign was waged. The other practice, also unlike Labour's procedure, was that the Leader did not attend the annual party conference in order to participate in its discussions but only to deliver the final address after conference debate had already adjourned.

Conservatives took considerable pride in their decorum. To be urged, as was one party conference, "to follow the lead of Mr. Churchill"[2] was not an unusual sentiment. In matters of foreign policy the party boasted that, as opposed to the opposition, it commanded "real unity."[3] Here, to be sure, the argument was strengthened by the unique authority on foreign policy that Churchill brought to the position. The party's respect for its Leader's opinions was all the greater because of Churchill's previous record both as a wartime strategist and as a prewar analyst of international events (especially in the 1930's when most Conservatives were pledged to a leadership whose foreign policy was at odds with Churchillian views). Although the disagreements of prewar years had left anti-Churchill resentments among the still-devoted friends of Baldwin and Chamberlain, there was hardly any Conservative disposition openly to question Churchill's postwar reputation for sagacity and knowledge in world affairs. It was hard, at any rate, to challenge greatness.

Consequently, a combination of factors tended to increase Churchill's influence in determining Conservative foreign policy and ordinarily to

---

1. See R. T. McKenzie, "Party Organization," in The British Party System, ed. Sydney D. Bailey (London: Hansard Society, 1952), pp. 115-1(

2. 68th Annual Report of the National Union of Conservative and Unionist Associations (London, 1947), p. 38.

3. 69th Annual Report of the National Union of Conservative and Unionist Associations (London, 1948), p. 91 (Anthony Eden).

submerge from public sight whatever dissenters may have existed. But Conservatives did not blindly or unwittingly accept the Churchillian lead. There were basic reasons, connected to conservatism itself, why they were more receptive to Churchill's international doctrine than was the rest of the British community. Or, stated differently, the background of Conservative thought was such as to provide Churchill an especially congenial political location. There was no need for him to go into the political wilderness as he had in the 1930's.

The theme of this chapter is that the most powerful Tory inclinations operated in the same direction as Churchill's advocacy of close Anglo-American co-operation. However, it does not follow that Conservatives always shared Churchill's (and Eden's) apparent enthusiasm about the English-speaking partnership. Among some of the party's right-wingers, the Churchillian line may have looked suspiciously like an overly loose internationalism—recalling Sir Winston's not entirely forgivable Liberal past. And at the other end of the party there could well have existed many of the reservations characteristic of independent and even moderate Labour attitudes. Then, too, conservatism had its eccentrics who developed their own international points of view. The fact that little attention is devoted to any of these deviations stems from the infrequency of their public expression. Undercurrents of opposition may thus pass unnoticed, but it is difficult to assign great significance to such undercurrents when they have not emerged at some level of intraparty discussion. To describe basic differentiation in Conservative foreign-policy thinking, when there exists so little evidence of it, would risk a greater error than that which may result from a straight account of the largely unchallenged official position. On the other hand, there have been important differences in emphasis, among Conservatives themselves as well as among their nominal press supporters, and these differences cannot be neglected in the analysis of the party's response to American policy.

Traditional Determinants

In its acceptance of the use of power in international relations, the Conservative party was at the opposite extreme from the attitude that pervaded socialist thinking. And in proudly proclaiming the validity of power politics, as a matter of principle, the Tory was also different from the liberal who more reluctantly accepted the employment of force.

It is true that the difference, as reflected by specific positions, tended to diminish in the last decade or two, since the pressure of events caused a more general appreciation of the neces.ity for policies based on armed strength. However, the doctrinal emphasis on power, in world affairs, belonged to the general stock of Tory traditions which, in Britain as on the Continent, had always been opposed from the left, whether by rationalism, liberalism, humanitarianism, or socialism. (The Leninist-Stalinist advocacy was, of course, a distinct departure.)

The Conservative based his case for military strength on the same pessimistic view of human nature as that on which he founded his preference for authority and order in domestic politics. Deeply imbedded in the Tory outlook was a suspicion that human material was not nearly so good or so trustworthy as his progressive opponents seemed to believe. A contemporary philosopher of conservatism, T. E. Utley, freely stated the basic assumption: "Human nature is violent and predatory and can be held in check only by three forces, the Grace of God, the fear of the gallows, and the pressure of a social tradition, subtly and unconsciously operating as a brake on human instinct, and imparted in childhood." From this point of view, there is no difficulty in assuming that "all politics is power politics" and that power is "an indispensable instrument of policy, and especially of foreign policy."[4] Philosophically, the Conservative approach rests, as Utley's statement indicated, on an Augustinian assumption of man's sinfulness. However, it is not probable that the theological conception as such has been widely influential in the thinking of Conservatives, despite the party's conscious links to the established religion. While many Tory convictions may have been bolstered by Utley's, or someone else's, reference to underlying philosophical assumptions, the party by its own admission was not primarily moved by doctrine.

Toryism's appeal was not so much philosophical, in the sense of being based upon the kinds of ideas it dismissed as "abstractions," as it was historical, in the Burkean manner of appealing to the sense of continuity in the community. Consequently, within the heterogeneous nature of its following, the party retained a hard core principally interested in preserving the existing order and in doing so in traditional ways. One of these ways was to rely on forceful discipline, which to a surprising

---

4.   Essays in Conservatism (London: Conservative Political Centre, 1949), pp. 2, 12, and 34.

extent remained in vogue in recent times. Its severities lingered in the
public schools and in the Regular Army, both of which furnished large
contingents of Conservative activists. While the preferences of some
Tories for the use of corporal punishment instead of jail sentences might
be overplayed by their parliamentary opponents, it remained true that the
Conservative tradition made for an absence of squeamishness about the
use of force. As a historian and Conservative member of Parliament
said of his party:

> They do not blush to recognize that politics imply essentially the
> use of force, that even between Englishmen good feeling is not always
> (nor likely for generations to be) enough, that good laws sometimes
> need physical compulsion. So they are not shocked (however re-
> gretful) to think that, between nations also, force must be occasional-
> ly necessary.[5]

Whether it is called "realism," "toughness," or some less attractive
name, this attitude toward world affairs has remained near the center of
the Tory position. Probably its appreciation was far from universal in
the party, especially during the recent large growth in Conservative
membership. The party's recruits often derived from social situations
whose traditions were less clearly defined than those of the prewar party.
But, despite notable accretions from the middle classes, especially at
the second rung of leadership, the Conservative party's tone was still set
by the aristocracy, in alliance with business wealth. Its traditional lines
of approach to foreign policy were well settled. There was less suscepti-
bility to modification from within than there was from without—that is,
from the need to appeal to liberal or independent voters.

Closely tied to the party's acceptance of power politics were its
patriotic motivations. It was in behalf of the national interest that Tories
were committed to the use of force in world affairs. "King and country"
represented values which, for Conservatives, were not impaired by a
looser, modern internationalism. Neither political nor class ideology
cut across the Tory consciousness of the British cause. Nationalism
was stated as a party principle, and all the more proudly because of the
suspicion that Labour's proclamation of national loyalty was less strenuous.
Emphasis at Conservative conferences on the patriotic motif was in contrast to Labour's symbols of socialism and working-class unity. If not
every Conservative was accustomed to use Churchillian phrases, like

---

5. Kenneth Pickthorn, "Philosophy and Principles," in the British Party
    System, p. 53.

"the British race" or "our island race," the party as a whole appreciated the distinction which the Leader drew in 1946: "Peering ahead through the mists and mysteries of the future so far as I can see it would seem that the division at the next Election will be between those who whole-heartedly sing 'The Red Flag' and those who rejoice to sing 'Land of Hope and Glory.' There is the noble hymn which will rally the wise, the sober-minded and the good to the salvation of our native land."[6]

The language had the master's own touch, but the spirit was demonstrably that of his party. Conservatives claimed no monopoly of patriotism, but their party was distinctive in its conspicuous devotion to a strictly national creed. It took various forms. Often it was highly romantic, as in Churchill's purple passages. Or it could be annoyingly superior in relation to outsiders; or (rarely) offensive in extreme, quasi-Fascist manifestations. But, in world politics, Conservative patriotism most meaningfully supported the uninhibited pursuit of the national interest. This, too, Churchill prominently illustrates.

What Conservatives meant by the national interest was not simply the protection of the United Kingdom. Theirs was the party not of "Little Englanders" but of a Disraeli-inspired tradition of building and maintaining overseas possessions. "The Conservative Party, by long tradition and settled belief, is the Party of the Empire,"[7] it was always insisted. The idea was not to be abandoned, although it might have to be acknowledged that the imperial system was not what it used to be. Even among those for whom the old days were really dead and for whom Imperial Preference was no magic formula, "Empire" was still an emotive word. If there was less to defend, it seemed that Conservatives were more anxious than ever to see it defended. Their view of Empire differed from the newer emphasis on a commonwealth of many nations, since it was not diversity that primarily appealed. "The idea of Empire," it was declared, "is the extension of the national unity overseas."[8] The Empire stood for the British tradition—its greatness and its contributions. When

6. Winston Churchill's address of October 5, 1946, contained in Conservatism: 1945-1950 (London: Conservative Political Centre, 1950), p. 84.

7. Britain Strong and Free (London: Conservative Central Office, 1951), pp. 10-11.

8. David Clarke, "The Conservative Faith in a Modern Age," in Conservatism: 1945-1950, p. 41.

the emphasis had to be modified, to suit the changing Commonwealth, it was done unenthusiastically.

This enlarged conception of nationality was the Conservative alternative to liberal or socialist internationalism, and it was valued accordingly. The sense of imperial responsibility served the Tory conscience as apparently more idealistic bonds met the needs of others. Furthermore, Conservatives felt that Empire was the more definite and meaningful enlargement of British overseas identification. "To the Conservative the practice of Empire is worth many times the theorizing over internationalism."[9] While the League of Nations and the United Nations were accepted pro forma, they did not come to play a vitally important role in the party's approach to foreign policy. "Collective security," even if its internationalist overtones had become less uncongenial to Conservatives than in times past, was hardly required to justify the party's acceptance of a defensive alliance. Power politics did not have to be dressed up as it usually was for Labour and Liberal audiences.

Publicly and officially, Conservatives by no means disapproved of what was called collective security. The party's foreign secretary, Anthony Eden, was himself associated with the doctrine and with the language of internationalism. But this was more closely related to his popularity in the nation at large than to his standing in the party. Of course, Eden's attachment to the principles of the United Nations did not vary with his audience, but he could tell the Conservative party, after voicing his own hopes for the United Nations, that because its authority was not yet widely accepted and respected it was necessary to organize other systems in order to achieve peace and security.[10] And Eden stripped a good deal of the vagueness from internationalist doctrine:

> Collective security is now based on the United Nations, as the Socialist Party rightly proclaim. But if we are in any degree honest, we must all admit that the presence among the United Nations of the United States —potentially the greatest military power in the world— makes all the difference to the reality of collective security.[11]

Superficially this may seem only a shade of difference from the way in which collective security was understood in the Labour party, but in

9. Ibid.

10. 69th Annual Report of the National Union of Conservative and Unionist Associations, p. 90.

11. 71st Annual Report of the National Union of Conservative and Unionist Associations (London, 1950), p. 31.

fact it reveals much of the traditional Conservative willingness to understand the national basis of power and its importance in checking the
power of other nations. In this particular sense, at any rate, it was
easier for Tories to see that an American alliance was one of the facts
of life.

The Conservative attitude with respect to rearmament presents
much the same pattern. Historically, the party had been more interested
in the maintenance and development of the fighting services than had its
political opponents. It was not always the party of preparedness, as it
claimed to have been in the early 1930's, as opposed to the then largely
pacifist-minded Labour movement. But there was no doubt that over
a period of time the Tories associated themselves with the building of
armed strength—if less diligently in the 1930's, at least more so than
other parties. Having many party leaders and members of Parliament
who had been Regular officers in the services was both cause and effect
of the Conservative attitude. Just as Labour considered itself the
guardian of social services, so Conservatives thought of their party as
chiefly concerned with the military establishment. "It is a permanent
characteristic of Conservatism," Utley remarked, "that it gives precedence to foreign policy and defense over all plans for improving the
material lot of the people."[12] This was more bluntly stated than was
usual among Conservative politicians, who were well aware of the electoral disadvantage of having military expenditures presented as a Tory-
sponsored rival to the social reforms of the Labour party. A Conservative government that cut welfare benefits in order to increase an arms
program would run even greater political risks than a Labour government doing the same thing.

But there was no doubt that the Conservatives themselves whole-
heartedly approved the principle of large-scale rearmament. The point
was plainly put in party literature: ". . . the sooner the West is con-
ventionally rearmed, while still retaining marked atomic superiority,
the better will be the chances of avoiding war and reaching a settlement."[13]
On this basis Conservatives supported the enlarged arms program of the
Labour government in 1951, and without the objections and reservations
evident in the Labour party. Tories were not only aware of the usefulness

---

12. Essays in Conservatism, p. 32.

13. A. H. Head, Pattern of Peace (London: Conservative Political
    Centre, 1951), p. 4.

of increased British power per se; they were also impressed, like the
liberals and right-wing Labour, with the importance of doing enough to
encourage the Americans to do more.[14] In this respect, Conservatives
were really in the vanguard of general opinion, as befitted their appreciation of power—American or British.

Ideology of the Right

Conservatives have often denied that their foreign policy was
fashioned by ideological considerations. Alliances, it has been held,
were rightly made only on the basis of their contribution to the British
national interest. In this way, Tories sought to establish their own
realism in accepting the Anglo-American alliance at a time when socialists displayed ideological inhibitions. Although the Conservative tradition and some of its contemporary exponents (notably Churchill) may
in fact be credited with ideological aloofness in the name of Realpolitik,
it would be off the mark to claim that the party's foreign policy was entirely uninfluenced by doctrinal preferences. Too much weight can be
assigned to the inconspicuousness of attempts to relate international
issues to the "Conservative way of life." True enough, there was no
Tory counterpart to the search for a "socialist foreign policy." But
there were ideological components of the postwar international conflict
which did predispose Conservatives to relatively favorable reactions to
the American connection. Like anyone else, looking at the world in terms
of his own concerns, the Tory was bound, despite a disavowal of internationalism, to project his likes and dislikes of various political systems,
especially as those systems appeared either favorable or threatening to
the principles and interests to which conservatism was committed.

Although the political attractions of American democracy, to cite the
obvious example, were not so heavily stressed by Conservatives as by
British liberals, there can be no doubt that a large section of the party
appreciated the basic similarity in institutions. Freedom and liberty
had not been the traditional slogans of Toryism, but they were important
in the twentieth-century liberalization of the Conservative movement.
The Conservative party was partially turned about from its old position
as the defender of state authority to the newer (but perhaps not fully
accepted) role of championing individual liberty against socialist

14. Ibid., p. 8. See also, for a typical Conservative response in the
    winter of 1950-51, the Yorkshire Post, December 22, 1950, p. 2.

planning and management. The inclination was not so strong as the advocacy of the American right, but it lay in that general direction.

Conservatives considered their antisocialist cause to be pointedly related to the fight against communism. On this score the party ranks often displayed a fervor which was absent in the community at large but which was entirely familiar in postwar America. For British Conservatives, anticommunism was less a new phenomenon than a carryover from the original antibolshevism that had been maintained through the interwar years. Particularly in the 1920's it had played a larger role in Conservative campaign tactics than it did after World War II. But its recent inconspicuousness did not necessarily indicate a diminution of the anti-Communist spirit among Conservatives. Rather, it was a matter of keeping in step with the public's apparent unreceptivity to what it stigmatized as "Red-baiting." In the elections of 1950 and 1951, at any rate, Conservatives were chary about the general employment of anything likely to produce an unfavorable reaction on the part of liberal and independent opinion. The party felt it had suffered in 1945 as a result of the Churchill-Beaverbrook campaign against Harold Laski, who, as chairman of the Labour party's executive, had been attacked as a sinister, totalitarian-minded influence.[15]

Since, in fact, a wide-open, sweepingly anti-Communist campaign tended to include Labour's near-Marxists as targets, such a campaign was inhibited by the public taboo against anything that resembled American crusades.[16] But within the Conservative party denunciations of communism were made with moral force and indignation, at least after the immediate postwar hopes for understanding Russia had vanished. It was doubtful that these hopes, though voiced by Conservative leaders, could have really softened the party's anti-Communist spirit. Conservative activists were frequently reminded of an ideological connection between

15. An account of the Conservative concentration on Laski is in R. B. McCallum and A. Readman, The British General Election of 1945 (London: Oxford University Press, 1947), pp. 142-43, 172-75, and 208-9.

16. Almost the only sympathy for American anti-Communist investigations was displayed in the Conservative press, although here, too, Senator McCarthy was spoken of unfavorably. For example, the column by "Scrutator" in the Sunday Times (December 14, 1952, p. 5) stated that it was silly to talk as though all American action against subversives was "witch-hunting." There were, of course, anti-Communist organizations like the Economic League, whose various activities were financed largely from Conservative sources.

their socialist opponents and the Communists. "We must never forget," R. A. Butler said, "that the Socialist faith is simply an off-shoot of the Marxist doctrine."[17] The specter of British Labour working gradually toward Russia's total elimination of private enterprise was put before Conservative audiences, and Winston Churchill declared that there was "no real difference between a full application of the Socialist system and Communism."[18]

Conservative conferences regularly discussed the dangers of Communist infiltration and passed resolutions deploring the existence of opportunities for subversive activities. In 1950 one proposal from the conference floor went so far as to ask for the strengthening of legislation against Communist treason, but this was withdrawn in response to persuasion from the party leadership.[19] Some of the fervor was linked to a consciousness of defending traditional religious as well as political and economic values against the left. For example, one rank-and-file speaker said: "In essence it is a struggle between the religion of totalitarian materialism on the one side and Christian democracy on the other. It is a struggle from which none of us can escape."[20] This crusading sentiment was not a usual note, but, in so far as it was present at all in postwar Britain, it seemed to have a home in the Conservative party.

Muffled as Conservative anticommunism often appeared to be, it undoubtedly affected the party's international outlook. Conservatives insisted, well before most of the rest of the community, that Britain was so unlike the Soviet Union that it could not provide a middle way between Russian and American systems. The notion of being an ideological bridge was never accepted.[21] Conservatives hardly shared the socialist or even

17. In Conservatism: 1945-1950, p. 91.

18. From an address of July 23, 1949 (ibid., p. 106).

19. 71st Annual Report of the National Union of Conservative and Unionist Associations, pp. 38-45. Passage of other resolutions, in 1947 and 1948, noted in 68th Annual Report of the National Union of Conservative and Unionist Associations, p. 29, and 69th Annual Report of the National Union of Conservative and Unionist Associations, p. 26.

20. 69th Annual Report of the National Union of Conservative and Unionist Associations, p. 102.

21. The farther right, the less attractive socialism and correspondingly the more antithetical the idea of the middle way (see F. A. Voigt, "Twenty-one Rebels and a Letter," Nineteenth Century and After, CXLI [January, 1947], 1-9).

the occasional liberal feeling of having a way of life that was somehow halfway between capitalism and collectivism. Nor did they relish the notion that Britain's future was to resemble Russia's economic system while maintaining a democratic political order. If Conservatives thought this possible, which they generally did not, they would have found it un- attractive anyway. Cultural distinctness from America may have ap- pealed to Conservatives, but there was an understandable rejection of the ideological uniqueness suggested by socialists.

In reacting to the challenge of Third Force ideas, Conservatives became more outspoken about the similarity of British to American political practices than might otherwise have been the case. Certainly, one member of Parliament said, we are not halfway "between the free- dom of conscience as enjoyed in the United States and the very negation of that freedom as practised behind the iron curtain."[22] It was the po- litical antithesis to communism that mattered, and in this respect demo- cratic principles as such were more attractive than their mixture with socialist economics. Conservatives often seemed closer to the pre- vailing American doctrine than to the philosophy held by the government of their own country from 1945 to 1951. Politically, it was not necessarily profitable to say so, and at any rate the words were hard for nationalist- minded Tories to utter. It was especially difficult in light of their long- standing charge that socialists had an unpatriotic yearning for the ways of the Soviet Union. Yet there was an open admiration, occasionally put in intellectual terms, for some American principles. This was a rather new pattern for Conservatives and not a traditional affinity.[23]

Conservative attachment was fostered during the six years of the Labour government by the party's desire to impress the British public with the virtues of an economic alternative to the socialism for which so much of the electorate had voted. Inevitably this meant pointing toward the striking postwar success of American capitalism, in spite of the fact that the Conservative party had never been—and was not now—the political champion of the American model of free competitive enterprise. How- ever, during the long decline of the Liberals, most big business, and a

---

22. C. E. Mott-Radclyffe (446 H.C. Deb. 501 [January 22, 1948]).

23. Fresh Conservative acknowledgment of compatibility with the United States may be observed in the first issue of a newly oriented Tory intellectual monthly, New English Review Magazine, Vol. I (September, 1948).

great deal of little business, had established itself in the Tory ranks. If aristocratic traditions, as well as the contemporary British environment, inclined Conservatives to describe their goal as neither socialist nor capitalist, but a "property owning democracy,"[24] that did not mean that the party failed to stand for the preservation of what was left of private capitalism. The language of the Conservative party's well-known Industrial Charter, with its emphasis on reconciling the need for central direction with the encouragement of individual effort, may have seemed tainted with socialism, but it was the closest that any British party, valuing its chances of electoral success, could come to the pronouncement of capitalist principles. The charter wanted, at any rate, a "system of free enterprise," even if it was to be "on terms with authority."[25] Relatively speaking, conservatism embraced the causes of business freedom from state control, of lower taxes, and of greater business incentives.

Therefore, since their own country seemed to be moving away from these objectives in most of the postwar period, Conservatives turned to the United States for favorable comparisons. This took place at several levels. Most blatant was the campaign of the Daily Express, which, while disowned as an official Conservative voice, undoubtedly aimed its mass-circulation editorials in the Tory cause at least at election time. In 1945, just after the end of the war and the advent of the Labour government, the Express inaugurated a series of conspicuous stories on American progress. The heading was "Watch America," and the theme was the era of plenty which the United States was beginning to enjoy because it had rapidly lifted government controls and demobilized its armed forces.[26] That Englishmen could have the same rich foods or luxurious goods, if they adopted the same economic policies, was always implied. In other quarters, less luridly and less irresponsibly, the American experience was cited to illustrate the potentialities of free enterprise. Apart from the evidently available material satisfactions, crudely appealing to a nation weary of austerity, American capitalism was also associated with

24. Broadcast by the Marquess of Salisbury, May 22, 1948 (in Conservatism: 1945-1950, p. 96).

25. Ibid., p. 50.

26. Illustrative of the campaign of the Daily Express were issues of September 28, 1945, p. 2; October 5, 1945, p. 2; and October 31, 1945, p. 1. However, so few examples do not convey the impact which derived from the frequent repetition of the "Watch America" line.

opportunities for business success. Here the appeal was likely to be strongest among ambitious but frustrated young Englishmen who sought to make rapid strides up the economic ladder. America might not appear so simply as a place to "get rich quick," but it was portrayed as a country where a new and enterprising business had better hopes of flourishing than in Britain.

In more general terms, Conservative political figures added their praise of the American economic system. This became unstinting at the time of the Marshall Plan. "The greatest asset," it was said, "to all the free peoples of the world at this moment is the miracle of American productive expansion under the impetus of freedom and economic incentives."[27] Similarly, in the intellectual counterattack against British socialism and the planning state the United States was the prize example. Its economic success was not to be attributed solely to natural advantages, one Conservative writer insisted. He pointed to Russia, also possessing abundant resources, but far behind America on account of the difference in economic systems. "It can scarcely be denied," he summarized, "that, judged by its results, the system of competitive free enterprise as it exists in America produces, by comparison with any other system, the greatest amount of wealth and the widest distribution of it."[28] As the United States distributed its wealth abroad, Conservatives were inclined to attribute these benign manifestations not only to the generousness of the American people but also to the advantages of their economic system. Conservatives went further than merely to refute the cries of capitalist imperialism. They could openly proclaim capitalist virtues.

Favorable Conservative impressions of American capitalism, and so to some extent of the United States generally, came under the influence of personal experiences. Over a considerable period of time, many British businessmen inevitably established relations, often of a social nature, with their American counterparts, particularly in eastern metropolitan centers with strong Anglophile traditions. These experiences, despite an occasional manifestation of British contempt for the nouveau riche, gave many Conservatives a sense of association with their "own kind" in the United States. American capitalism was less of an abstraction and more a collection of

---

27. Sir Arthur Salter (457 H.C. Deb. 548 [November 1, 1948]). At the time, Salter was an "Independent" member of Parliament, but he subsequently established his conservatism.

28. Richard Law, M.P., Return from Utopia (London: Faber & Faber, 1950), p. 26.

important and influential friends.

However, it is easier to account for the avidity with which Conservatives became public proponents of the American economic system by the special political circumstances of the first six postwar years. In attacking the record of the government, it was useful to argue that what Labour claimed as its accomplishments, especially full employment and social welfare, were made possible only by the munificence of American help. From the beginning of the European aid program, Churchill, for instance, always stressed the greatness of the help being received, while he chastised his opponents for not acknowledging American generosity more warmly.[29] His party liked to taunt socialists for their inability to do without "huge loans from a capitalist country."[30] For campaigning purposes, crediting the United States was the alternative to admitting socialist success; or, as a party pamphlet stated in late 1950:

> The Washington Loan and Marshall Aid from American are, of course, the two factors which ever since 1945 have buttressed the British economy and shielded it from the more disastrous consequences of Socialist incompetence and misrule. Without these generous aids from America there is not the slightest doubt that widespread unemployment and general privation would have been added to the other hardships and misfortunes which the nation has endured.[31]

There was every political advantage to be gained by emphasizing the generosity of the United States, plus an ideological point to be scored by reference to capitalist productivity and beneficence.

So long as their opponents, rather than themselves, appeared dependent on American aid, Conservatives had special cause not only to praise capitalist largess but also to welcome any antisocialist pressures originating in the United States. The New World's ideology was called in to redress the Old World's socialism. The party could not go so far as to urge, in its official line, that the United States make its economic assistance conditional upon Britain's return to capitalism. That would have been too direct a challenge to the cherished belief in the right of elected representatives to frame national policies. As mistaken as Tories re-

---

29. 443 H.C. Deb. 705 (October 28, 1947).

30. Oliver Lyttelton (453 H.C. Deb. 66 [July 5, 1948]).

31. Conservative Research Department, Developments in Socialist Policy (London: Conservative and Unionist Central Office, 1950), pp. 14-15. See also, from the same source, Conservative Party Conference (London, 1950), p. 12, and Notes on Current Politics, September 17 and October 1, 1951.

garded the socialist program, there was a limit to the methods they were prepared to advocate against that program. But there was a Conservative tolerance of the American right-wing view that it was wrong to subsidize a socialist administration. Space in the party's widely distributed magazine was given to the expression, by an American, of just that opinion.[32] At least, conservatism made it clear that Americans joined in holding that socialism was responsible for Britain's ills. Americans, said David Eccles, a future Tory minister, "believe in European recovery under a free system and so do we on these benches."[33]

Less prominent Conservatives, voicing their own sentiments, were inclined to push the point somewhat farther. One member of Parliament asked whether it was honest of the Labour government to accept Marshall aid and "to use it for a process of nationalisation which is intended to destroy the very way of life for which America is making this sacrifice."[34] Another, much more extreme Tory member, insisted that the United States should specifically refuse Britain any more dollars unless the Labour government "promise not to nationalise iron and steel."[35] This was hardly the language of the responsible party leadership, but that did not mean that it was far from the wishes of zealous Tory activists in local party organizations—that is, the opposite numbers to the left-wing extremists of the constituency branches of the Labour party.

If their top leaders were necessarily inhibited from overtly welcoming American pressure on British policies, others could afford to reflect some of the underlying, extremist feeling. This was more likely with respect to general European rather than purely British issues. For example, a Conservative could hopefully ask whether the United States was going to oppose Labour's evident preference for the nationalization of German industries in the Ruhr.[36] Criticism of Labour for trying to attach "strings of socialism" to European union included this admonition:

32. Tory Challenge, I (October, 1947), 9, and April, 1948, p. 4.

33. 453 H.C. Deb. 214 (July 6, 1948).

34. Beverley Baxter (449 H.C. Deb. 811 [April 13, 1948]).

35. Sir Waldron Smithers (456 H.C. Deb. 344 [September 16, 1948]). Sir Waldron's opinions, in this as in almost all political matters, were both so far to the right and so individual that his party in no way could be associated with what he said.

36. Viscount Hinchingbrooke (437 H.C. Deb. 1790 [May 15, 1947]).

"Either this country is with the United States, or she is against the United States. Socialists must really understand that American contempt for Socialism runs right through the economic scale of American society."[37] The significance of these remarks lay partly in their being directed at the section of the Labour party which, coincident with its enthusiasm for the Marshall Plan, began to count the Democratic Administration and much of its following as embryonically socialist in character. Conservatives, naturally, did not like the then entirely popular American bounty to be converted from capitalist to socialist inspiration. It was eccentric for a Tory to agree, in effect, with Labour that America's program for European recovery had ceased to foster private enterprise.[38] Overwhelmingly, Conservatives were assured that the American weight was antisocialist and, as such, to be warmly approved.

Conservative ideology was also related to the acceptance of other American policies about which leftward-oriented political groups had serious doubts. The outstanding example was provided by Spain. Unquestionably the Tory tradition of Realpolitik itself worked powerfully in favor of willingness to come to terms with Spain, as with Tito's Yugoslavia. But it was also important that there were few, if any, political sentiments among Conservatives that had to be overcome. In fact, Conservatives often appeared anxious that Spain should become more of a full-fledged ally than the United States openly advocated. Spain, said the quasi-official Tory newspaper, the Daily Telegraph (in late 1950), "should be invited into active membership of the Atlantic alliance. To sacrifice to ideological prejudice the security which she can help to underpin would be a moonbeam from the larger lunacy."[39] Surely this editorial comment went beyond the mere desire to ally with Spain in spite of its political system. That would have been more like the liberal position. In dismissing political objections as a "prejudice," the Telegraph made it fairly evident that the Franco regime, while unadmired, was not

37. Lord John Hope (450 H.C. Deb. 1145 [May 4, 1948]).

38. Only Viscount Hinchingbrooke seems to have gone so far as to say that the American Administration had been affected by socialist influence to the extent of no longer insisting on a free economy in Europe (see 460 H.C. Deb. 1193 [January 27, 1949] and "The Course of Conservative Politics," Quarterly Review, CCLXXXVII [July, 1949], 285). However, Hinchingbrooke's defense of free enterprise was much more of a crusade than was typical of his party, and he tended to go his own way on this issue and also, by 1952, on foreign policy as well.

39. December 29, 1950, p. 4.

the anathema it was to socialists and many liberals.

Conservative party opinion in Parliament, although not showering praise on Franco (any more than had the Telegraph) and not even going so far as to urge Spain's admission to the North Atlantic Treaty Organization, was noticeably warmer in response to American dealings with Spain than was the Labour party. For instance, it was argued, in mid-1951, that since the unilateral American moves were detracting from Allied unity, the Labour government should have been willing to join in arrangements with Franco.[40] The need to prevent Spain's economic collapse was stressed, as was the country's strategic importance.[41]

The relative caution among parliamentary spokesmen, and also in official party literature on relations with Spain,[42] was in significant contrast to opinions emanating from the extreme right. Without suggesting that the strongly pro-Franco views of the latter exercised any direct influence on Tory foreign policy, they are nevertheless worth noting in the account of various Conservative attitudes. Frank sympathizers with the Spanish regime were not so conspicuous as they were in the United States, and they did not appear prominent in the postwar Conservative party. But their opinions were presented in a few traditional right-wing publications through most of the postwar period. It was declared, at various times and places, that Spain should be included in the Marshall Plan,[43] that Spain was linked to Christian civilization's fight against Communist tyranny,[44] and that the Western powers should win the good will and respect of Spaniards.[45] To some extent, these really pro-Franco views represented the revival of associations made during the Spanish civil war. Conservatives, as a party, had not declared themselves for Franco as British Labour had for the Spanish Loyalists, but the more consciously anti-Communist elements no doubt had had some

---

40. R. A. Butler (491 H.C. Deb. 487-89 [July 25, 1951]).

41. Duncan Sandys (491 H.C. Deb. 504-11 [July 25, 1951]).

42. Head, op. cit., pp. 19-20.

43. Arthur F. Loveday, "Even Spain," Quarterly Review, CCLXXXVI (July, 1948), 310-24.

44. George Glasgow, "Foreign Affairs," Contemporary Review, CLXXVIII (September and December, 1950), 182-89 and 373-79.

45. Major General J. F. C. Fuller, "The Defense of Europe," English Review Magazine, IV (March, 1951), 161.

basis for an ideological attachment to Franco's cause. This did not mean
that the Tory right wing was Fascist or pro-Fascist, any more than the
Labour Left was necessarily Communist or pro-Communist. At most,
there was a predisposition to sympathy.

Generally, it is necessary to avoid too heavy an emphasis on Conservative identification with outside political forces as a factor in determining the party's approach to foreign policy. Although anticommunism
and procapitalism constituted important leanings, Toryism was too nationally minded to link itself to the credo of a particular political movement in another country. British socialists and liberals had their international, or European, organizations, but not the Conservatives. Neither
did they associate their cause with that of any American party. Their
inherent disinclination to do so was reinforced by specific facts. No
American party threatened the modified capitalist order which Conservatives defended. Although Fair Dealism was not close to their hearts,
they would have been happy if Britain had it and no more. Democrats as
well as Republicans were nonsocialist, and that was comfort enough.[46]
A section of the Labour party might claim the Democrats as friends,
but that was no cause for Conservatives to view Republicans with special
favor. The emphasis of postwar Toryism, especially at the party's central
office, was well to the left of Republicanism. Equally important was that
the G.O.P. was suspect among Conservatives as well as the rest of the
British community because of its isolationist reputation.

There was a difference between the response of Conservatives to the
1952 presidential campaign and that of the liberal press, for example. It
was not entirely an accident that the one quality daily newspaper which
could not be accused of pro-Stevenson reporting was the Daily Telegraph.
Its American correspondents displayed nothing like the degree of disapproval of Eisenhower's campaign that characterized so much of the rest
of the press. The Telegraph's largely Conservative readers were not
prepared to be so disappointed, if they were at all, by Stevenson's defeat.

Many Tories undoubtedly shared the general British hope for Democratic success, and especially for Stevenson's, but it was conspicuously
easier for them to adjust to Eisenhower's election. The Tory Daily Mail,
for instance, admitted that there was British misgiving about the Republican

---

46. The short-lived Labour attempt to portray the American Adminis-
    tration as "socialist" was ridiculed by Conservatives; e.g., by
    Lord John Hope (475 H.C. Deb. 2138 [May 24, 1950]).

campaign but expected great things of Eisenhower's presidency.[47] The
Beaverbrook press looked forward to fruitful understandings between
Eisenhower and his friend Churchill.[48] And in a study of the American
election, published in a Conservative journal, the Washington correspondent of the Daily Telegraph, Denys Smith, expressed some positive approval concerning the actual result.[49] This was the kind of statement
which was not made outside of Conservative circles, and it was unusual
even there. Probably the most accurate general description was that
Conservatives were better prepared than any other political group to
assume an attitude of especially benevolent neutrality toward the Republican Administration, assuming its continuation of policies not much
different from those of the Truman Administration. More than benevolent neutrality was very doubtful. Even if the Democrats should really
become a socialist party and so resemble the opposition at home, Conservatives were likely to show their customary restraint concerning
political controversies in the United States.

American Policies of Strength

Since an international position based on the employment of power
against Communist aggrandizement so well suited the Conservative
temper, the trend of postwar American policy under Truman was more
appealing in many ways than Franklin Roosevelt's had been. Churchill
had not been alone in disliking softness, anticolonialism, and personal
charm as methods for getting along with Russia. His views were shared
by his party, which was less lured by the possibility of appeasing Stalin
than it had been by the appeasement of Hitler in the 1930's. Incidentally,
the difference between the party's attitude toward Communist advance
and that toward the prewar Fascist gains may not be completely explained by the Conservative's more obviously polar opposition to left-
wing totalitarianism. There was also a Tory consciousness of the nineteenth-century effort of British statesmen to check the Middle Eastern
extension of the Russian Empire. And, more generally important, the
party's traditional respect for power and a flair for its use were now

47. November 6, 1952, p. 1.

48. Evening Standard, November 5, 1952, p. 4; see also Daily Express,
November 6, 1952, p. 4.

49. "President Eisenhower," National and English Review, CXXXIX
(December, 1952), 344-48.

symbolized by its leadership in a way that had not been typical of the 1930's.

All things considered, it was not surprising that relatively early in the postwar period there was voiced in a Tory source a clear-cut preference for the development of a tougher American policy than the optimistic one displayed at Yalta.[50] In time, Englishmen of other political persuasions became similarly, though reluctantly, convinced. But in the beginning of the "get-tough" moves only Conservatives, among coherent groups, appeared in wholehearted agreement. This was illustrated by the reception of the Truman Doctrine. While Labour was either openly hostile or quietly critical, and the liberal press was ambivalent, Conservatives took a positive line. "The United States," said a popular Tory paper, "has embarked upon this new, forceful phase in foreign policy in order to call a halt to Russian expansion." There was nothing to indicate that Tories had ever expected any other method to succeed. "Power and not cooperation is still the elemental force in international society."[51] America had become realistic, and this Churchillian note was echoed in the Conservative press.[52] Absent from Conservative commentary was any fear for the consequences of the President's announcement. On the contrary, it was assumed that a strong stand was the only way to halt the Russian aggression that would otherwise lead to war.[53] Furthermore, there was a special satisfaction among those who had, as members of the wartime government, been concerned with Britain's anti-Communist policies in Greece. These had been under heavy fire from both the American and the British left in 1945, and now that the United States was to assume the same responsibility it seemed, as one Conservative former minister said, a "vindication of British policy" in that part of the world.[54] And generally Conservatives were happy about the Truman Doctrine as a sign of definite American participation in world affairs.

Even more than the rest of the community, Conservative opinion was inclined to view the new development of forceful policies as the result of

50. Malcolm Muggeridge, "American Foreign Policy," New English Review Magazine, I (September, 1948), 19-24.

51. Daily Mail, March 14, 1947, p. 1.

52. Daily Telegraph, March 15, 1947, p. 2.

53. The Conservative press in Scotland took this same view (Glasgow Herald, March 14, 1947, p. 4).

54. Harold Macmillan (437 H.C. Deb. 1945 [May 16, 1947]).

original British inspiration—although not the Labour government's. Churchill, specifically, was considered an important source, and with considerable justice. Instead of thinking of themselves merely as the willing followers of the "get-tough" line, Conservatives tended to consider the influence as running quite the other way in the first four or five postwar years. This was more than a manifestation of the consciousness of superiority of the British ruling class to American newcomers in world affairs. In 1949 a direct line could be traced to the new military alliance from the Fulton address. "It was this famous speech," a party pamphlet declared, "which pointed the way to the Atlantic Pact."[55] Conservatives wanted to encourage, it was added, all such co-operation. Churchill himself took an understandable pride in the course of developments, especially upon the completion of the Atlantic Pact, when he could taunt many of the Labour critics of his Fulton speech as "converts" to his program. Always his references to "the decisive strength of the United States as expressed by the Atlantic Pact" served as a reminder that it was he who had most prominently called America to its new role.[56]

Absence of Conservative dissent from the Churchillian emphasis on the American alliance was a striking phenomenon in light of the early postwar burst of animosity toward the trade policies of the United States.[57] Even the most strenuous defenders of Imperial Preference against Yankee traders appreciated the need for Anglo-American solidarity in international politics. L. S. Amery, to cite the first apostle of Empire, said in 1947 that he too believed that the peace and freedom of the world depended on understanding and partnership with America. Only, he thought, it was all the more likely to be successful if Britain were freed from its ties to mistaken American trade doctrine.[58] Similarly, Oliver Stanley, representing a milder variety of the same school of thought, referred to the wrongheadedness of American economic policy but insisted on the importance of the transatlantic friendship: "In the cooperation of the United States and the

---

55. Conservatism: 1945-1950, p. 220.

56. 464 H.C. Deb. 2024 (May 12, 1949) and 473 H.C. Deb. 190 (March 28, 1950).

57. See chap. iv.

58. 68th Annual Report of the National Union of Conservative and Unionist Associations, p. 64.

British Empire lies the best hope for peace in the world."[59] The advocate
of Imperial Preference saw no inconsistency between his program for
strengthening the British Empire and at the same time joining in a fuller partnership with the United States. He was not so unrealistic as to
think that the Empire was going to be made strong enough to face Russian
power without America. Consequently, there was no separatist imperialist line on foreign policy. America's role in world politics could be
welcomed and commended, whatever the continuing complaints about
international trade.[60]

Conservative leaders found it possible to be more openly laudatory
about the new American assumption of responsibility than did the spokesmen of the Labour party. Officially, Labour ministers also noted their
pleasure with the American activity which followed upon the Truman
Doctrine, but Conservatives tended to have greater interest in calling
attention to the "immense significance," as Eden described it in May,
1947, of "the development of American foreign policy, and the shouldering
by that great nation of responsibilities commensurate with her power."[61]
At the time, this relatively greater enthusiasm was associated with the
virtual monopoly by Conservatives of uninhibited enthusiasm for the
Truman Doctrine. But the position then adopted was the beginning of a
pattern, so that, even with the subsequently widespread British acceptance
of the Marshall Plan, Conservative attitudes appeared more thoroughly and
consistently favorable to the United States. No Labour leader was likely,
before or after the Marshall Plan, to use the same encomium as did R.
A. Butler in referring to the United States as Europe's "powerful friend
and economic saviour."[62] Nor would many of his opponents have sub-
scribed to Churchill's reiterated belief that only America's atomic
monopoly, or clear superiority, prevented a Russian conquest of Europe
in the early years of the postwar period. "Nothing," Churchill told his
party in 1948, "stands between Europe today and complete subjugation to
Communist tyranny but the atomic bomb in American possession."[63]

---

59. Ibid., p. 68.

60. E.g., the National Review, in the forefront of the advocacy of Imperial
     Preference, said: "Being acutely critical of American policy in the
     field of international trade, we are glad to praise its wisdom in this
     other field without reserve" (CXXXII [April, 1949], 367).

61. 437 H.C. Deb. 1756 (May 15, 1947).

62. 456 H.C. Deb. 923 (September 22, 1948).

63. 69th Annual Report of the National Union of Conservative and Unionist
     Associations, p. 151.

Emphasis on the significance of the American alliance was apparent beyond the ranks of the party leadership. It seemed popular at Conservative conferences, much more evidently so than at Labour conferences, for speakers to eulogize Britain's relations with the United States. "Above all," it was typically urged in 1948, "we must march hand in hand and step by step with the United States."[64] Or, as another member of Parliament declared a year later, "we do have certain common interests and common bonds which are forged every day more tightly as the pressure of world events threatens the very existence of all freedom-loving peoples."[65] Similar sentiments came from the Conservative back benches in Parliament, and with greater frequency and intensity than from the Labour side. Conservatives were not necessarily more highly aware of the importance of American power, but they could speak of it in relation to Britain without the popular limitation imposed on Labour politicians by socialist traditions.

There was probably always a limit to the growth of pride in the alliance, given Britain's lesser role in it, but Conservative leaders had little reason to fear that their own followers were likely to charge them with subservience to the United States, least of all to American capitalism. In fact, public opinion polls indicated that Conservative voters, like their party spokesmen, were more prone than the rest of the population to a close American attachment. In 1949, for example, 57 per cent of polled Conservative voters thought the British government should take "quite a lot" of trouble to get on well with America, while the corresponding Labour figure was only 40 per cent and the Liberal 49 per cent. And, in the same poll, the number of Conservatives who thought the government "should not bother at all" to get on well with America was significantly lower than that registered by those with other party allegiances.[66] Again in the spring of 1952, to take results from a different period and from a different research organization, 31 per cent of Conservative-inclined voters said that America and Britain were "natural allies and should always stick together," while the Labour percentage was 16 and the Liberal 18. Also roughly parallel to the earlier poll, only 8 per cent of the Conservatives chose the least

64. C. E. Mott-Radclyffe, M.P. (ibid., p. 87).

65. Michael Astor, M.P. (70th Annual Report of the National Union of Conservative and Unionist Associations, p. 62).

66. Poll by Research Services, Ltd., as reported in International Journal of Opinion and Attitude Research, III (winter, 1949-50), 632.

pro-American alternative—in this case, that British relations with the
United States should be "on the same footing as with other countries"—
compared with 22 per cent of the Labour voters and 13 per cent of the
Liberals who preferred "the same footing" to either the highly preferen-
tial alternative or the middle suggestion that Britain should act with the
United States in most things but should remain independent.[67]

Perhaps the marked desire of Conservative voters for close American ties was partially a reflection of the party line, during Labour's
tenure of power, to the effect that the government was not doing enough
to foster Anglo-American relations. The idea was that any Labour slack-
ness in this regard diminished the chance for Britain to exercise an influence on American policy. Notably, when critical international decisions
were being made, Conservatives scolded the Labour government for not
being in close enough touch with the United States. As the Korean campaign began, for example, one journal held that Prime Minister Attlee
"should have flown to Washington within a week to show that the two
Governments were prepared to act in absolute concert and to agree upon
the best means of making joint plans."[68] Subsequently, Conservatives
frowned upon any attempt to separate Britain from America and expressed
concern that the Labour government might be giving the impression that
Britain was "not really after the same things" as the United States.[69]
In 1951 the Conservative party pledged to work more closely with America
than had the Attlee administration. Campaigning (successfully) in that
year's general election, the party charged that Labour had "allowed rifts
to develop between the United States and Britain," whereas "the surest
hope for peace" lay in the close association of the two.[70]

In the early 1950's, as at the time of the Truman Doctrine in 1947,
Conservatives did not reflect all the characteristic British chariness about
the exercise of American strength. "Peace through strength" remained
the party's foreign-policy prescription, and consistent with that stand
individual Tories had often indicated an acceptance of strong measures

67. Poll by British Institute of Public Opinion, press release of May 6,
    1952.

68. National and English Review, CXXXV (August, 1950), 168.

69. Richard Law, "Korea and Western Unity," National and English Re-
    view, CXXXVI (March, 1951), 148.

70. Britain Strong and Free, pp. 5 and 8.

that were otherwise apparently abhorred in Britain. That "the third world war" had in some sense already begun was stated in 1948 by a Conservative who later became an undersecretary in the Foreign Office.[71] And, in the critical winter of 1950-51, when so many feared that stronger American measures might lead to an enlarged war, the Daily Telegraph, while not specifically approving any proposed American measures, nevertheless was more concerned to caution against Britain showing "a spirit of appeasement."[72]

How far the Conservative party, as such, was prepared to join in any American suggestions of anti-Communist counterattacks is difficult to estimate. No such ideas were emphasized in Conservative pronouncements, and it might be misleading to seize upon a stray fire-breathing speech here and there. The most that can safely be said is that Conservatives showed an inclination to go farther than the bulk of their compatriots in supporting a militant stand against Soviet imperialism. That much was assuredly illustrated by these words from the party's 1951 statement of policy: "We cannot accept as permanent the loss of political freedom imposed by force upon the countries of Central and Eastern Europe. These peoples must be given the hope that their rightful place awaits them among the free nations."[73] Perhaps "liberation" was not even implied, but still this was strong talk in the British environment— so strong that it was rare indeed.

Bases for Reservations

In presenting the Conservative approach, a picture of relatively willing agreement with American foreign policy (if not of acquiescence in American leadership) has been given. But this is to speak generally and to leave temporarily out of account the outstanding differences over Far Eastern issues. Also the impression of Conservative attitudes is derived largely from the party's six years out of office, when Tories may occasionally have felt that American policy was more promising than some of the suspected predilections of the Labour government.[74] Once again

---

71. Anthony Nutting (446 H.C. Deb. 412 [January 22, 1948]).

72. November 28, 1950, p. 4. Often the Daily Telegraph took a stronger line than was typical of Conservative spokesmen generally.

73. Britain Strong and Free, p. 8.

74. There was an important distinction between the Conservative view of Labour in general and that of Foreign Secretary Bevin in particular. Whatever the Tory attitude toward Bevin's knowledge of inter-

settled in positions of power and responsibility, Conservatives were subject to some change in perspective. Not only was there no political reason
to paint the United States in relatively glowing colors, but in so far as
Britain's interests clashed with America's the Conservative government
was bound to defend the national position. Ineffectiveness in this respect
would inevitably produce party resentments. While the Churchill-Eden
leadership was unlikely to aim these resentments at the United States,
the future emergence of other and different party voices could not be
discounted completely.

In addition to these speculative, and perhaps remote, considerations,
a few causes did exist for Conservatives to refrain from identifying too
clearly with American policies—apart, that is, from the fact that Conservatives themselves might dislike some of those policies. Since the party
needed the support of marginal voters who feared the United States was
too bellicose in dealing with Communist nations, it was hardly profitable
for Conservatives to appear without a distinctive international position.
On the contrary, some political advantage was probably gained by
Churchill's renewed suggestions of negotiating with Russia, although
such advantage may, in fact, have been incidental to his purpose in pro-
posing big-power talks. Well before Churchill's announced wish to meet
Malenkov in 1953, he had indicated that his policy included at least the
hope of negotiating with the Soviet. Churchill had dramatically advanced
this conception during the 1950 general election campaign. And just afterward, repeating a phrase from his campaign address, he voiced his hope
that "another talk with Soviet Russia upon the highest level" might be useful in forestalling the dread prospects of another war.[75]

Conservatives, in 1950-52, did not really present themselves as a
"peace party." Rather they were seeking to dodge the label of "warmonger."
Refuting this Labour accusation became of first-rank importance in the 1951
campaign, when Conservatives were charged with provocativeness in connection with their occasional preference for stronger methods in Britain's
dealing with Iran. However, the warmonger issue was set against a wider

---

national affairs, there is no question that he was, on basic matters
of foreign policy, considered by Conservatives to be more nearly
representative of their approach than he was of Labour party
tendencies. It was virtually a point of pride among Tory members
of Parliament that their party had backed Bevin more consistently
and more wholeheartedly than had Bevin's own side of the aisle.

75. 473 H.C. Deb. 199 (March 28, 1950).

suspicion, fostered by Labour, that Churchill and the Conservatives were generally less able, by habit or temperament, to preserve the peace. The campaign was expressed in terms of whose finger was to be "on the trigger," culminating in a graphic portrayal of that theme in a pro-Labour newspaper.[76] Without any question, the Tories felt they were hurt, electorally as well as personally, by the warmonger label. Their own campaign literature showed indignant concern,[77] and after winning a narrow election victory the party magazine expressed the belief that "the base charge" had lost the party many votes.[78]

In documenting the campaign on the warmonger issue—which, for all its lack of official Labour sanction, was carried on by individual candidates—the Conservatives noted that a few Labour attacks had had connotations relating to American relations. For instance, Churchill had been likened to MacArthur in type.[79] But, even without any specific connection of the 1951 campaign to Conservative friendship for American policies, the frightening political disadvantage of the warmonger label was cause for Conservatives assiduously to avoid providing a future pretext for its revival. This meant that the Tory party had major political reasons for appearing moderate relative to America's international policy.

There was also a more particular political reason to avoid a "pro-American" label. No matter what British attitudes might be with respect to foreign policy, the United States was too rich and too powerful to be widely popular in postwar Britain. Even outside socialist ranks, and in the public to which Conservatives had to appeal for votes, America was bound to be associated with capitalism and big business. The fact that Conservatives were also so associated did not mean they wished the stereotype to be strengthened in the population at large. However favorably Conservative leaders may themselves have regarded American capitalism, they were presenting their party to the mass of voters on a platform which promised retention of practically all the popular features of the Labour

76. D. E. Butler, The British General Election of 1951 (London: Macmillan & Co., 1952), pp. 118-28. See reproduction opposite p. 134.

77. Conservative Research Department, All the Answers on 100 Vital Issues (London, 1951), pp. 137-39.

78. Tory Challenge, Vol. V (November, 1951), inside front cover.

79. Notes on Current Politics, November 26, 1951, pp. 24-28.

government's legislation. It would have been, and would be in the future, political folly to seem to agree too much with a nation which was conceived to be hostile, for example, to a socialized health service. And, more pointedly in later postwar years, Conservatives wanted to avoid the appearance of sympathizing with the more strenuous antisubversive campaigns in the United States.

Conservatives objected as politely as possible to being dubbed "the American Party." A Tory publication once took some pains to indicate the unfairness of the title: "While the Conservatives are the 'American party' in that they have striven throughout the postwar period to sustain the cooperation and fellow-feeling of the War years as a cardinal principle of foreign policy, they have never done so on a party-political basis."[80] Nor did Conservatives ever intend to carry their program of American co-operation so far as to neglect their traditional emphasis on the importance of Britain's role in the world. Special cordiality to America was one thing, but drawing "so close as to destroy Britain's identity" was quite another.[81]

Specifically, the Conservative consciousness of Empire provided a potential source of grievance against American policies. It was felt that the United States had an inadequate appreciation of the strategic importance of British imperial interests and that Americans retained a historical prejudice against colonialism in general and British interests in particular. Consequently, in the postwar period, Conservatives thought that they should point out to Americans that their true interests now lay in protecting what had been traditional British positions. As already noted, the Truman Doctrine had been welcomed because it represented, among other things, an apparent American acceptance of an Empire, and Tory, policy. But Conservatives were not completely assured of an American change of heart, and at a period of crisis, such as that provided by events in Iran and Egypt in 1951, Americans were again suspected of not understanding the importance of preserving the British stake. This was in spite of the fact that Churchill, as he said in mid-1951, had been trying to persuade Americans that "their main interests are engaged in the Middle East at least as much as they are in any other part of the

---

80. Conservative Research Department, A Monthly Survey of Foreign Affairs, March, 1951, p. 4.

81. Utley, op. cit., p. 39. Also Conservative Political Centre, Imperial Policy (London, 1949).

world outside their own country."[82] He remarked that he had desired, ever since the war, that the United States should be more interested in what was taking place in Iran and Egypt. It was assumed that Americans did not yet know much about these places.

In light of this general outlook, Conservatives were especially unhappy about the American assumption of an in-between negotiator's role in the Iranian oil dispute. The United States might be well intentioned, it was said, but its ambassador's actions in Iran were "very misguided."[83] It was also in America's interest for Britain to stay at the Abadan refineries, one Tory member of Parliament declared, and therefore the United States should support the British position.[84] When it was thought that America failed to do so, there was a feeling that the United States was not "backing up" Britain. Tories, because of their Empire sensitivity, were quick to jump to this criticism, although it was shared by others in the community.[85] Since the Iranian affair, as well as Middle Eastern troubles in general, persisted well after 1951, the grievance against the United States did not die away. The gentle reference to it was unmistakable in Foreign Minister Eden's 1952 speech to the Conservative conference, when, after noting Britain's backing of the American partner, he said: "Wherever we have difficult work to do, and there are some places I need not mention, I hope we can count in turn on wholehearted support and understanding. Without it, the partnership cannot claim the deep loyalties of our peoples."[86]

Probably the plaintive note that America failed to back the Empire was less important in itself than as a symptom of a continued fear that the United States would, out of its relative inexperience, adopt mistaken lines of policy which were injurious to Britain and to the West generally. Imperial-minded Conservatives believed that Americans were no match for the oriental wiles with which British diplomats had learned to cope.

---

82. 491 H.C. Deb. 981 (July 30, 1951).

83. 489 H.C. Deb. 804-8 (June 21, 1951). However, at this time Labour spokesmen showed some signs of a similar complaint against the United States, not surprisingly since their party was in office when the Iranian withdrawal was undertaken.

84. Ibid., cols. 769-71.

85. E.g., the Economist indicated disappointment with any absence of full American "loyalty" (CLX [May 5, 1951], 1019, and CLXI [October 6, 1951], 779-80).

86. 72d Annual Report of the National Union of Conservative and Unionist Associations (London, 1952), p. 36.

The United States was not yet sufficiently skilled or cautious. Americans might inadvertently give away too much or (quite inconsistently) take so firm a position as unnecessarily to provoke a war.

Here Conservatives were usually more charitable than America's other British critics, since they were satisfied with the main postwar direction of American policy. If there were mistakes in that policy during the first six years, Conservatives liked to say that it was because there had been "an almost complete vacuum in experienced British leadership."[87] When in office, the Conservatives assumed that they provided the experienced leadership. Glad as they still were to have the United States exercising its power, they expected Americans to take counsel with British wisdom. Far Eastern affairs may be observed as a case in point.

---

87. Notes on Current Politics, May 14, 1951, p. 8.

British responses to American Far Eastern policy were more striking for their similarity of theme than for their differences. The various
political groups did retain their own approaches to Asian issues, but in
the main these were reflected as shades of the same basic coloration of
attitude, especially toward China. American policy was suspect; with
few exceptions, the range of British opinion ran from acutely hostile to
cautiously critical. The degree of disapproval was significant, since it
showed the extent to which a given ideological group accepted, or rejected, the American alliance. Such differences cannot be ignored in the
analysis, but in this case their description must be second in importance
to the explanation of the generality of criticism. Far Eastern issues
shook the entire community, in addition to setting the stage for the
Bevanite mobilization of left-wing resentments. China proved as much
of a stumbling block to Anglo-American harmony as it was to satisfactory
relations between the Truman Administration and the American public—
though for very different reasons.

It can be granted at the outset that America's China policy, or often
the lack of a defined policy, was vulnerable to attack from two opposing
points of view. The Administration's opposition to the Chinese Communists, especially after their defeat of the Nationalists, was too slight
for Republican critics in the United States but too strong in the eyes of
most British observers. American policy toward China, refusing
either to recognize or to attempt the destruction of the Communist regime,
was seldom defended on the basis of intrinsic merits. In so far as the
American Administration's line was defended at all in Britain, it seemed
that it was done only on the ground that it was the best that could be expected given the state of opinion in the United States. The British alternative, or at least that which characterized the stand of both the Labour and
the Conservative governments, may not have been better in any sense now
ascertainable, but it did have the same kind of advantage for the British
public that the MacArthur alternative had in the United States: it was
more clear cut in its preferences than was the position of the American
Administration.

204

The Administration's policy toward China, as it developed under President Truman and Secretary Acheson, appeared both unsettled and ambiguous. Or perhaps it seemed ambiguous because it was unsettled. What the British public was responding to was less a concerted policy than a series of expedients—though not necessarily inappropriate expedients. Thus, before the outbreak of the Korean war, the United States did not recognize the Chinese Communists, but neither did it make evident any serious intention of protecting Formosa as a Nationalist bastion. Even in the summer of 1950, during the first stages of the Korean fighting, the Administration's "neutralization" of Formosa did not constitute a definite commitment to the long-run championship of Chiang Kai-shek so much as it indicated that the United States might inadvertently end up with such a commitment. Only after the massive Chinese intervention in the Korean war, in late 1950, did it seem likely that the United States would, more or less permanently, keep Formosa out of the hands of Mao Tse-tung; and by that time the maintenance of the Nationalist island forces had become mingled with the conception that it was impossible for the United States to conclude any peaceful settlement with Communist China.

Whether the latter assumption was in fact determining American policy may be doubted, particularly in light of the official persistence in two years of truce negotiations and eventually, in 1953, of the willingness to make the concessions which appeared necessary to secure a truce. Nevertheless, the American role in the truce negotiations did not clarify long-run policy toward China. It still remained open to doubt whether the American approach to a full-scale peace conference was to be based on an unalterable nonrecognition of the regime of Mao Tse-tung. Perhaps no American Administration could or should have adopted a clear-cut position, at least after 1950, on an issue that depended so much on the conduct of Communist China itself. But even if in this circumstance the most intelligent course should turn out to be the indefinite one presented by the United States, there can be no doubt that this very indefiniteness, however advisable, contributed to the volume of criticism directed at the United States.

Background for Disagreement

It is easy enough to say that British interests in the Far East did not coincide with America's. How these interests, or their evaluation, differed from those of the United States presents a problem that is not so simple. The generalization that Britain, because of losing its consciousness of great power status, was no longer concerned about the Far East (or anything else remote from home) is highly dubious. The most that might reasonably be argued along this line is that Britain, as a nation, felt less responsible than America for the consequences of Communist aggrandizement outside the nation's sphere of customary political influence. But this did not mean that Britain was unconcerned about Asia. For example, there was no lack of continued vigilance in dealing with Communists in Malaya; nor was there any protest, except from the fellow-traveling left, to the strong measures that were adopted. Here, it is true, the government moved to protect the lives of British residents and the imperial stake in the rubber industry, but that is only another way of indicating that Britain was prepared to act in given Far Eastern circumstances.

More significant than Malaya as an illustration of the foci of Britain's Asian interest is that of India. Its place in the British consciousness more than rivaled the prominence of China in the American mind. India was the Asian problem with which Englishmen had been concerned for generations. The involvement had been so great and of such long standing that, even if India had completely severed its ties to Britain in the postwar period, it is likely that British attention would have only diminished and not evaporated. However, there was no cause for a sharp decrease in interest in the recently held Indian subcontinent. India, while asserting its independence (under what turned out to be gracious British auspices), elected, like Pakistan, to become a member of the Commonwealth, although on a more tenuous basis than Canada, Australia, and New Zealand. As a republic, India did not acknowledge the same loyalty to the monarch; and, largely as a concession to Indian sensibilities, the Commonwealth ceased to be legally the "British" Commonwealth. But India was a member of the same family of nations and in terms of population by far the most impressive. Its presence, along with that of Pakistan and Ceylon, meant that the Commonwealth—in Britain still often thought of as the British Commonwealth (or, more anachronistically, as the British Empire)[1]—had a very large Asian component. The very fact that this component was not securely tied to the Commonwealth meant that Britain, desirous of maintaining the bond, was sure to be sensitive to Indian viewpoints. To offend India, especially on an Asian issue, was

---

1. In addition to the use of the term "Empire" in some quarters as a synonym for Commonwealth, it is also applied, more narrowly, to the non-self-governing territories under British rule.

something Britain ordinarily had reason to avoid.

Furthermore, Britain was intimately concerned with India's future prosperity and stability. Economic assistance to India, as a member of the sterling area as well as of the Commonwealth, tended to help solve Britain's larger problems, and it was, for example, considered important that American aid programs be politically acceptable to India. This was part of a general concern quite different from any traditional imperial attitude. Labour and liberal groups were more conspicuous than Conservatives in responding sympathetically to Indian views. The fact that the Labour government had, in the first place, made the arrangements for the entry of India into the Commonwealth gave its supporters a special reason for wanting to preserve the attachment. There was considerable Labour pride in what was considered the fruits of an enlightened and moderate policy with respect to imperial relationships. Conservatives did not usually share this sense of satisfaction, but, while troubled about the new looseness of the Commonwealth, they were also bound to cherish what ties remained.

Being absorbed in the maintenance of the Asian Commonwealth did not preclude other British interests in the Far East. Japan is a case in point. From almost the beginning of the occupation, and perhaps from the last stages of World War II, there were complaints that Britain was being excluded by the American hegemony in relation to Japan. At first, however, the supreme authority of General MacArthur was seldom subjected to openly hostile criticism. More typical were gentle comments about America's "short-sighted policy" in seeking to monopolize occupation responsibilities.[2] Only leftists were immediately shrill in denouncing "Shogun MacArthur," and from 1947 to 1950, when Far Eastern affairs did not command a great deal of popular attention, they maintained an intermittent attack on America's and MacArthur's "imperialism" in Japan, as well as in Asia generally.[3]

In the more moderate line of complaint, which did accept the validity of an American priority of interest as an outgrowth of the war against Japan, what was mainly stated was a growing dissatisfaction that Britain

2. Lewis Einstein, "The Next Allied Talks," Fortnightly, CLXV (January, 1946), 15.

3. Jonathan Grant, Tribune, November 16, 1945, pp. 9-10. Cf. 433 H.C. Deb. 2367-72 (February 27, 1947), 437 H.C. Deb. 1906-12 (May 16, 1947), 457 H.C. Deb. 476-83 (October 29, 1948), and 473 H.C. Deb. 304-6 (March 28, 1950).

had no way of finding out what was going on. Conservatives contributed to this criticism, although they did not necessarily direct it against American authority. In mid-1946 one back-bencher declared that there was a "curtain hanging over Japan, and that curtain is one of fog."[4] R. A. Butler, later in the same year, questioned whether British interests were being adequately represented.[5]

Considerations, to be sure, were mainly economic, and they involved the previously discussed fear that America might rebuild a ruthlessly competitive Japanese industry in textiles and other fields.[6] America's desires for a solvent Japan, and later for a Japanese military ally, were not shared in Britain. In this sense, the British attitude toward American policy in Japan was essentially negative, but it was nonetheless real. It did not so much indicate an absence of interest as a rather different and partially conflicting interest from that which the United States appeared to promote.

Probably, in broad perspective, this British attitude toward Japan was not so highly responsible as that of the United States. Political and strategic factors were not usually taken into account. The same was often true with respect to the early differences in approach to China's postwar problems. During the Chinese civil war and just afterward there was comparatively little concern for the noneconomic consequences of the struggle for power in China. Reports on the course of Chinese events, in the columns of the internationally conscious quality press, did not treat the outcome with indifference; but the British position in world politics did not appear to be seriously affected. The United States, it was known, was much involved, but that, say, in 1945 or 1946, did not necessarily interest Englishmen. They probably felt no more attached to the American interest in Chiang Kai-shek than, at the same period, Americans felt to the British stake in India or elsewhere in the Middle East. As serious a paper as the Economist treated the renewed outbreak of the Chinese civil war without a word about British interests but primarily as a reflection of "Far Eastern Rivalries" between American and Russian spheres of influence.[7] As late as the end of 1946, the same publication spoke of a

4.   423 H.C. Deb. 1879 (June 4, 1946).

5.   427 H.C. Deb. 1523-24 (October 22, 1946).

6.   See chap. iv.

7.   CXLIX (November 10, 1945), 667-68.

"direct confrontation of American and Russian power in the Far East."[8]
This was not in the nature of an attack on American imperialism, or
even a matter of equating the United States and Russia (which perspective was then rife in left-wing circles), but it did indicate a detachment
from Chinese developments.

Britain's relative unconcern is sometimes attributed to a lack of the
geographical proximity felt in the United States by virtue of facing China
across the Pacific Ocean. So broad a generalization is qualified by a
traditional British participation in China, but in its trade and not so much
in its politics. Whatever political control Britain exercised among Chinese,
notably in Hong Kong, was primarily for reasons of Commerce. Instead
of assuming responsibility for China's political future, as Britain had
morally and otherwise for India's, that role was largely left to the United
States. Although British missionaries did participate in Chinese educational and philanthropic ventures, their impact on the national consciousness was not large when compared with the totality of similar experiences elsewhere. The Chinese endeavor was, for Britain, only one
of many instances of overseas activity and not a uniquely important one.

More particularly, the British outlook was different from the American in that no great expectations about China's role as a great power had
been cherished during the war years. Treating China as one of the Big
Five, both in the peace settlement and in arrangements for the United
Nations Security Council, was regarded as a peculiarly American, or
Rooseveltian, fancy. Britain did not think of Chiang Kai-shek as an important ally (at least not of Britain), and the preservation of his regime
was of no intimate significance. Certainly no British government was
going to be charged with success or failure on the basis of the outcome
of a civil war in China. This comparative aloofness made it hard for
Englishmen to comprehend why American emotions rose in response to
results in China. Any reflection on how they would have reacted to apparent failure of British policy in an area of traditional British political
interest might have been helpful in understanding the political repercus-
sions in the United States after 1949.

In so far as notice was taken of early postwar developments in China,
the American role was usually subject to adverse comments. And these
came from virtually every angle, so as almost classically to reflect
British lack of confidence in American diplomatic wisdom, steadiness,

8.   CLI (December 7, 1946), 901.

and maturity. Even the very small fraction of British opinion that was aware of the dangerous realities of Chinese communism found no satisfaction with American policy—any more than did their much more vocal and numerous opposite numbers in the United States. Incidentally, the few Englishmen who believed in the importance of backing Chiang did not fail to emphasize the widely accepted faults of his regime.[9] At any rate, there was the implication that the United States was not providing consistent leadership, Or as Brigadier Fitzroy Maclean, Conservative member of Parliament and free-lance commentator on international affairs, said in 1949, it was no use for Britain to try to follow American policy in China because America had no policy—it was "a case of the blind leading the blind."[10]

However, almost no other British pronouncements on American policy stemmed from the militantly anti-Chinese Communist position of Maclean. Middle-of-the-road opinion seemed so much impressed with the inadequacies of Chiang that it was felt that the United States faced a dilemma in which there was nothing worth backing[11] or that it had been a mistake to place too much money on Chiang in the first place.[12] During the civil war the liberal Guardian already regarded Chiang as one of the "shady allies" with whom the United States foolishly chose to co-operate in an effort to do anything to hinder Russia.[13] If liberals did not suggest that Chiang was worse than the Chinese Communists, there were left-wing statements to that effect. American intervention was said to be on the wrong side, thus fitting the conception of dollar imperialism in the Far East which had been propagated from the beginning of the post-1945 period.[14]

As the civil war drew to a close, there was at least general pleasure that Britain was not identified with the losing side. This was especially evident in the Labour party, where there was no inclination to be pessimistic about future relations with the Chinese Communists even after

9. National Review, CXXX (March, 1948), 187-88.

10. 467 H.C. Deb. 1656 (July 21, 1949).

11. Economist, CLI (July 27, 1946), 125-26.

12. L. D. Gammans (Conservative) (464 H. C. Deb. 1301 [May 5, 1949]).

13. Manchester Guardian Weekly, November 11, 1948, p. 9.

14. New Statesman, XXXII (November 23, 1946), 371-72; cf. 446 H.C. Deb. 580-83 (January 23, 1948).

their attack on the British ship "Amethyst" in the Yangtze. One Labour member of Parliament declared at that time: "We have not made the fatal error which the Americans made of endeavoring to bolster up the corrupt, rickety, ramshackle power of the Kuomintang, and thereby incurring the hostility of the Chinese Communists by doing so."[15] Coupled with this satisfaction was the belief that Mao Tse-tung's party was somehow different from other Communist movements. Sometimes this assumption reflected the characteristic left-wing belief in the beneficent potentiality of any new Communist movement, but more often it was based on the idea that Mao might be (or might become) independent of Moscow. Already, in mid-1949, recognition of the Communist regime was widely anticipated. Rather than Mao's evident antagonism acting as a deterrent, it tended to confirm the British in believing that a sympathetic stand should be adopted as an alternative to the unsuccessful American policy.

Although the decision on recognition was a responsibility of the Labour government, it was frequently advised by independent opinion in the name of facing "realities."[16] Asian nationalism was considered one of these realities, and the protection of British trading interests was another. Establishment of diplomatic relations, it was stressed, did not mean approval of communism, Chinese or any other style. Recognition, according to the Times, was to be "a purely pragmatic act."[17] The other side of this view was that it was "absurd" to treat the Chiang Kai-shek regime as the legal government of China. American backing of Chiang in Formosa was regarded as unwise. It would, the Manchester Guardian Weekly editorialized in early 1950, "cement Communist China and Soviet Russia."[18] Otherwise, it was insisted, they might not become allies at all.

Whether this brand of thinking played a greater part in the original desire for recognition than did the admitted hope of maintaining trade connections is open to question.[19] Whatever the reasons, recognition

---

15. W. Wyatt (464 H.C. Deb. 1260 [May 5, 1949]). Cf. ibid., cols. 1224-1349, for other remarks on China.

16. Spectator, CLXXXIII (October 7, 1949), 451-52.

17. January 2, 1950, p. 7.

18. January 5, 1950, pp. 8-9; ibid., January 12, 1950, p. 8.

19. Illustrative of interest in trade prospects was the Scotsman, January 7, 1950, p. 6.

was widely approved when it was announced early in 1950. Virtually no case was made against dealing with the Communists because they were Communists.[20] The only significant objections openly raised, in this period, related to the timing of the recognition. Foreign Minister Bevin was criticized for moving so soon, especially before full Commonwealth consultation and without the participation of the United States.[21] It was not claimed, for instance, in Eden's objections to Bevin's method, that the United States was right to refuse recognition. Eden only urged that moving "in step with our partners" was important.[22] Presumably the United States would have been expected, if more time had been allowed, to come around to the British view.

In the six months or so before the Korean war began, it was assumed that America was not really intransigent on the establishment of future relations with Communist China. Foreign Secretary Bevin spoke only of the "very aloof attitude" of the United States, at the time when Britain was contemplating recognition. Quite evidently, Bevin believed that the United States was not going to veto the admission of Communist China to the United Nations Security Council. He told the House of Commons in May, 1950, that the American attitude on this was "very fair," in agreeing neither to vote for nor to veto China's admission. Bevin also said that the United States was opposed to Chiang's blockade of the Chinese mainland and that America wanted to co-operate "to give China a chance."[23] In effect, he was hinting that it would not be so long before the gap between British and American policies toward China would narrow. This reflected the widely held estimate that the American Administration was only temporarily inhibited from facing the "realities" by Republican attacks on the State Department. The Labour government (without any apparent dissent from the Foreign Office) was confident of the wisdom of its own China policy. Most Englishmen seemed to agree. And "responsible" Americans, it was thought, really agreed as well.

---

20. The possible exception was provided by Brigadier Maclean (475 H.C. Deb. 2160 [May 24, 1950]).

21. Economist, CLVIII (January 7, 1950), 1-2.

22. 475 H.C. Deb. 2071 (May 24, 1950).

23. Ibid., cols. 2082-86.

The Korean War: First Stage

Before the assumption as to eventual American policy toward China could be tested over an ordinary course of time, the Korean war intervened. For the moment, existing disagreements about China did not forcibly intrude, and there was a virtually unanimous British praise for the immediate American action against the North Korean aggression. However, given the firm conviction that Mao's regime was a fait accompli, the action in Korea was never viewed as the beginning of a campaign against communism in Asia. Also what was happening in Korea lacked, for Britain, the dramatically energizing qualities typified by America's large-scale participation and hugely expanded rearmament program. British interest was largely indirect, and the original enthusiasm was a reaction to American implementation of the general principle of a United Nations stand against military aggression. Willingness to take action in Korea served notice of the serious intention to do the same elsewhere, notably in Europe. This was the keynote of Prime Minister Attlee's announcement of the American military moves: ". . . the salvation of all is dependent on prompt and effective measures to arrest aggression wherever it may occur."[24]

To this theme, British parliamentary opinion, save for strict pacifists, voiced no objections. The principle seemed universally popular, and the most the extreme Labour Left did was to question whether the United States was really acting within the limits of the United Nations Security Council resolution. Although enthusiasm diminished as one moved to the left in the parliamentary ranks, there was very little open opposition especially in the early weeks of the war.[25] A member of Parliament whose foreign-policy views were ordinarily hostile to American policies gave vent to no more than "misgivings" about the Korean commitment.[26] Even among those who feared that the Americans might extend the war by protecting Formosa, there was a desire that Britain should join in sending troops to Korea.[27] Tribune, for example, was vigorous in its support of the Korean campaign in its first few months and specifically

24. 476 H.C. Deb. 2160 (June 27, 1950).

25. See the parliamentary discussion on Korea (477 H.C. Deb. 485-596 [July 5, 1950]) for some of the strongest pro-American sentiments ever expressed.

26. Tom Driberg (477 H.C. Deb. 569-78 [July 5, 1950]).

27. R. H. S. Crossman (478 H.C. Deb. 718-19 [July 27, 1950]).

critical of the rare left-wing case for United Nations withdrawal.[28] And moderate editorial opinion was filled with praise for American promptness. The sentiments of the Economist were fairly typical: "To those who wondered whether the United States really would come to the assistance of any victim of aggression, the answer is now on the record."[29] By the early fall, with military success, confidence in America was higher than ever. Crossing the thirty-eighth parallel did not appear to cause any more stir in Britain than in the United States.[30]

Yet there was at the same time and in the summer of 1950 a manifest uneasiness about broader American Far Eastern policies in relation to the Korean war. At the extreme was the New Statesman, which coupled, almost from the beginning, its support of United Nations action against aggression with the fear that it provided "American Imperialism just the opportunity it desired."[31] It was in this light that the unilateral American neutralization of Formosa was suspected; President Truman's order to the Seventh Fleet did not appear to the left as a move to localize the conflict. It seemed even less so when General MacArthur paid his famous midsummer visit to Chiang on Formosa, and the left declared that the American Administration should remove the General from his command.[32] Tribune was insistent on such action, since at this stage it still had hopes that Truman and Acheson were not really interested in Formosa. The Administration was called upon to save itself and everyone else from the consequences of appearing hostile to Communist China.[33]

The Labour Left was not alone in being disturbed about the American commitment concerning Formosa. In August, 1950, the liberal Manchester Guardian Weekly spoke, though in a different key, to the same effect: "The Western world is horrified at the thought that by the Presidential declaration about Formosa the United States may have laid herself open to pos-

---

28. Outstanding among Tribune's editorials in support of the Korean war was that of July 28, 1950, pp. 3-4.

29. CLIX (July 22, 1950), 153.

30. A good sample of the equanimity at this stage was provided by the Spectator, CLXXXV (October 6, 1950), 361.

31. XL (July 1, 1950), 1-2.

32. Ibid., August 12, 1950, p. 161.

33. September 1, 1950, pp. 3-4.

sible war with Communist China, the very thing the Russians most want
to provoke."[34] The Formosan issue, it was thought, threatened the whole
exemplary enterprise of enforcing collective security in Korea.[35]
Moderate critics did not hint at bad American intentions but rather at
what the Economist called "the insufficient care" taken to explain
Formosan policy at the outbreak of the Korean war.[36] It was not argued,
as it was on the left, that the United States should have neglected to neu-
tralize Formosa but only that it should have been done without appearing
to champion Chinese Nationalists as opposed to Chinese Communists.

The welcome for Truman's disavowal, in August, 1950, of MacArthur's
Formosa views was general. More than ever, the British divided American influences on Far Eastern policy into good and evil, and there was no
doubt that MacArthur now symbolized (beyond strictly left-wing circles)
what appeared dangerous in American handling of foreign affairs.[37] In
addition to his representing, in fact, a policy with which almost all Britain
disagreed, MacArthur was in other respects ideally cast for the devil's
role in the British mind. The General's histrionics contrasted with the
restrained behavior Britain liked in its own generals (and in Eisenhower),
and his rhetoric was of exactly the kind which was out of fashion in Britain.
Furthermore, MacArthur's publicized behavior in relation to civil authority was at odds with customary British circumspection. American habits
in this respect had never been admired, and MacArthur's seeming adoption of his own political course confirmed the unfavorable stereotype.
After MacArthur, every other American general, at the slightest hint of
political expression, was suspected of being "out of control."

Not entirely dissimilar criticism of MacArthur's attitude concerning
Formosa was, at the time, also vocal in the United States. What was different was the absence of anything approaching the nearly universal character of the objections in the British community. These objections were but
slightly mitigated by occasional praise for MacArthur's military abilities
(by Churchill, for instance, after the victories of the early fall of 1950).
Even Churchill, while not identifying the General with any unpopular

---

34. August 17, 1950, p. 8.

35. Ibid., August 31, 1950, p. 8.

36. CLIX (August 12, 1950), 298-99.

37. E.g., London Times, August 30, 1950, p. 5; News Chronicle, October
     17, 1950, p. 2; and Spectator, CLXXXV (September 1, 1950), 258-59.

policies or even referring at all to such policies, expressed, relatively early, the British anxiety that was always present in connection with the Korean campaign. We must hope, he said, that "the forces of the free peoples of the world will not become too deeply involved in the Far East. . . ."[38]

It was not the mere desire to avoid an enlarged Asian conflict that meaningfully set off British opinion from that of most Americans (who, after all, preferred a small war too). What was relevant, though so careful a champion of Anglo-American harmony as Churchill would never have said so, was that Britain was prepared to believe that further involvement would be attributable to mistaken American policies. There was a virtually unanimous feeling even in mid-1950 that the United States had already alarmed the Chinese Communists by its nonrecognition, by its continued attachment to Chiang, by its ambiguous attitude about Formosa, and by MacArthur's apparent intentions. Only very rarely was there any-one who justified the American anti-Chinese Communist moves by the strategic concern for Formosa that actuated MacArthur defenders in the United States; and no one in Britain did so out of regard for Chiang. The only point in British dispute was whether America's China policy resulted from honest error or deliberate malice (as the left urged more and more). Americans, it will be remembered, were also divided on China issues in the summer of 1950, but hardly along the same lines.

Trauma of Chinese Intervention

In view of the British state of mind during, as well as before, the first part of the Korean war, it is not surprising that the massive Chinese intervention of November, 1950, was viewed very differently than it was in the United States.[39] It would be too much to say that Englishmen, or a large portion of them, excused the Communist aggression by the theory that America provoked it. Ideas, except on the extreme left, were not so clear cut as that. The Economist typified the reaction of the press that had ordinarily been forebearing in criticism of America's China policy. It did not want to pardon "the clear aggression of the Chinese Communists,"

---

38. 71st Annual Report of the National Union of Conservative and Unionist Associations (London, 1950), p. 107.

39. The general nature of this difference was described on the basis of firsthand observation by Ernest Borneman, "The British Disagree with Us," Harper's, CCII (May, 1951), 35-42.

but it asked whether the American-led campaign in Korea had really kept in view its limited United Nations purpose or whether it had been transformed into a program of winning a complete Far Eastern victory. So vital was it to avoid a major entanglement in Asia, the journal said, "that everything possible should have been done to avoid it—and certainly everything possible was not done."[40] This stinger was aimed at MacArthur's large-scale drive to the Yalu River as well as at previous American policies. A less restrained liberal paper spoke of MacArthur having committed "the military folly of stampeding forward without really knowing what he has let himself in for."[41] Another and decidedly Conservative source said that talks with China should have been tried before MacArthur's offensive.[42]

The meaning of British criticism of MacArthur was different in kind as well as degree from the corresponding tendency of some Americans to charge that the advance to the Yalu caused the Chinese to intervene. For the British to hold MacArthur responsible meant that they believed that a foreign general, over whom they could not even hope to exercise direct control, had by actions (of which Britain generally disapproved anyway) brought about results they considered disastrous. The climate of opinion was such that rather than being inclined to ignore possible past errors in American policy, in the name of meeting the Chinese onslaught, there was, at first, an open season for shooting at the United States in general and MacArthur in particular. Ordinary British decorum seemed to have been put aside, and so ardent a believer in Anglo-American unity as the venerable Liberal, Lord Samuel, talked about the difficulties caused by MacArthur's pronouncements and by his ignoring what was claimed to have been the prior Chinese notice of reactions to having Western armies near their border.[43] And this was soft language relative to that of the Labour peers who participated in the same House of Lords debate on the Chinese intervention.

By comparison, strictly Conservative commentary seemed almost to defend the American point of view, but this appearance was deceptive. Most Conservatives did omit personal attacks on MacArthur, and, con-

---

40. CLIX (December 2, 1950), 926.

41. News Chronicle, December 6, 1950, p. 2.

42. Daily Mail, November 29, 1950, p. 1.

43. 169 H.L. Deb. 1003-4 (December 14, 1950).

sistent with their belief in the importance of a policy of strength, they
were not inclined to accuse American policy of anything like warmon-
gering.[44] But Conservatives were unlikely to credit the United States
with wisdom, especially in carrying the war as far north as the Yalu
River. [The point was made, with usual Churchillian concern for
saying nothing too offensive to American sensibilities, in the notable
parliamentary speech of late November, 1950: ". . . I had hoped that
General MacArthur's advance in Korea . . . would stop at the neck or
wasp waist of the peninsula and would leave the country between the
neck and the Yalu River and the Chinese frontier as a kind of No-man's
land which allied air power would dominate."[45] Churchill repeated this
same strategic preference a few weeks later when he criticized the absence of high-level Anglo-American talks upon the crossing of the thirty-
eighth parallel. At that time, he said, stopping at the narrow waist should
have been urged.[46]

This point seemed prominent in the Tory thinking that was otherwise most nearly in agreement (or least far removed from agreement)
with general American policy toward China. The Marquess of Salisbury,
the highly respected Conservative leader in the House of Lords, had
never, for example, been sympathetic with British recognition of Communist China or with the view that American recognition would have
prevented the Chinese aggression. Yet, in mid-November of 1950, he
suggested that the United Nations position was dangerous because "we
have, if anything, advanced too far."[47] Essentially, in his view, as
evidently in Churchill's, there was concern for the consequences of a
mistaken military policy. The cause was not assigned to political motivations, whether of MacArthur or of anyone else.]

This sharply contrasted with the approach of the Labour Left, especially that portion which had previously been openly suspicious of
MacArthur. Its immediate reaction to Chinese intervention was to pro-

---

44. Typical of many Conservative comments was the restraint of the
Yorkshire Post, November 29, 1950, p. 2.

45. 481 H.C. Deb. 1336 (November 30, 1950). The military sagacity of
the advance was also questioned by Brigadier Head (481 H.C. Deb.
1204-5 [November 29, 1950]).

46. 482 H.C. Deb. 1363-64 (December 14, 1950).

47. 169 H.L. Deb. 281 (November 15, 1950). See also Salisbury's speech
(ibid., cols. 988-97 [December 14, 1950]).

claim the justification of the worst socialist fears. The New Statesman
took for granted the "appalling role" of MacArthur's advance in provoking the Chinese and exclaimed that what had begun as United Nations
resistance to aggression "ended in an insane American gamble in the
diplomacy of power politics."[48] The same theme was echoed by parliamentary spokesmen of the Labour Left and by the periodical outlets for
socialist views on foreign policy.[49] The all-out critics of American
policy in China were now having their day.

Popularly the United States was presented as an aggressive power
in a wider sense than had been indicated by the left-wing belief in Mac-
Arthur's provocation of China. [In the few months of crisis following the
Chinese intervention, Americans were almost invariably observed to be
demanding relatively strong retaliatory measures, in contrast to the
pacifying role assumed by British diplomats. Newspaper headlines
tended to fix the stereotype of Americans ready for large-scale war.
The tabloid of largest circulation—pro-Labour, but not pro-left—was
illustrative. It provided headlines, day after day in January, 1951, which
presented its millions of scanners with an almost entirely unrelieved,
and unexplained, picture of American belligerence, only barely restrained
by the efforts of British Labour statesmen.[50] Other mass-circulation
papers were similar, if less lurid. It was no wonder that, in an opinion
sample taken at the time, while 58 per cent said that if a war came it was
likely to come through Russia, as high as 21 per cent chose America as
the likely source. Of Labour voters taken alone, 25 per cent pointed to
the United States. The corresponding Conservative figure was only 8
per cent.[51]

For suspicion of the United States to have mounted so high was truly
a distressing sign of the crisis in British confidence that was caused by
the Chinese intervention and particularly by the American reaction to it.
Undoubtedly there was genuine fear of what the United States was going

---

48. XL (December 2 and 9, 1950), 528 and 576.

49. 481 H.C. Deb. 1251-60 (November 29, 1950), 482 H.C. Deb. 1419-24
    (December 14, 1950), and 169 H.L. Deb. 319-26 (November 15, 1950);
    cf. Reynolds News, December 3, 1950, p. 1, and Glasgow Forward,
    December 2, 1950, p. 1.

50. Daily Mirror, almost daily front-page stories through January, 1951.

51. British Institute of Public Opinion, press release, January, 1951.

to do. Reports of MacArthur's preference for strong measures were disturbing enough, but they were not new to British ears. What was really shocking was the first interpretation of President Truman's press conference statement that the use of the atom bomb in Korea was under active consideration. That meant only war and destruction to the British, and the left made the most of the report from Washington.[52] Moreover, alarm was sufficiently general so that Prime Minister Attlee journeyed to the United States to communicate, as his supporters understood it, the British horror of precipitating large-scale war not only with China but with Russia as well. Since, following Attlee's American visit, no atom bomb was dropped, it became part of Labour lore that their leader had saved the peace of the world. The converse was that the United States, left to its own devices, would have started a major conflict.

Furthermore, it would have been a conflict against a nation with whom the Labour government (apparently supported by most British opinion) still felt it should deal in its previously determined diplomatic course. The official British view was reiterated by the Undersecretary for Foreign Affairs just after the Chinese intervention had taken place:

> In our view, and it is unquestionable, the People's Government of China is the effective Government of China and the Nationalist representatives [at the United Nations] today do not represent anything but a small section of the Chinese people. If it were suggested that the representatives of the People's Government should not represent China in the United Nations, as long as that situation prevails it means that hundreds of millions of Chinese are going without true representation in the United Nations.[53]

That the British government still preferred Communist China in the United Nations was clear enough, although admission was not to be officially pressed for the time being. The "enlightened" character, as the Daily Mirror called it, of Britain's attitude toward China seemed widely accepted as the proper course for settlement of the conflict.[54] The Manchester Guardian Weekly considered the admission of Communist China to the United Nations one of the indispensable conditions for success of the peace negotiations it hoped for in December, 1950.[55] To

---

52. 481 H.C. Deb. 1382-91 (November 30, 1950), and 482 H.C. Deb. 544-51 (December 7, 1950).

53. Ernest Davies (481 H.C. Deb. 1357 [November 30, 1950]).

54. November 30, 1950, p. 12.

55. December 7, 1950, p. 8.

another independent journal, trading a United Nations Security Council seat for Korean peace seemed entirely reasonable.[56]

It followed from this position that American attempts to have the United Nations name China as an aggressor were bitterly opposed from the very beginning. The antithesis of Britain's peaceful approach was to "brand" China as an outlaw.[57] Hopes persisted through the winter of 1950-51, despite Chinese intransigence, that a soft policy would dissuade China from aggression. When finally a modified condemnatory resolution was passed by the United Nations, there was either satisfaction that Britain had succeeded in toning down the original American language or continued feeling that any harsh words were mistaken. The exceptions to the preference for a soft policy were, at this stage, so few as to be noticed for their apparent eccentricity in the British community. The Daily Express took one of its own distinctive lines in urging Britain to joir in condemning China as an aggressor.[58] And there was a rare defender, on strategic grounds, of the American insistence on strong measures.[59] No doubt, the paucity of public utterances along this line understated the number of Tories who did sympathize with America's distrust of Chinese intentions. These were not days when it would have been popular, in Britain, to appear to agree with MacArthur.

There was another, very different side to the general British distress over America's position in China. No matter how wide the divergence in national viewpoints with respect to the Far East, the majority opinion seemed to cherish no less the need for Britain and America to stick together. In fact, the desire grew as the dangers of a split in the alliance became more obvious. There was no time when greater stress was placed upon Anglo-American unity than during the crisis period when the intentions of the United States were most feared and doubted. Except for the militant left, whose estrangement from the alliance was now under way, British disapproval of American policies toward China was almost invariably coupled with the fervent hope that existing disagreements would not drive the allies apart on larger matters. This was a principal theme of Prime Minister Attlee, both before and after his sudden trip to Washington.

56. Spectator, CLXXXV (December 15, 1950), 684-85.

57. W. Wyatt (481 H.C. Deb. 1341 [November 30, 1950]).

58. January 19, 1951, p. 4.

59. G. F. Hudson, "The Privileged Sanctuary," Twentieth Century, CXLIX (January, 1951), 4-10.

Maintenance of "cordial" relations with the United States was at once his obvious policy and his political defense against the Conservative view that Churchill would have maintained a stauncher tie.[60] Attlee's position, after talking with President Truman, was that Britain's recognition of Communist China (and desire to have Mao eventually represented in the United Nations) could be retained consistent with friendship and cooperation with the United States. If anything, there began, in mid-December, a tendency by Labour leaders to minimize the importance of the China disagreement as an impediment to close relations with America.[61] As Labour's daily newspaper said, at the height of the crisis, a split between the United States and Britain must never take place.[62] That was Britain's policy. The Labour government was long since committed to it as a first principle in foreign affairs, and some of the most confirmed party critics of American policy in China now reaffirmed their adherence to the alliance.

Strong emphasis on the Anglo-American unity theme was connected to the concern that the United States contemplated abandonment of Europe. Never was this more poignant than when America seemed likely to become preoccupied with Asia. It was in Europe, as the Times insisted, that the British believed the greatest danger lay. The British government was supposed to convince America of "the abiding truth that Europe must remain the chief defensive base of the free world." The Attlee-Truman meeting, it was thought, had confirmed this, along with "their two countries' great and unshakable solidarity of interests." For the sake of preserving this united front, the Times subsequently admitted, there was a virtue in British agreement to the modified version of the United Nations condemnation of Chinese aggression; otherwise, this quasi-official voice had remained, as expected, totally unconvinced of the wisdom of the American approach.[63] Liberal commentary generally took very much the same line, in no way retreating from the preference for Britain's softer China policy, but prepared to give way, without complete surrender, in order to avoid the disaster of a break between Britain and the United States. As the Economist stated:

---

60. 481 H.C. Deb. 1434-40 (November 30, 1950).

61. 482 H.C. Deb. 1350-62 (December 14, 1950). The general debate following Attlee's trip to Washington took place at this time (ibid., cols. 1350-1464).

62. Daily Herald, December 18, 1950, p. 4.

63. December 4, 1950, p. 7; December 9, 1950, p. 7; January 20, 1951, p. 7.

There is every reason for using the plainest possible language to the Americans—and not merely to the Administration but to American public opinion. But when it comes to action, first things must come first. And incomparably the first thing for Britain is that the Atlantic Alliance should hold fast.[64]

Conservative views in the winter of 1950-51 were not very different.[65] The Daily Telegraph saw considerable harm to Anglo-American relations stemming from the Labour Left's criticism of the United States. This was not the time, the Conservative organ said, to attack MacArthur.[66] Perhaps this, while mainly reflecting a concern for subsequent American reactions, also indicated that Conservatives were less certain than others that America was entirely wrong and Britain's Labour government entirely correct about China. However, most Tories gave no sign of being closer to the American position than to Britain's, and, as a general rule, they too merely argued that the differences ought to be accepted as they were and that unity be preserved anyway. Conservatives joined in the British feeling that a larger war should be avoided in China and that the United States should be urged to concentrate on the defense of Europe.[67] Satisfactory Anglo-American relations were required for this purpose, and it was also typical of Conservative comment to add that "upon it our survival absolutely depends."[68]

A special word needs to be devoted to the Labour Left's response at this point. Its criticism of the United States, immediately after the Chinese intervention, was mainly distinguished by a stridency and by a "told-you-so" quality. But a larger difference arose a few months later. Then, instead of moving with the rest of British opinion to a concentration on preserving the Anglo-American alliance, the Labour Left continued to harp on the irreconcilability of existing differences and the horrors of

---

64. CLX (January 27, 1951), 178; cf. also News Chronicle, January 23, 1951, p. 2, and Manchester Guardian Weekly, February 1, 1951, pp. 8-9.

65. Conservatives criticized, as usual, Labour's capacity to maintain cordial American relations and tabled a motion to this effect (484 H.C. Deb. 623 [February 15, 1951]).

66. Daily Telegraph, December 5, 1950, p. 4.

67. R. A. Butler (481 H.C. Deb. 1424-34 [November 30, 1950]). Press comment was similar, i.e., Glasgow Herald, December 4, 1950, p. 4.

68. This was the phrase of Robert Boothby, who, on occasion, has been independently critical of America's trade policy and foreign policy generally (484 H.C. Deb. 109 [February 12, 1951]).

yielding to the American view.[69] Although this tendency did not at first amount to a full-fledged departure from the Labour party's commitments, it was preparatory to the subsequent break. The events of the winter of 1950-51 released the flood of ideological objection which had been dammed during the preceding two years.[70]

Recurrent Alarms

During the next two years of the Korean war, while the left concentrated on the evils of American policy, most of the rest of Britain still hoped for the best but frequently feared the worst. Always the barest hint of strong American measures against China created alarm. On the other hand, the fears were occasionally alleviated by apparent American acceptance of stalemate, as well as by renewed hopes of a negotiated peace satisfying the United States and China. Thus, spirits rose with the removal of General MacArthur (which was widely and sometimes wildly approved), with the persistence of the Truman-Acheson-Bradley policy that emerged from the MacArthur hearings, and with the willingness to negotiate at the Korean battle line. So much was entirely to the good, in the British perspective, and most of the press had nothing but praise for the American Administration's determination not to fight "the wrong nation in the wrong war and in the wrong place." These words were echoed by many British defenders of the Anglo-American alliance; at favorable moments, right-wing leaders must have felt

69. The growing left-wing emphasis on the divergence in Anglo-American policies may be plainly observed in the writings of R. H. S. Crossman, whose shifting attitudes previously (in chap. v) provided a case study. In the mass-circulation Sunday Pictorial (where he put in words of fewer syllables what he pronounced, at the same time, in Parliament and in the New Statesman), Crossman's columns between November, 1950, and February, 1951, reflected the hostility which was then characteristic of those who had not yet fully declared their opposition to the conditions of the alliance.

70. Alienation of the left proceeded unevenly. Compare Tribune (January 12, 1951, pp. 3-4, and January 26, 1951, p. 4) with the more pessimistic New Statesman (XLI [January 27, 1951], 88). The latter also published the most sensational of all socialist declarations against American Far Eastern policy—that of G. D. H. Cole. Not only did Cole say that he had regarded the Korean war as a civil war which, despite his avowed dislike of communism, he had wanted the North to win, but he made the dramatic statement: "If Great Britain gets dragged into a war with China by the Americans, I shall be on the side of China . . ." (ibid., February 3, 1951, pp. 120-21). This statement may well have articulated the implicit preferences of a large segment of the British left.

almost certain that they, and not the left, had turned out to be correct about the United States. Perhaps in 1951 and 1952 this was the predominant feeling and representative of the nation's basic commitment.

Yet it was less impressive, on the surface, than the manifestations of continued British hostility to policies the United States was suspected of contemplating or adopting. Statements by individual Americans were capable of causing sharp reactions. The speech by the State Department's Dean Rusk in May, 1951, because it came from an official source, caused more consternation than most. To Britain, Rusk had appeared to imply that the United States would only deal with a Chinese regime which overthrew the Communists. This, like any American move closer to Chiang, meant, in British opinion, a prolongation if not an extension of the conflict with China.[71] Similarly, advocacy by various American sources, official and unofficial, of a total trade embargo, or of the bombing of China, reactivated British fears for the consequences of strong measures previously thought to enjoy American favor.[72]

It was ordinarily expected that British statesmen should urge mildness and caution upon their American colleagues. The barest suspicion of British diplomatic neglect in this regard was the signal for complaint. The prime example was the discussion that followed Prime Minister Churchill's first visit to Washington, in January, 1952, after his return to office the previous autumn. Among his usual American activities, Churchill had addressed Congress. In that environment he had said that he was glad that the United States did not allow the Chinese anti-Communists on Formosa to be invaded and massacred and that, if the prospective Korean truce should be subsequently broken by the enemy, United Nations action should be "prompt, resolute and effective."[73]

This language was taken by some Americans but by many more Englishmen to mean a change in British Far Eastern policy in the direc-

---

71. Illustrated by the Manchester Guardian Weekly, May 31, 1951, p. 8; and the Conservative National and English Review, CXXXVI (June, 1951), 327.

72. London Times, January 29, 1952, p. 5; Economist, CLXII (January 26, 1952), 189-90.

73. The full sentence containing these disputed words was: "We welcome your patience in the armistice negotiations and our two countries are agreed that if the truce we seek is reached only to be broken, our response will be prompt, resolute, and effective" (98 Cong. Rec. 277 [January 17, 1952]).

tion of support for stronger measures. A close reading of the speech betrays no such intention, and the Times, in praise of Churchill, pointed out that there was no basis for deducing that a new threat or setback in the Far East meant "an automatic engagement of wider war with China."[74] But Churchill had given his Labour opponents enough upon which to presume that the Prime Minister had deserted Britain's stand. To have pleased both the Labour party and the American Congress by remarks on China was too much to expect. The Prime Minister had some parliamentary explaining to do, and, while in the end he routed his opponents, the nature of the discussion revealed how fully a policy of extreme caution was prized in Britain. Churchill's original defense of his speech was that in view of the high American casualties in Korea he had been most anxious that "we should make the United States Government feel that we meant to be their good comrades at the council board. . . ."[75]

This did not satisfy the Opposition, which obviously felt it had seized a useful public debating point. Attlee, for instance, chided Churchill for appearing to have represented Britain as an ally in an American war and to have indicated agreement with Americans who wanted to use Formosa as a spearhead against the China mainland. The Labour leader added that it was necessary to be careful in speeches not to lend support to those people whose minds were turned in the direction of an anti-Communist crusade against China. Pointedly, Attlee said: "I think it is up to us to be a steadying influence here which will help the Administration in the United States of America."[76] Some of Attlee's left-wing colleagues thought the American Administration was already beyond help, but that made them no less eager to object to any appearance of British agreement with strong Far Eastern measures.[77]

Finally the Labour party presented a motion of censure which expressed regret that the Prime Minister had failed to give adequate expression to British policy with reference to Korea and China. Specifically, it was claimed by Herbert Morrison, speaking for the motion, that Churchill had encouraged the possibility of extending the Korean war.[78] The Prime

74. January 18, 1952, p. 5.

75. 495 H.C. Deb. 197 (January 30, 1952).

76. 495 H.C. Deb. 841 (February 5, 1952).

77. As Aneurin Bevan (496 H.C. Deb. 982-94 [February 26, 1952]).

78. Ibid., cols. 945-63.

Minister's reply was one of his tactical masterpieces, turning for its success very largely on surprise revelations. The previous Labour government, Churchill said, had itself given assurances to the United States
that "in the event of heavy air attacks from bases in China upon United
Nations forces in Korea they would associate themselves with action
not confined to Korea," and that, in certain other circumstances, action
"of a more limited character" could be taken without consultation. Thus,
implied the Prime Minister, in talking to Congress about "prompt, resolute, and effective action" he was only communicating established policy.
Amid the confusion of the Labour Opposition, both on the part of the
many who had never known of the earlier commitments and on the part
of the few who had not expected them to be revealed, Churchill scored
a considerable triumph.

This cannot concern present purposes so much as the things which
Churchill said in the course of explaining his China policy and its relationship to that of the Labour government. He was adamant in his own long-
standing "opinion about the danger of our getting involved in China," and
he declared that he had never departed either publicly or privately from
his views, expressed at the time of Chinese intervention, that "the United
Nations should avoid by every means in their power becoming entangled
inextricably in a war with China." If this was not enough for his suspicious British critics, Churchill also indicated his profound disagreement with some Americans who had contrary opinions. He reiterated
that he had not departed in any way from the Labour government's policy
"with regard to the Korean conflict and the relations between Great
Britain and China." What he had told Congress about Formosa, Churchill
insisted, carried with it no change of policy in that particular. Few adventures, he said, "could be less successful or fruitful than for Gener-
alissimo Chiang Kai-shek to plunge on to the mainland."[79] Churchill,
it was plain, still adhered to the general British view of Far Eastern
policy on every major item. The fact that he was said to think otherwise
must be attributed either to Labour's own sense of being even farther
removed from the American position or to a belief that the public was
so fearful of surrendering to American policy that an advantage was to
be gained by attacking the Prime Minister. The latter was probably close
to the political truth, and Labour might have won some votes if their

---

79. Ibid., cols. 969, 973, 968, 978, and 982 for specific references.

opponent had been any less the master of parliamentary debate.

It was exceptional that Churchill or anyone else gave British opinion any basis, however slight, to suspect an alignment of London's Asian preferences with those of Washington. Consequently, criticism illustrative of Britain's abhorrence of dealings with Chiang Kai-shek was usually directed at American policy itself. The barrage was continuous but heaviest in connection with an incident like that of the Yoshida letter. This letter from the Japanese prime minister to John Foster Dulles (in his capacity as negotiator of the Japanese peace treaty) was published in January, 1952, and it appeared, in Britain, to indicate that Japan had been subject to American pressure to recognize Nationalist China. Such a policy had only recently been resisted by Britain, whose participation in making the Japanese treaty had been based on a compromise which excluded both Chinese Nationalists and Chinese Communists from the conference table. The compromise, allowing the Japanese subsequently to choose which Chinese regime they wanted to deal with,[80] had not mollified left-wing criticism, but as a pis aller it had been accepted by the wider band of opinion that was mainly concerned lest Japanese industry be driven by American policy from markets on the Chinese mainland to undercutting British commerce in other places.[81]

Not only did the British believe that in the treaty itself this had been forestalled, but it was also widely understood, though perhaps incorrectly, that John Foster Dulles had given assurances that Japan was to be free from American influence so far as Chinese recognition was concerned. In light of this, the Yoshida letter was bitterly provocative. If the United States were now urging Japan to deal with Chiang, was Dulles to be accused of bad faith or were the former British negotiators to confess that they had never had any definite assurances about the American policy?[82]

80. This feature was stressed by Kenneth Younger, who was charged with defending the former Labour government's role in negotiating the treaty (494 H.C. Deb. 886-97 [November 26, 1951]).

81. Anxiety about Japanese competition was expressed by a Conservative, W. Teeling (ibid., col. 951), as well as by Labour members of Parliament noted in chap. iv.

82. The belief that Dulles had given assurances was assumed by press commentary, as in the Manchester Guardian Weekly, January 17, 1952, p. 8, and the Spectator, CLXXXVIII (January 25, 1952), 97-98, and it was thereafter taken for granted in a great deal of subsequent public discussion. Nevertheless, the truth was not really established, and it was possible that former Foreign Secretary Morrison only thought that he had been given assurances. Lack of certainty did not

Either way, the Anglo-American split on China was again revealed, and
more starkly than usual. Foreign Minister Eden restated what he said
had always been the British view: that Japan should be free, after the
treaty came into force, to decide its own relations with China. He assured left-wing critics that Britain had tried "to persuade the Americans
to take our view" on Chinese policy but that the agreement to differ remained.[83]

Equanimity could hardly exist about this agreement to differ; the
British too greatly feared the consequences of America's policy toward
Communist China. American military moves were always disturbing on
a wide front. The most prominent illustration in the two years after the
MacArthur offensive was provided by the bombing raid, in June, 1952,
on the Yalu River power stations. If the reaction to the raid was disproportionate to the deed or to the consequences, it thereby illustrated
British sensitivity all the more abundantly. The attack itself was not on
Chinese territory, and it took place after an entire year of patient American participation in truce talks. Yet the raid gave the Labour Left an
issue which was most embarrassing to the British defenders of the
Anglo-American alliance. They did not agree with the extreme socialist
views that the air attack made "complete nonsense of the efforts of the
negotiators" or that it was a "course of madness."[84] But it was difficult
for right-wing Labour, independent, or Conservative spokesmen to reply
effectively to such charges. Not only was the adoption of a strong military measure in Korea unpopular on its own account, but this particular
measure was further complicated by the fact that the British government
had not been informed in advance of the raid. Attlee and Eden, for example, did not join the left in disapproving the very idea of the raid, but
they did deplore the absence of consultation.[85] Even the rare member
of Parliament who enthusiastically welcomed the air attack (which the party
leaders did not do) thought that Britain should have been informed.[86]

---

prevent the charge of bad faith being revived as part of attacks on
American policy and on that of Dulles, in particular, when he became secretary of state.

83. 495 H.C. Deb. 166 (January 30, 1952).

84. New Statesman, XLIII (June 28, 1952), 757; Tribune, June 27, 1952,
p. 1.

85. 502 H.C. Deb. 2247-62 (June 25, 1952).

86. Ibid., col. 2308.

This was more than a display of injured pride. The British expected to be consulted about any change of policy in the Korean war, and it was believed, although not unanimously, that the Yalu raid represented such a change. The Manchester Guardian Weekly, for instance, said it was not only a change but a bad change.[87] Most of the moderate press was not so sure on either point, and the Economist was more typical in urging that the bombing did not go beyond the general bounds of agreed Korean policy. Still it was a "capital blunder" for there to have been no consultation.[88] Apparently the raid on the Yalu power stations looked enough like a shift in policy so that the British thought there should have been an Allied rather than an exclusively American decision. This was one way of saying that the British public would have been more likely, if its own government were involved, to have accepted the bombing as representative of the policy of limited war rather than as an ominous portent of American willingness to risk extension of the conflict.

The trouble was that the United States was widely suspected of being willing to court dangers that Britain, on its own, would not contemplate. The frequency with which individual but important Americans called for strong measures served as a reminder of the difference between the American and British attitudes toward the conflict with China. [Almost no one in Britain, during the two years following the Chinese intervention, spoke out for a more forceful policy.] Among newspapers, the Daily Telegraph was occasionally close to being an exception. It had sympathized with MacArthur's complaint about allowing the Communists "free sanctuary" in Manchuria, and it editorialized, in May, 1951, in favor of the American as opposed to the British attitude concerning Formosa.[89] But it was still some distance from urging the drastic measures that were generally unpopular in Britain. Brigadier Maclean, in the House of Commons, was nearer to doing so, but in his emphasis on the need to adopt a strong line in order to deter Communist China he represented no more than a very small section of the Conservative back benches. From Maclean's advocacy, Churchill clearly dissociated himself (and the party leadership). Thus, he took pains to say, at the time

---

87. June 26, 1952, p. 8.

88. CLXIII (June 28, 1952), 861-62. The London Times, June 26, 1952, p. 9, and the Spectator, CLXXXVIII (June 27, 1952), 841, made similar observations.

89. May 12, 1951, p. 4; ibid., April 7, 1951, p. 4.

of the Yalu bombings, that he could not go along with the general statement that hitting the aggressors hard was the best way to get an armistice.[90]

Underlying Expectations

The continued British aversion to strong measures against Communist China was bolstered, though less prominently as time went on,
by the original expectancy that Mao Tse-tung's regime was actually or
potentially an independent power capable of amicable relations with the
West. This hope underlay both the desire to avoid antagonizing China
in the early stages of the Korean war and the advocacy, even after the
Chinese aggression, that the Peking regime should be admitted to the
United Nations. The latter always appeared the British recipe for ob-
taining a general settlement in the Far East. And while, for example,
a moderate journal granted, by early 1951, that Communist China could
not be rewarded with a United Nations seat while persisting in aggression, the characteristic view was still expressed: "It is essentially
arguable that, as de facto Government of China, Mao Tse-tung's administration is fully entitled to the Chinese seat on the Security Council,
and if that had been conceded at the time when Great Britain recognized the administration all the present trouble might have been obviated."[91]

This had the attractiveness of a proposition seemingly incapable of
being disproved (or proved). The believers in the value of a soft policy
toward Communist China claimed that it had not been tried. To the
argument that Britain had tried it and failed to obtain even an ordinary
diplomatic response, it was answered that a really fair trial would have
required American participation. That is, the British contended that
the United States should have agreed originally to give Mao's regime a
place in the United Nations. This proposition, in the face of persistent
Chinese recalcitrance at the peace table, probably lost much of its appeal in 1951 and 1952, at least to liberal opinion and to Conservatives
(who had never been very optimistic about the Chinese Communists).
But hope was capable of a ready revival upon the achievement of a truce
in Korea.

Labour always kept the belief alive. The party's leadership,

---

90. 502 H. C. Deb. 2041 (June 24, 1952).

91. Spectator, CLXXXVI (February 9, 1951), 164.

not merely the left wing, prided itself on the Labour government's author-
ship of Britain's policy toward China. It was conceived to be part of the
same benign enlightenment which had prompted postwar dealings with the
nationalism of India and Burma, and its virtues were proclaimed long
after it was an issue in the winter of 1950-51. For instance, in November,
1951, Kenneth Younger (speaking as a former minister of state for foreign
affairs) reasserted the Labour position:

> I have always believed that the Central People's Government
> should have been admitted to the United Nations soon after it got
> control, in fact, of China. I agree also . . . that in viewing the very
> unfortunate situation in the Far East we should be wrong to think
> that it is only Communist policy which has caused these difficulties.
> I believe there have been serious errors on the part of the United
> States over the last 18 months or more.[92]

Refusal to admit Communist China to the United Nations was the
American "error" which was explicitly referred to in other official
Labour comments at this same time. Herbert Morrison, recently foreign
secretary, still insisted, as a matter of fact, not only that China should
have been admitted earlier but that he favored admission as soon as
possible. On the other hand, Morrison did acknowledge that the Americans had reasons to be opposed while their soldiers were being killed by
the Chinese in Korea. He understood that argument, Morrison said,
"though on a balance of considerations" he did not agree with it.[93]

Labour's repetition of faith in its own previous China policy almost
always carried with it the implication that America's different policy
might be blamed for the course of events. A former undersecretary for
foreign affairs suggested as much even in 1952: "Had Britain's policy
been accepted by the U.S.A. it may well be that the Korean incident would
have been avoided, or at least, settled earlier."[94] The idea had been
perpetuated that the United States Administration, as represented by
the State Department, had really wanted to accept Britain's attitude
toward Communist China. As a Labour pamphlet said, after noting the
customary disapproval of American policy in Asia: "It should be added
however that in diverging from British policy the American Government
was often acting under heavy pressure from Congress contrary to its own

---

92. **494** H.C. Deb. 331 (November 20, 1951).

93. **494** H.C. Deb. 991 (November 26, 1951).

94. Ernest Davies, "Some Aspects of Labour Foreign Policy," Political
Quarterly, XXIII (April-June, 1952), 129.

opinion."[95] This served to fortify Labour's conviction that it had been right all the time, since whatever the United States did under congressional pressure was assumed to have had unfortunate results.

Neither subsequent events, nor the conversion of others to the views attributed to the American Congress, dissuaded Labour from its belief in the virtues of recognizing Communist China. Through 1952, at any rate, it remained a fixed principle. When convinced that Secretary of State Acheson, for example, was really against recognition, his opinion was denounced along with that of other Americans.[96] It was not always said that recognition of Communist China by the United States would bring peace in Korea, but it was declared that peace was impossible without it. The Labour party adopted this as its policy in the fall of 1952:

> It is clearly a travesty that the delegate from the rump regime of Chiang Kai-shek should speak in the United Nations in the name of the Chinese people who have rejected him, and the Labour Party believes that there can be no lasting political settlement in the Far East which is not based on the recognition that the Peking Government is the effective government of China and, as such, should represent that country in the United Nations.[97]

Upon this the party seemed agreed. The statement originated with the Labour executive and was accepted by the party conference without dissent.

Initiation, while in office, of the policy of recognition was not the only reason for Labour's staunch adherence to it. Socialists, of various persuasions, specialized in understanding revolutions in other countries. Chinese communism, like the Russian model in its early stages, struck responsive chords in the Labour tradition. Usually this was openly revealed only on the left. Elsewhere it was expressed more hesitantly, as when an official spokesman for the party advanced the claim that Labour had shown "understanding for the Chinese revolution, though the fruits of this policy will be slow to mature."[98]

---

95. Problems of Foreign Policy (London: Labour Party, 1952), p. 6.

96. As by John Strachey, former Labour minister, as reported by the London Times, July 7, 1952, p. 2. Members of Parliament, meeting informally, had been addressed by Secretary of State Acheson apropos of the Yalu River raid.

97. Labour's Foreign Policy (London: Labour Party, 1952), pp. 6-7.

98. Denis Healey, "Power Politics and the Labour Party," in New Fabian Essays, ed. R. H. S. Crossman (London: Turnstile Press, 1952), pp. 164-65.

The left wing had greater confidence than this in the process of under-standing revolutionary China. That the United States failed to accept the Chinese revolution was given as the reason for the prolonged war in Korea. American "counterrevolutionary" activity was, in the eyes of the Labour Left, the cause of China's continued intervention.[99] Aneurin Bevan went so far as to declare, in June, 1952, that "a Korea truce could be reached tomorrow if the United Nations informed Communist China that they recognized the Chinese revolution as an accomplished fact."[100] By November of the same year, he said much the same thing, only then he thought it would take "a few weeks" to end the war.[101]

Not only did Labour Leftists conceive, along with much less extreme opinion, that the United States could, by changing its policy, produce a Titoist revolt, but they also believed that a continuation of American non-recognition was going to drive an "embittered China" into further depend-ence on Russia.[102] This suited the familiar socialist conception of what caused a left-wing revolution to go wrong. Just as Bevan, for ex-ample, imagined that earlier Western rebuffs had caused Russia to be-come a repressive dictatorship, so he thought that the United States was "going to repeat the same folly in China."[103] Given this conspectus (which was too adamant for the party leadership), the more totalitarian and the more Kremlin-minded the Chinese Communists became, the more it was all the fault of the United States.

This was indeed a drastic example of the tenacity with which the preference for the British policy toward China could be championed. After two years of unrepentant Chinese aggression and hostility, one had to have a very thick ideological crust to be so sure that China would have responded favorably to Western, or specifically American, sympathy. The fact that most of the British public was much less certain (and many outside the Labour party not certain at all) did not mean, however, that the contrary American views were acceptable. The hope for getting along with China was national in character, and, if not

---

99. Aneurin Bevan (502 H.C. Deb. 2264-71 [June 25, 1952]).

100. As reported by the London Times, June 16, 1952, p. 4.

101. Ibid., November 24, 1952, p. 3.

102. Desmond Donnelly, M.P., in a letter to the London Times, December 5, 1952, p. 9.

103. In Place of Fear (New York: Simon & Schuster, 1952), p. 44.

articulated by all sections of opinion so long as actual fighting continued, it was almost bound to come to the surface upon the slightest sign of pacific Chinese intentions. At any future conference table the British public was as likely to prefer conciliatory concessions as it had been anxious, earlier, to favor nonprovocative military measures in Korea.

Even where optimism about Communist China no longer exercised an influence of any sort, the national disinclination to accept American views remained staunch and largely unmitigated. The adoption of strong measures against China was unpopular for other reasons, not necessarily related to the policies or the character of Mao's government. For example, the Conservatives, who had never luxuriated in the general hopes for "understanding" Communist China, were seldom more likely than Labour to approve of anything that risked, or seemed to risk, a larger war in the Far East. This was not a matter of forfeiting Tory better judgment for the sake of catering to the electorate. There may have been some such motivation, but it did not, in fact, check individual back-bench members of Parliament from expressing sympathy for a more forceful Asian policy. Despite this sympathy, stemming from the Conservative's traditional and ideological bent, the party's view of British national interests dictated moderation. For a few, the important influence may have been that an enlarged Asian conflict posed an immediate threat to the British trade position in Hong Kong. But overwhelmingly important was the strategic consideration that an American concentration in the Far East would expose Europe to Communist aggression.

The essence of Britain's Asian policy was assumed without socialist underpinning. Perhaps, in consequence, Conservatives were less deeply committed to the policy than was the Labour party, but for practical purposes their position was the same. Political ideology was not the decisive factor in determining British attitudes toward China. It was reasonable to expect the gulf between official British and American policies to remain as wide with the Churchill government in office as it had been in the days of the Labour government.

In the circumstances created by the Asian conflict, left-wing hostility to American foreign policy became solidified in an organized political movement. This organization, under the name of "Bevanism,"
only exacerbated the already reanimated hostility; it did not have to
create it. As a matter of fact, in disapproving of America's policy toward China, Bevanites differed little in substance from the rest of the
Labour party—and not much more from liberal opinion in the British
community. But, being equipped with the full socialist bias against the
United States, Bevanites were able to maximize propagandistically the
existing Anglo-American disagreements over events in the Far East.

However, this was only one aspect of Bevanism. There were other
causes, some of them more fundamental, that divided the Labour party
and gave to Aneurin Bevan's revolt of 1951 a durability that had been
lacking in earlier protests against the Anglo-American alliance. Although Bevanism may be recognized ideologically as but another indication of the attitudes of the Labour Left, it was also a political force whose
development was significant on its own account.

Initial Development

Simultaneous with the left-wing's shift from the glorification of the
Marshall Plan to the deprecation of Far Eastern military moves, American policy came to be associated with the enlarged British rearmament
program. In what looked like responses to American suggestions, the
Labour government had proposed one major increase in defense expenditures not long after the start of the Korean war and another following
the Chinese intervention and the consequent alarm concerning prospective Communist aggression elsewhere. No matter what was said in behalf of rearmament for the protection of Britain, the entire program was
linked, notably in Labour Left consciousness, with American policy and
its recent manifestations in the Far East. Thus a new psychological
obstacle to acceptance of arms expenditure was created, in addition to
the usual socialist reluctance to believe that providing the weapons of
power politics was virtuous or useful (especially in competition with
expenditure on economic welfare measures).

The Labour Left had been wary of a stepped-up rearmament program for some years before it arrived. When the need for European defense was discussed in 1948, for example, the left-wing tendency was to regard a really large force as economically impossible. British military commitments, it was argued, had to be kept to a minimum and the Americans made to pay for them.[1] Britain was to go ahead with its social reconstruction program—also financed by the United States. The old "Keep Left" critics gave occasional warnings during the period of good feeling that they had not been converted to an Anglo-American alliance that was going to require large British armament expenditures.[2] These, it was emphasized at the beginning of 1950, would imperil the economic recovery and security which were claimed to be the most important European defenses against communism.[3] In so far as the validity of further military preparations against aggression was admitted, the Labour Left thought that the responsibility was America's.[4]

No wonder, then, that the Labour Left was unhappy about the pressure for rearmament that followed the outbreak of the Korean war and especially about the irresistible pressure in the winter of 1950-51. Nevertheless, when an enlarged rearmament program appeared to be the price of maintaining the American alliance, Leftists had no choice but to go along with some increase in arms expenditures. They were not at first prepared, any more than the rest of the community, to risk the loss of American power in Europe. However, this did not preclude an argument about how much larger the arms program was to be. The Labour Left continued to insist that the welfare state should not be threatened in the process of building military defenses.[5] There was no doubt where it figured the priorities lay.

This represented the pre-Bevanite position on rearmament, or where the Labour Left already stood before Aneurin Bevan gave it political momentum. Also, by early 1951, the familiar ideological ground swell had taken place. The suspicions of Wall Street and the Pentagon, which had

---

1. R. H. S. Crossman (456 H.C. Deb. 1155 [September 23, 1948] and 467 H.C. Deb. 1606 [July 21, 1949]).

2. Keeping Left (New Statesman pamphlet [January, 1950]), pp. 19-27.

3. New Statesman, XXXIX (January 14, 1950), 27-28.

4. Jennie Lee (478 H.C. Deb. 1016 [September 12, 1950]).

5. New Statesman, XL (December 16, 1950), 616.

been quiescent for a few years, were again in the open and were thriving
in the climate of recent events. There was, almost classically, an em-
bryonic political movement, and Aneurin Bevan put himself at the head
of it.

The reasons for Bevan's importance to the cause of the Labour Left
were connected both with his personal reputation in the party and with
the special circumstances of his resignation from the Labour cabinet
in April, 1951. Bevan was the only front-rank Labour leader who seemed
a kindred spirit to the socialist militants. He had earned a place in their
hearts by a substantial record of rebellion against the official party line
before his entrance into the Labour government in 1945. In fact, Bevan
had rebelled so strenuously in prewar days that he was temporarily
ousted from the party. He carried on his socialist militancy, unbound
by the wartime party truce, and earned a considerable reputation both
as a parliamentary debater and as a dramatic platform speaker. After
his wartime readmission to the party, Bevan's popularity was evidenced
by repeated election at the head of the poll for members of the Labour
party's national executive. Unquestionably, Bevan had, besides his own
gifts of oratory and personality, a background which was politically helpful. He was the son of a miner, and he had himself worked in the coal
pits and otherwise temporarily earned his living and education by manual
labor. These constituted advantages not only for working-class voters
but also for the middle-class devotees of socialism; to them, Bevan was
the prototype of a working-class leader.

He combined a militant and melodramatic repetition of cherished
socialist slogans with the achievement of status as a cabinet minister.
He had been minister of health during most of the period beginning in
1945 and so had been identified first with the enactment and then with the
administration of the health service program. Politically, this was the
most directly appealing of the Labour government's legislative measures.
Although Bevan's methods of championing the health service may have
earned him the special enmity of doctors and of various other critics of
the new scheme, there is no doubt that he firmly established himself,
among socialists, as a man who could get things done. This position he
enhanced by employing the debating skills, developed over two decades
of parliamentary service, to defend his policies colorfully and effectively
against Conservative critics in the House of Commons. Bevan's style of
address was, it is true, considered too heavily class-angled for the taste

of marginal voters (so that he was not put forward as a radio speaker during general election campaigns), but for enthusiastic socialists he had the charismatic quality they found wanting in other, less dramatic leaders of the Labour party.

During five and one-half years as minister of health, Bevan had managed at one and the same time to retain his reputation as a man of the left and also as a responsible member of the Labour government which was increasingly under party attack for alleged right-wing tendencies. Partly, this dual role was possible because Bevan had not been personally associated with the government's foreign policy when, in 1946 and 1947, it was most unpopular among socialists. Indeed, the Labour Left had regarded Bevan as potentially sympathetic to their complaints, since his wife, Jennie Lee, was a Tribune editor and prominent among the earliest critics of the Anglo-American alliance. Also, on the domestic issue of nationalization, where the left suspected (after about 1948) that the government was backsliding or about to backslide, Bevan was assumed to be on the side of the advance-to-socialism school of thought. For instance, it had been widely bruited about that Bevan had led the successful inner fight for going ahead with the nationalization of steel when some of his fellow-members of the cabinet were most reluctant to do so. Therefore, it could be supposed by socialists that Bevan was disturbed by the fact that the very slim Labour majority returned in the 1950 election was really committed to no further nationalization beyond the final implementation of the measure to take over the steel industry.

There was little happiness in the Labour party over the plight of its second postwar government. Its parliamentary grip was tenuous, its public support was probably diminishing, and its prospective policies consisted mainly of the difficult carrying-out of a large rearmament program while enforcing wage and price restraints. There was nothing here to gladden socialist hearts. And there was no bounty for Aneurin Bevan when, in a reshuffle of the cabinet in January, 1951, he was named minister of labor and charged with the unpopular task of maintaining industrial peace without being able to make substantial wage concessions. The trade-union leaders, with whom he had now to deal, did not, by any means, always share the left-wing enthusiasm for Bevan's leadership ability.

Bevan was no longer to have it both ways; either he had to appear

as one of those responsible for the rearmament program that his left-
wing admirers already disapproved or he was going to have to abandon
his membership in the government. The consequences of his position
became partially apparent during the parliamentary debate in mid-
February, 1951, when he was among the Labour ministers charged with
speaking in behalf of the defense program. This was one of the rare
times that Bevan had openly to declare his positive support for a government measure outside the safer domestic field. However, he was replying specifically to a Conservative motion of no confidence in Labour's
ability to carry out the projected program, and Bevan's speech could
loosely appear as a case against a faster rate of rearmament as well
as a defense of the program itself. Thus there was something for the
boys on the left: ". . . if we turn over the complicated machinery of
modern industry to war preparation too quickly, or try to do it too
quickly, we shall we do so in a campaign of hate, in a campaign of
hysteria, which may make it difficult to control that machine when it
has been created." This mistake, Bevan said, had been made "in other
places," where a campaign for increased arms production was accompanied by "a campaign of intolerance and hatred and witch-hunting."[6]
But he thought, despite some doubts, that Britain would be able to keep
its principles while rearming. Bevan, if not very enthusiastically, did
seem committed to the defense program. At this stage he was like many
of his prospective followers who were not yet in rebellion against the
party policy; they did not like rearmament, but they were stuck with it.
Attack on the policy was still in the sniping stage.

The signal for the pre-Bevanites to emerge in full force was Bevan's
resignation of April, 1951. He shrewdly chose his immediate cause: the
budget introduced by Hugh Gaitskell, the still new Labour chancellor of
the exchequer. Gaitskell had imposed, as one of the methods for meeting
the requirements of the government's 4,700 million pounds rearmament
program, a charge of one-half the cost of dentures and spectacles hitherto
furnished free by the National Health Service. This provided Bevan with
an ideal political issue. A completely free medical service and no retreat
from social welfare for the sake of rearmament were principles to which
the Labour party was bound to be devoted in the long run. Bevan, in his
letter of resignation, was able to sound the socialist tocsin by saying that
the budget was wrongly conceived because it failed to "apportion fairly

---

6. 484 H.C. Deb. 736 (February 15, 1951).

the burdens of expenditure as between different social classes."[7]

Yet, no matter how the burdens were distributed, Bevan now seemed to say the rearmament program was too big. This point was made by Bevan and by two colleagues who resigned with him—Harold Wilson, president of the Board of Trade, and John Freeman, parliamentary secretary to the Ministry of Supply. These three together, but especially Bevan and Wilson, gave the left-wing case against the government's policy the respectability it had previously lacked. In statements following their resignations, Bevan and Wilson stressed the belief that the rearmament program of 4,700 million pounds was impossible and that it was wrong to distort Britain's economy in an effort to attain it. From the beginning, the Bevanites placed the blame on the United States, both for instigating Britain's proposed scale of armament and for purchasing raw materials in such quantity and at such prices that Britain was unable to buy what was needed for its civilian or defense industry. Aneurin Bevan declared:

> It is now perfectly clear to anyone who examines the matter objectively that the lurchings of the American economy, the extravagant and unpredictable behaviour of the production machine, the failure on the part of the American Government to inject the arms programme into the economy slowly enough, have already caused a vast inflation of prices all over the world, have disturbed the economy of the western world to such an extent that if it goes on more damage will be done by this unrestrained behaviour than by the behaviour of the nation the arms are intended to restrain.[8]

The raw-materials shortage was but the first of many troubles the Bevanites were to impute to the United States. Like most of their subsequent complaints, this one was not solely the property of the left. There was, in fact, a shortage of raw materials; and other critics, though more gently, had placed some of the onus on American stockpiling practices.[9] The acute shortage turned out to be relatively brief, but it was enough of an issue at the time of the April resignations for it to be harped on for a few months.[10]

Bevan's resignation statement showed that the revolt was to involve foreign-policy matters much broader than the level of rearmament or

7. London Times, April 23, 1951, p. 4.

8. 487 H.C. Deb. 36 (April 23, 1951).

9. 484 H.C. Deb. 2515-2619 (March 2, 1951).

10. Ian Mikardo (487 H.C. Deb. 1106-14 [May 1, 1951]); Harold Wilson (489 H.C. Deb. 1442-50 [June 27, 1951]); also in Aneurin Bevan, In Place of Fear (New York: Simon & Schuster, 1952) p. 168.

the charge on dentures and spectacles. He also challenged the terms of
the Anglo-American alliance in the language already made familiar by
the smaller fry of the Labour Left. The government, Bevan declared,
had allowed itself "to be dragged too far behind the wheels of American
diplomacy." There was even the appeal to Third Force sentiment: "This
great nation has a message for the world which is distinct from that of
America or that of the Soviet Union. Ever since 1945 we have been engaged in this country in the most remarkable piece of social reconstruction the world has ever seen."[11] This, needless to say, was what Leftists,
at least, had believed all the time. Bevan had only to say the words to become the champion of their cause.

In the first six months following their resignations, the Bevanites
operated in fairly limiting circumstances. The Labour government,
if it was to remain in office until it chose the least inopportune time for
an election, required the parliamentary votes of the rebels. Any organization of votes against government policy would have forced a premature
dissolution and have brought down on Bevan's head the charge of helping
the Conservatives to gain power. Consequently, before October, 1951
(when the Conservatives did win the general election which was called in
Attlee's own good time), the Bevanites had relatively few opportunities
to display their strength. The Trades Union Congress in September provided one occasion, and here, in defiance of the major union leaders,
nearly enough votes were mustered to pass a resolution deploring the
Labour government's imposition of charges for dentures and spectacles.[12]
This particular cause was the most popular of Bevanite issues—appealing
even to some who did not necessarily oppose the rearmament program
itself. In fact, removing the health service charges was so popular in
the Labour party that it was not left for the Bevanites to exploit. Once
out of office, the Labour leadership made no effort to defend the charges;
but in the meantime, before the general election, retreat on even so narrow an issue was tactically impossible. In consequence, the Bevanites
reaped a considerable temporary advantage among the rank and file.
They presented themselves as the true defenders of socialist accomplishment.

Because the Labour party's 1951 conference took place on the very

11. 487 H.C. Deb. 38 (April 23, 1951).

12. 83d Annual Report of the Trades Union Congress (London, 1951),
pp. 501-5.

eve of the parliamentary election, there could be no direct contest on the rearmament issue.[13] The ranks had to be closed for the electoral combat that lay directly ahead. Nor in the general election was it possible to test Bevanite against non-Bevanite. The apparently larger struggle between Labour and Conservative concealed the internal disagreement. There were, at the time, less than thirty members of Parliament who were known, in inner circles, as supporters of Bevan's revolt, and their election campaigns were necessarily directed against Conservative opponents and not against their own party leaders. Since the voters were thus ordinarily unimpressed with Bevanites as such, the fact that all of them won their seats (in an election where Labour lost altogether only twenty-one members of Parliament) did not mean that they were helped by the stand they had taken against rearmament. Nor was there any statistical evidence to indicate that they were hurt by being Bevanites.[14] This was probably the important point, since it was coupled with the fact that a few Bevanites had retained marginal seats. It gave heart to any Labour member of Parliament whose wavering to the Bevanite cause may have previously been checked for fear of the response of the independent or "swing" voter.

By concentrating their attack on the rearmament program during most of 1951, the Bevanites were not entirely out of step with public sentiment. The level of that program was also questioned by sources well to the right of Aneurin Bevan. Without agreeing with the Bevanite advocacy, the Times and the Economist, for example, hinted that America had set too fast a pace for Europe.[15] Remarks of this sort reflected only doubt, never clear-cut objection, but they were very much part of the British atmosphere surrounding the Bevanite revolt. In fact, the case against Britain carrying the full projected arms program was officially granted by the Conservative government, in 1952, when it took a series of steps to diminish the intensity of the rearmament effort.[16] Nothing

13. Discussion of the rearmament program played a relatively minor part in the proceedings (50th Annual Report of the Labour Party [London, 1951], pp. 100-101, 110).

14. David E. Butler, The British General Election of 1951 (London: Macmillan & Co., 1952), pp. 272-73.

15. London Times, July 25, 1951, p. 5; Economist, CLXI (October 6, 1951), 780-82. The latter made a distinction between the admitted need in 1951-52 for rapid rearmament and the huge scale contemplated for 1954.

16. Prime Minister Churchill's statement (508 H.C. Deb. 1775-82 [December 4, 1952]) was the last of several announcements of a "stretch-out" of the British effort.

was conceded to Aneurin Bevan in the process, since it was declared that he had been right for the wrong reasons. Furthermore, the Bevanites seemed to stand for greater reductions than those announced—or at all likely to be announced in any future cutback by the government.

By ideological compulsion, if nothing else, the Bevanite argument against British rearmament assumed a distinctive form. The narrowest point of attack was that the American guaranty of Western Europe, after its reassertion through the North Atlantic Treaty Organization in early 1951, was the real military deterrent, sufficient to render unimportant the size of any European nation's build-up.[17] Even this argument, made by a moderate Bevanite, presented a challenge to basic assumptions about the Anglo-American relationship. It questioned the prevailing belief that a large-scale British effort was necessary in order to retain a significant American participation in European defense. Bevanism really suggested a new self-willed British position in relation to the United States.

Another aspect of the Bevanite protest against the rearmament program was that Britain was burdened with more than its fair share of the Western defense effort. Britain's allies, one Bevanite declared, were "stealing a march on us," and "cashing in on the industrial dislocation caused in this country by our higher level of rearmament, to their own benefit."[18] The statistical support for this statement may have been dubious, but, regardless of the figures, there was always an appeal in the claim that Britain was disproportionately sacrificing. Whether that was now the case many socialists considered irrelevant, since what they had in mind were the economic sacrifices of the early years of World War II. In this perspective it was easy to believe that the Americans should shoulder a larger portion of the new load.

In addition, Bevanites presented a special economic argument to justify a higher American armaments burden, relatively as well as absolutely, than that of Britain. Their leading spokesman was Thomas Balogh, the Oxford economist. Writing late in 1951, Balogh granted that by about 1952 the American ratio of arms expenditure relative to national income would be greater than Britain's (18 as compared with 15 per cent), but this, he said, was not enough of a difference between the two countries. Britain could not afford anything near an equal drain, imposed by re-

17. W. T. Williams, "Outlook in the Cold War," Fabian Journal, February, 1952, pp. 19-20.

18. Ian Mikardo (491 H.C. Deb. 75 [July 23, 1951]).

armament, on its capital investment program, since the nation (as well
as the rest of the world) was already so far behind the United States in
industrial plant. By devoting its limited resources to arms production,
it was argued, Britain was destined to drop farther behind the long competitive lead enjoyed by the newer and more modern American manu-
facturing facilities.[19] In this sense, rearmament was thought to post-
pone, perhaps irrevocably, the rehabilitation of British civilian industry
so that it could compete successfully in world export markets.

Here the argument against large-scale British rearmament was
joined to the popular desire for economic independence. This was a
theme the Bevanites regularly played upon.[20] They sought to broaden
their support by implying that without the arms program Britain could
manufacture and sell enough machinery and other export items to solve
its international balance-of-payments problems.

Opposition along these several lines to the high level of British arms
production was the bench mark of Bevanite doctrine—the one issue on
which a fairly diverse following could unite in opposition to the official
Labour line. Beyond this, Bevanites were agreed only in standing, in
varying degrees, to the left of the rest of the party. In foreign affairs
this meant hostility to the United States. The nature of this hostility was,
as always, shaped by aspects of socialist ideology, but its volume and intensity depended on the availability of international grievances as well as
on the political means for expression. The events of 1951-52 provided
the issues in abundance, and Aneurin Bevan furnished the political vehicle.

German Rearmament

Before examining the general enlargement of the Bevanite case
against American foreign policy, the question of German rearmament
deserves special consideration. It seemed well suited for Bevanite exploitation, since American pressure was intimately associated with a policy
that was almost completely unpopular in Great Britain. German rearmament, in any form, had no ready champions, as it had in the United States.

On the other hand, before the Bevanite revolt, neither had there
been a concerted opposition to the Labour government's apparently re-

---

19. "Rearmament and International Social Policy," Fabian Journal,
   October, 1951, pp. 10-16.

20. See chap. iii.

luctant and conditioned acquiescence in German rearmament.[21] Disapproval remained largely beneath the surface so long as a political motive for its activation was absent. Conservatives, despite some misgivings, were not likely to object to a further build-up of European military strength.[22] Independent opinion, while adopting an attitude best expressed as openly unenthusiastic, was, as usual, ready to pay the price demanded by the exigencies of Anglo-American relations. At least, it was said, American agreement to German rearmament within a European defense community was better than what, at various times, seemed to be the proposed alternative of an independent German army.[23] That, presumably, was also an influence in securing support originally from the Labour government, but when Ernest Bevin, late in his tenure at the Foreign Office, agreed to German rearmament, the question was not widely discussed in the Labour party.

However, by 1952 the increased American pressure had made the issue of German rearmament politically relevant. There seemed an advantage in attacking what no one in Britain would defend as more than a pis aller. Fears concerning the emergence of a new German power were, if anything, more widespread than ever. The reluctant British supporters of German participation in a European army shared none of the American anxiety for the completion of treaty arrangements. The Economist, for instance, responded to the Franco-German disagreements of early 1952 with a desire for a "creative pause" for reflection on the whole problem.[24] This, of course, was some distance from opposition to the proposed rearmament scheme.

Open opposition was much more likely to come from within the Labour party, whose reactivated socialist foreign-policy conceptions included the distrust of rebuilding Germany, under a right-wing government, as a counter to Communist Russia.[25] The United States was now

---

21. The New Statesman (XXXIX [April 8, 1950], 392) did voice strong pre-Bevanite objections.

22. While admitting that German rearmament was merely the lesser danger in a choice of European policies, it was frankly accepted by the Conservatives, as indicated by the remarks of their Research Department's publication, Foreign Affairs, August, 1952, p. 6.

23. London Times, July 28, 1951, p. 7; Manchester Guardian Weekly, November 9, 1950, p. 8, and February 7, 1952, p. 8.

24. CLXII (February 16, 1952), 379.

25. J. Baird (491 H.C. Deb. 545 [July 25, 1951]).

cast in the role the left had formerly assigned to the Chamberlain government. The Bevanites did not have to stir socialist feelings on this score
so much as merely to give vent to them. This was done from almost the
beginning of the left-wing revolt.

The question was whether the Bevanites were to have a virtual monopoly on the opportunity for mobilizing the widespread Labour dislike for
German rearmament. On the surface, it looked as though the party's
official leaders were stuck with their previous German commitment,
however unpopular, just as they were to the high level of British rearmament which they had themselves proposed. However, once out of office,
the Labour party found a formula by which it could at least temporarily
criticize the current program for rearming the Germans and still contend that the party had not turned its back on former agreements.

This shift was not necessarily accomplished in order to deprive the
Bevanites of sole possession of a popular cause. It cannot be established
that Bevanite political pressure was sufficient, on its own account, to
compel the leadership to make a tactical concession. There were also
genuine anxieties among right and center Labour leaders about the
wisdom of German rearmament in general and about the particular plan
for minimizing the dangers of a resurgent German national power. For
example, Hugh Dalton, in announcing the party executive's new policy in
late 1951, expressed "grim doubts" about the revised framework in which
German strength was to be contained within a European community.
"Would not Germany," he asked, "soon burst it asunder, as her strength
grew, or dominate it and use it for her own ends?"[26] This, incidentally,
was an appealing consideration well beyond the confines of the Labour
party. To many in Britain, Germany was still the European enemy in a
way that was not possible for Americans to comprehend. The intimacy
of the German threats in two great wars, particularly the most recent
one, was a potent memory, readily reinforced by the remaining marks of
the air blitz.

The specific point which Dalton attacked in the current proposal for
a European defense community was the change from the original idea of
having only small German units to the conception of what he thought was
really a German national army within the European force. The present
scheme, it was argued, was more dangerous than that which Labour had

---

26. Party political broadcast reported in the London Times, December
17, 1951, p. 3.

approved in the first place. It did not adequately guard against a resurgent German military power. However, the Labour party's national executive called only for a postponement of final British agreement to the treaties relating to the European Defense Community. Officially, this was not coupled with a denunciation of German rearmament under all circumstances or with an attack on the United States for urging the general policy. Consequently, there was some distinction in tone between the limited critique of regular party spokesmen and the more violent blasts of the Bevanites. There was, in fact, a considerable variety of Labour opinion on the subject, and a few adhered throughout the discussion of 1952 to the position that Labour was bound to approve the EDC and the Bonn contractual agreement.[27]

Nevertheless, the Parliamentary Labour party, as a body, took essentially the same stand as had the national executive and thus voted against immediate approval of the treaties when Foreign Minister Eden presented them to the Commons at the end of July, 1952. Labour's opposition was merely symbolic, of course, since the Conservative government had the requisite votes. It was entirely possible that if the Labour party had been the responsible government of the day it could not have afforded the indulgence of opposing, even if its members had wanted to, the program to which it had once agreed in principle and which was now pressed so hard by the United States. But, in the actual circumstances, the charge of reversing its previous position, which Labour brought upon itself, was a small price to pay for adopting a line that reflected considerable party feeling and the genuine convictions of many Labour leaders themselves. It also went a short distance to remove the stigma (so valuable to Bevanite rebels) of Labour's constant bipartisan acquiescence in Conservative and American foreign policy.

To accomplish all this, and yet avoid the appearance of flagrant inconsistency, Labour leaders tabled a carefully worded amendment to the Conservative government's motion to approve the treaties. The amendment accepted the aim of including Germany and a German armed contribution in a European defense community, but it rejected the current proposals as "inopportune."[28] In the arguments for the amendment (and thus against approval of the treaties) there was something for every kind of opponent of German rearmament. The narrowest ground was provided

27. 500 H.C. Deb. 1448-1585 (May 14, 1952).

28. 504 H.C. Deb. 1725 (July 31, 1952).

by what were now called the "Attlee conditions," previously stipulating the kind of arrangement to which a Labour government could give its approval. Three specific conditions were repeated by the former Labour defense minister, Emanuel Shinwell. Besides the safeguard of first having the other European nations adequately armed vis-à-vis Germany, Labour would also have required a delay until the German people themselves consented to rearmament and until another attempt had been made to negotiate with Russia over plans for uniting Germany.[29] The last two conditions involved specifically socialist considerations, and the idea of negotiating with the Russians before going ahead was heavily stressed by the Bevanites. They claimed the United States was too ready to override negotiation as an alternative to German rearmament. Both on this score and on the matter of consulting the German people, the Labour party derived comfort from the fact that it was in accord with its ideological friends, the German Social Democrats.

Despite the efforts of some Labour leaders to disavow the more extreme root-and-branch arguments against German rearmament, the party's stand against the treaties had a distinctive left-wing flavor. Indeed, here in the midsummer of 1952, Bevanite foreign-policy views appeared to be at a high point of popularity. The left was able to mobilize its own maximum strength on German rearmament, while opponents within the party found this an issue on which they had neither the inclination nor the facility to take a strongly favorable position. When the party wavered into moderate disapproval of German rearmament, it was natural that broader, simpler, and more drastic arguments would have their day. The moderate right-wing objections, regardless of their official status, did not loom so large as the more thorough Bevanite denunciations with which they were mingled in parliamentary opposition.[30]

Although, at this time, opposition to German rearmament seemed popular among active Labour supporters, and occasionally elsewhere in the community, the party leadership showed little subsequent inclination to emphasize its stand on this issue. The Labour party, as a whole, did continue through 1953 to reiterate its desire for a postponement of German rearmament, specifically until after another attempt to settle the German problem in a Big Four conference. But political propaganda relating to German rearmament was carried on mainly by the Bevanites

29. Ibid., cols. 1725-38.

30. Ibid., cols. 1699-1840 and 1869-1960 (August 1, 1952).

and their allies. The target was the continued American determination, often painfully obvious, to secure French and German approval of the treaties allowing rearmament. Along this line, the Bevanites had already advanced the view that the United States was plotting to rebuild German power at the expense of Britain and to use German strength against Russia.[31] This was related to the left-wing bogy that the United States favored Germany, as opposed to other European allies, and that American capitalists enjoyed a right-wing kinship with the Ruhr industrialists— particularly Herr Krupp.

These appeals, imputing essentially evil intentions to American policy, were probably irrelevant to those who merely distrusted the wisdom of German rearmament. The underlying fear of a neo-Nazi power was general enough, in the right and center of the Labour party, for example, but that was not the same as believing that the Americans were deliberately plotting the results which were feared. Having misgivings about rearming Germany was not enough to make one a Bevanite. If it were, there would have been many more Bevanites.[32]

It is in this light that one should question the view that Labour was converted to Bevanism in the process of opposing the German treaties in 1952. Arming the Germans was, after all, an especially unpopular policy for its proponents to maintain once Labour was freed from the responsibilities of office-holding. The party leadership was not yielding to Bevanites alone, but to them and to other substantial elements prepared to join the Bevanites on this issue. Furthermore, there is great significance in the fact that Labour's apparent retreat on German rearmament was not labeled as a permanent change of policy. The way was left open, despite strong internal party pressure, for the leadership to reassert support for German participation in Western defense. In fact, such reassertion was made early in 1954 after the Berlin meeting of the Big Four foreign ministers.[33] Thus from the record on the uniquely

31. New Statesman, XLIII (March 29, 1952), 361.

32. Certainly the one Conservative member of Parliament, Lord Hinchingbrooke, who spoke against his party's support of German rearmament and abstained from voting on the approval of the Bonn treaties, did not qualify as a Bevanite. His was a highly individualistic line.

33. The decision of the Labour leadership to make support of German rearmament again the official party policy was taken on the ground that the party's previously stated conditions, particularly with respect to a Big Four conference on Germany, had been met. However, this

charged German issue it cannot be concluded that moving in the Bevanite direction was inevitably the party's fate.

Expansion of the Bevanite Critique

Exactly what it would have meant to move "in the Bevanite direction" was never very clear. On foreign policy, Bevanism was a bundle of objections sufficient to rally the Labour Left on the basis of its original dislike for the Anglo-American alliance but with only an overtone to suggest an alternative to the maintenance of Britain's tie to the United States. That overtone was evidently enough to please the most dogmatic left-wing socialists who had never accepted the need for joining Britain to the American power, and yet it was not too much for many who had, though reluctantly, recognized the international exigencies requiring the alliance. The latter group appeared much the larger. It consisted of the numerous Labour Left who had, in previously going along with the United States, often done so against their inherent preferences and therefore with reservations. As one leading Bevanite remarked informally (in 1952), he had been unable to offer reasons against the Atlantic Pact, but he had, at the time of its approval, been emotionally and instinctively against it—and he still was.

From this standpoint, Bevanism was understandable if not cogent. Its strong hostility to American policy appealed to basic left-wing feelings about the alliance, yet without openly rejecting the British need for the United States. Bevanism represented a claim for American power on socialist terms. The unattainability of the terms might logically have led to an outright disavowal of the alliance, but the left seldom carried its case so far. To do so would have been to expose the Bevanite position at its weakest point.

What Bevanism did was to couple denunciations of the United States with the contention that Britain, backed by sufficient socialist purpose, should and could modify American policy. This was the theme of One Way Only,[34] the first and most nearly complete statement of the Bevanite

decision secured only a very bare majority in the Parliamentary Labour party and a surprisingly unsubstantial majority in the party's national executive (London Times, February 24, 1954, p. 8; and February 25, 1954, pp. 4 and 6). Whether the policy could be maintained in a party conference remained open to some doubt. Bevanite criticism of German rearmament continued unabated.

34. Published as a Tribune pamphlet (London, 1951).

international attitude. At times, especially after 1951, this theme was somewhat muted in the louder volume of complaint about what the Americans were doing, but it was always at least implicit that by "standing up to the Americans" a British government could influence the course of events. Aneurin Bevan, in his confidence and in his strong language (from British platforms), personified this socialist desire.

Mainly what the Bevanites wanted was less emphasis on military strength. Often this took the form of urging, as in One Way Only, that rearmament should be subordinated to a "world plan for mutual aid" along the lines of the proposed Point Four program. But, even when such an alternative was not suggested, the United States was charged with undertaking too large a military build-up. This was a step beyond objecting (mainly for economic reasons) to British rearmament. The Bevanite case also stressed the belief that American rearmament was on so large a scale as to become an aggressive threat. As always in left-wing socialist ideology, military strength was assumed to be a cause of war, and the Bevanites contended that by 1953 the United States might be tempted to use its acquired strength to start a war against Russia. This was consistent with One Way Only's vision of the consequences of America's "wild anti-Communist crusade." And it was the background for the reiteration of the need to restrain the United States. For example, the Bevanites argued that Britain should make it clear that it held the veto (which it did) over the use of British bases by American bombers.[35] Thus any plan for an atomic attack on Russia was to be nipped in the bud by British firmness.

The Americans whom the left would thus have restrained were sufficiently particularized so that they did not include the mass of people in the United States or Labour's erstwhile friends in the Truman Administration. These were usually pictured, equally with the rest of the world, as the victims of a relatively few aggressive-minded military planners. Partly to help the "good" Americans resist the machinations of the "bad" ones, Britain was urged to take a firm stand against the Pentagon, which now, even more than Wall Street, was the focal point of left-wing fears. The Pentagon was charged with the "bold and grandiose" plan of building "a position of dominance" from which to threaten the Soviet Union with war unless it gave way to American desires.[36] The United States, it was

35. Pp. 4, 10, and 11.

36. New Statesman, XLII (September 29, 1951), 327.

argued, was building toward an armed strength which was not designed to encourage negotiations but rather to try to compel Russian agreement to American conditions. "The fulfilment of American policy," Tribune declared in 1952, "would mean the formation of a solid alliance dedicated to a crusade against Communism. Firmly implanted within that alliance would be the forces of Chiang Kai-shek, General Franco and a rearmed Western Germany."[37] These forces were assumed to be potentially aggressive, and Chiang and Germany especially so because of their interests in regaining territories previously lost to Communists.

However, the United States was vaguely suspected on its own account as well as on account of its allies. The collection of allies—and sometimes Japan was added to the list—was supposed to be a consequence of the desire by some Americans to build a military combination preparatory to having a showdown with the Communist bloc. This was an enlargement of the stereotype of potential American aggression that had appeared during the most acute stage of the China controversy in 1950-51. But the general conception also had links to the earlier postwar socialist view that the United States, rather than Britain (or the West generally), was the enemy of Russia and communism. The idea of a war growing out of Russo-American antagonism had been rife in 1946 and 1947, and the deduction that Britain did not share all the aspects of that antagonism survived the acceptance of the American alliance. In suggesting that the United States was adopting a tough policy that might lead to war, the Bevanites were sounding a familiar note.

This was done most frequently with reference to Far Eastern affairs, where every divergence of American policy from Britain's provided an opportunity to stress the relatively aggressive character of the United States.[38] The very continuation of the war in Korea was, as already noted, charged to the Americans, on the ground that their support of Chiang Kai-shek prevented a settlement with the Chinese Communists. Furthermore, it was this policy and its ramifications which were supposed to risk spreading the conflict. Because it was believed that the United States was deliberately pursuing a dangerous line, the good faith of the American

---

37. April 4-17, 1952, p. 1.

38. Going Our Way (Tribune pamphlet [London, 1951]), p. 16; Tribune, January 25-February 7, 1952, pp. 1-2; 488 H.C. Deb. 985-86 (June 6, 1951); and 496 H.C. Deb. 1034-40 (February 26, 1952).

desire for a Korean cease-fire was impugned.[39] Bevanites were at least as ready to blame the United States as the Chinese for the delays in achieving a truce. That suited the left wing's picture of America's insistence on its own terms rather than being willing to compromise for the sake of peace. It was this which the Bevanites believed would prevent a larger settlement with Russia as well as the particular truce in Korea.

Always there was the underlying belief that peace was what the Communist nations wanted. About China, the Bevanites seemed certain; and about Russia, only slightly less so. Charitable views of Communist intentions had to be taken (if not often stated) in order to portray the United States as the likely cause of war. If American sponsorship of large-scale military preparation were to be considered inherently and deliberately aggressive, it was necessary to assume that Russia lacked either the will or the means to undertake a major conflict.

The generalized picture of the United States as the potential aggressor was accepted with various shades of conviction in the Bevanite ranks. Not every follower of Aneurin Bevan (or always Bevan himself) carried left-wing suspicions of American power politics and American capitalism to the same extreme position. But the tendency to regard the United States as a provocative force was strong enough so that Bevanism was almost invariably characterized by an alarmed insistence on the need to deter the Americans from consciously setting off a conflict with the Soviet Union. Bevanites wanted Britain to offer the United States more than friendly advice. They recommended forceful threats.

But what Britain should significantly threaten was uncertain so long as the Bevanites refrained from advocating the end of the alliance. Perhaps that drastic step was what the left yearned to take, especially as the chances of Britain exercising a socialist influence on America became dimmer and dimmer. The trouble lay in finding a policy substitute for the Anglo-American relationship. Nothing had ever commanded a left-wing following except the faded alternative of the Third Force. Although sentiment in favor of forming such a socialist bloc had never died, as a

---

39. Barbara Castle, "What Has Gone Wrong in Korea," Tribune, December 14, 1951, pp. 5-6; 494 H.C. Deb. 25-29 (November 19, 1951); Tribune, January 11, 1952, p. 3. Also, related to complaints about truce negotiations, were criticisms directed at American handling of prisoner-of-war camps, as at 501 H.C. Deb. 6-12 (May 19, 1952); ibid., cols. 625-36 (May 21, 1952); ibid., cols. 919-25 (May 26, 1952); 502 H.C. Deb. 186-89 (June 11, 1952); ibid., cols. 2222-26 (June 25, 1952).

policy it now lacked even the semblance of reality it had had for the Labour Left in an earlier day. Lack of substance did not prevent the continued hankering for a Third Force,[40] but it did ordinarily preclude Bevanites from proclaiming it as the basis of their foreign policy. When the language of the Third Force was employed—as in loose statements about joining India in a neutral bloc—it merely demonstrated the depths of socialist frustration over the alliance with the United States.

Political Force

Bevanism's lack of a positive alternative to the foreign policy it criticized so heavily was no barrier to its active bid for control of the Labour party. The struggle that erupted in 1952, while by no means ended, constitutes a useful case study in the possibilities and the limitations of a campaign to commit one of Britain's major parties to a left-wing opposition to American foreign policy.

Although emphasizing this aspect of Bevanism, its other and probably more important objectives must also be taken into account. One aim was to pledge the Labour party to a thoroughgoing socialist domestic program, analogous to the nationalization proposals of 1945. Another was to gain power in the party not only for Aneurin Bevan personally but for his entourage as well. Bevan's campaign was joined principally by Labour back-benchers whose chances to achieve future ministerial office rested mainly with the success of a left-wing revolt. Excluded by the prevailing leadership from the fruits of office, as well as from the determination of policy, their only course was to upset the leadership. This meant challenging both the prestige of their established party leaders and the strength of the principal unionists—that is, the combined power embodied in Transport House, the headquarters for the Labour party and the Trades Union Congress. The task was formidable, and it had been far too much for previous left-wing revolts. But the time seemed especially opportune. Not only were there outstanding socialist issues on which to press a campaign among the party faithful, but the occasion of Labour going into opposition had great advantages. No longer were left-wing aspirations bound either by a general sense of responsibility that went with being a majority party or by the magnification of the powers of leadership that accompanied the formation of a cabinet. Coincidentally, the postwar generation of party and union leaders was aging or approaching retirement.

---

40. See chap. vi.

The most obvious battle line was within the Parliamentary Labour party, whose leadership had eventually to be secured if Bevanism was to have real effect. No matter what resolutions were adopted by a Labour party conference, in order for them to be carried out it was necessary to have a majority within the parliamentary ranks. But here the Bevanites were nowhere near success. The maximum strength ever displayed in open rebellion was 57 out of a total of 295 Labour members of Parliament. The occasion on which the 57 rebels emerged to be counted was in March, 1952, when that number broke with the party leadership's policy of continuing (in opposition) to approve the government's rearmament program. The Bevanites were not satisfied to go along with their party's purely formal objection to the Conservatives' ability to carry out the program; they voted against the program itself.[41]

Among the 57 there were probably a few who objected to the rearmament level on such limited grounds that their Bevanism was rather dubious.[42] While allowing for such cases, it is evident that the list of 57 dissidents coincided closely with the body of parliamentary sentiment identified, in other ways, with a left-wing position in the Labour party. The great majority had indicated, in speeches or writings over a considerable period of time, that they accepted the traditional socialist outlook on international problems. Many of the same names had appeared in connection with the abortive revolt on foreign policy in November, 1946. There were a few additions, but none was of consequence beyond the trio who had resigned from the government in the previous spring. More notably, some of the rebels of 1946 were now on the other side of the fence, having achieved office and party status in the interim.

Since Labour members of Parliament could be affected, though not readily controlled, by pressure from outside the parliamentary organization, the Bevanites tried to rally rank-and-file Labour supporters to their cause. This was in the tradition of left-wing revolts, and the Bevanites were different only in the thoroughness with which they captured the constituency parties. That they were able to do so was demonstrated by the results of the selection of constituency party representatives to

41. 497 H.C. Deb. 559-60 (March 5, 1952). Personal supporters of Bevan were evidently a little more numerous. Bevan received 82 votes in 1952 and 76 in 1953 when he stood unsuccessfully against Herbert Morrison for the deputy leadership of the Parliamentary Labour party (Economist, CLXIX [October 31, 1953], 320.

42. As W. T. Williams (497 H.C. Deb. 511 [March 5, 1952]).

sit on the national executive. This selection, limited to seven of the twenty-seven executive seats, was solely in the hands of the local parties, and the preponderance of trade-union votes was not brought into play as it was in determining conference policies (and in choosing the remaining members of the executive). The manner of voting had other special aspects tending to increase the importance of hard-core socialists. Although each local organization was entitled to a number of votes roughly proportionate to its own membership, the arrangement tended to favor the smallest units—where the party was often only a zealous band of "intellectuals." Furthermore, some local units did not instruct their delegates on how they should vote at the party conference. The result was often to leave the choice of candidates to the most eager party workers who were willing to pay their own expenses in order to attend the annual conference and vote for members of the executive.

Even in 1951 the Bevanites, still largely unorganized, had won a minor victory in this Labour popularity contest. Aneurin Bevan and three of his already recognized supporters were returned by the local parties, but, since all save one of these had previously represented the constituencies on the executive, the net gain was slight.[43] Principally what was noticed was that the one defeated sitting member was Emanuel Shinwell, whose prestige among socialist militants had been tarnished while he held the defense ministry.

These results were only a portent of what was to come in 1952. By then the Bevanites had mobilized their followers through an extensive campaign conducted by discussion teams at the constituency level. And they had obtained support for a strictly Bevanite slate of six candidates for the executive. All six were in fact elected, eliminating both Herbert Morrison and Hugh Dalton from their long-accustomed places and leaving only one non-Bevanite to represent the constituency organizations.[44] Most impressive was the defeat of Morrison. He had been the chief organizer of the political sector of the party and the recognized electoral tactician of Labour policy. Also he was the deputy leader of the Parliamentary Labour party and presumably in line of succession to Attlee's position. Morrison's identification with the Labour government's policies had only been made more complete by his brief (and rather unhappy) tenure as

43. 50th Annual Report of the Trades Union Congress, p. 98.

44. 51st Annual Report of the Trades Union Congress, p. 87.

foreign secretary, following Ernest Bevin. In defeating Morrison, the local parties were clearly repudiating their moderate leadership.

However, this was not the same as repudiation by the party as a whole. For that purpose, the Bevanites sought to upset the commitment to the rearmament program—that is, to get the party conference of October, 1952, to take a stand directly opposed to that which the Parliamentary Labour party had reaffirmed a few months before. In making this challenge, the Bevanites needed more than the support of the constituency parties. They had to win an appreciable number of unions to their cause, at least on the rearmament issue.

Therefore the principal conflict was within the unions. The Bevanites had the advantage of an undoubtedly popular cause, but their confirmed opponents in the Trades Union Congress had, on their side, the established lines of organizational loyalty. These lines were defended against Bevanites almost as vigorously as against Communists. In fact, from the point of view of many union leaders any left-wing attack on their policies was intertwined with the Communist threat to infiltrate and capture sections of the Labour movement. Although that threat was much less potent than in times past, the Communists did have local and regional centers of influence in addition to the control of enough unions to constitute an organized force within the TUC. This was joined to the Bevanite opposition on the rearmament question in such a way that it was not always clear how large Aneurin Bevan's own following actually was. Certain unions, like the Union of Shop, Distributive, and Allied Workers, were considered predominantly Bevanite, but others taking similar positions, like the Amalgamated Engineering Union, were suspected of being influenced by the Communist party line.[45]

Despite the defection of individual unions, on varying bases, the resistance of the TUC leadership was, in 1952 as before, sufficient to hold the line where it counted most—in the two massive general unions and in the National Union of Mineworkers. They were supported by enough smaller and medium-sized unions so that at the Trades Union Congress, held a month before the Labour party conference, the anti-Bevanites were ready for a showdown fight. This took place over left-wing efforts to alter the strong support for rearmament that had been reiterated in May

---

45. For the accounts of major unions opposing rearmament see the London Times, April 14, 1952, p. 6; May 10, 1952, p. 6; and July 9, 1952, p. 3.

by the General Council of the Congress. This policy statement represented no retreat whatsoever from the program initiated by the Labour
government in the previous year. And, when it was presented to the
congress for approval, it was indorsed by the general secretary of the
TUC, and by other spokesmen, in language that was entirely unyielding
to the Bevanite point of view. There were no concessions to avoid a
head-on collision with the left-wing opposition. What was asked for was
indorsement for the "greatest possible measure of rearmament" within
Britain's power.[46] Approval was gained by an overwhelming majority
of the congress. Delegates representing only about one and one-half
million members openly declared their opposition (with about one million
listed as abstentions), compared with the total of five and one-half
million supporting the position of the General Council.

Although this result was undoubtedly impressive, it displayed the
general left-wing potential at something less than its full force. In addition to the one million abstainers, who might have been wavering
Bevanites, there were doubtless antirearmament minorities within unions
which, en bloc, had supported the General Council. The conversion of
these minorities into controlling majorities, especially in the largest
unions, had been thwarted in large part by the leadership's appeal to the
delegates' traditional loyalty to established policy. Large-scale rearmament was thus not supported entirely for its own sake but because it represented the TUC's previous commitment. Interestingly, the leadership
did not, at the same congress, stem the leftward pressure on the issue
of further nationalization. The 1952 congress actually overrode the
evident desire of the General Council to avoid being committed to proposals for the extension of social ownership.[47] But this was not a clear
case of Bevanites (and Communists) scoring an organized victory against
a determined official resistance. The fact that the left had been unable to
do so when the battle lines had been sharply drawn, on the rearmament
issue, indicated that the power of the leadership was still largely unimpaired.

---

46. 84th Annual Report of the Trades Union Congress (London, 1952),
    pp. 190 and 355-82.

47. Ibid., p. 448. At the congress held the following year the TUC
    leadership did secure a favorable vote on its "go-slow" attitude
    toward further nationalization and at the same time again defeated
    the left's opposition to rearmament (London Times, September 10,
    1953, p. 8; ibid., September 12, 1953, p. 9).

Since the same power was to be reflected at the Labour party conference, the results were almost a foregone conclusion. With most of the union strength pitted against the Bevanites, they had no hope of overturning the party policy on the conference floor. In votes, the unions had almost five times the number allotted to the constituency parties. After subtracting that portion of the union strength which had displayed either a Bevanite or a Communist preference at the Trades Union Congress, there was still a considerable margin of support for the established party leadership. This was decisive in defeating the key opposition motion for a re-examination and reduction of the rearmament program, although the result (3,644,000 to 2,288,000) was not so overwhelming as that which had been scored at the Trades Union Congress.[48]

Again the Bevanite cause was mingled, despite an effort at dissociation, with more far-reaching arguments than the simple opposition to the level of rearmament which the relatively moderate sponsors of the resolution insisted was their only aim. Although fellow-travelers, pacifists, and purveyors of extreme Bevanism had their own favorite resolutions, they also supported the most popular opposition line. Consequently, the debate was striking because so many who spoke for the mild Bevanite resolution indicated that they were either against rearmament altogether or against its present purposes.[49]

This appearance derived in part from direct Communist influence in some unions and some constituency parties, but even the largest estimates of Communist participation indicated that the major role was played by the socialist outlook of the Labour Left.[50] This outlook was, of course, basic to Bevanism, and it inspired the attack on the foreign policy of which the rearmament level was only a part. The way in which left-wing international sentiments had been revived, especially in the constituency parties, was revealed not only on the floor of the conference but even more particularly by the resolutions which the local organizations

48. 51st Annual Report of the Trades Union Congress, p. 154.

49. Ibid., pp. 142-54.

50. One of the few public statements concerning Communist infiltration of the 1952 conference was made by Hugh Gaitskell: "I was told by some observers that about one-sixth of the constituency party delegates appear to be Communists or Communist-inspired. This figure may well be too high; but if it should be one-tenth or even one-twentieth it is a most shocking state of affairs to which the national executive should give immediate attention" (London Times, October 6, 1952, p. 6).

had submitted prior to the annual meeting.[51] These displayed, in many instances, a wholesale dislike for the Anglo-American alliance and an insistence on the pursuit, by the Labour party, of a "socialist foreign policy." In a way, this was only one aspect of a resurgent "advance to socialism" spirit that was manifest among the rank and file in 1952. It had been reflected by the TUC's resolution pressing for more nationalization proposals. Similarly the party conference also passed a resolution which, more specifically than the leadership desired, required the national executive to prepare a list of key and major industries to be taken into public ownership when Labour returned to office.[52]

This apparent socialist revival among party activists did not necessarily make for Bevanite power and influence. Having challenged the leadership of the TUC and of the party so directly, Aneurin Bevan and his followers had exposed themselves to the charges of disloyalty and disunity. There was a special grievance against what was called a "party within the party"—that is, the concerted effort by the Bevanite members of Parliament to organize the constituencies in their own behalf. They had, by their very success in electing six members of the executive and in defeating Morrison, overplayed their hand.

Now there was talk of party discipline. Although a purge by the national executive of the Labour party was tactically improbable (with six Bevanites on the executive), the Parliamentary Labour party could exercise a degree of control over the Bevanite organization in its ranks. A measure had already been adopted to prevent any repetition of the revolt by the 57 Bevanites against the defense program, and attention was directed to Bevanite group meetings and related propaganda activities.

51. Resolutions for the 51st Annual Conference of the Labour Party (London, 1952). In this publication there were included all the resolutions submitted by the various local components of the party, and it was striking to note the heavy emphasis on issues of foreign policy and rearmament as well as the almost entirely critical tone of resolutions locally adopted on these subjects. The significance of this was minimized by Labour officials on the grounds that many of the resolutions, particularly the most extreme ones, came from constituencies where there was only a small organization and that, even where the resolutions came from a large local movement, the attendance at the time of adoption was likely to be slight and unrepresentative.

52. 51st Annual Report of the Trades Union Congress, pp. 91-112. This resolution did not, however, cause the executive to adopt any far-reaching nationalization proposals (see the Labour party's policy statement, Challenge to Britain [London, 1953]).

It was not long after the party conference that a decision was made to suppress the Bevanite apparatus. The proposal to do so was made by Clement Attlee, whose own prestige if not his actual post as party leader, had by this time come under strenuous attack. The backing of the overwhelming majority of Labour members of Parliament, especially of those sponsored by trade-unions, was secured for the adoption of a resolution ordering the abandonment, within the Parliamentary Labour party, of all group organizations not officially recognized. In a further provision aimed at limiting Bevanite activities, members were called upon to refrain from making attacks on one another.[53]

While these moves could not in themselves put an end to Bevanism, they did place its growth under the handicap of being officially branded as factional and divisive—a handicap of considerable import in a movement prizing loyalty. Also, it was now clear that the rebels had become no stronger in the Parliamentary Labour party because of their success in elections to the Labour party executive. They only mustered 51 votes against the 188 who supported Attlee's cease-and-desist order. The 188 were obviously determined opponents of Bevanism, and the estimated 25 or so who abstained were not likely sympathizers but merely foes of what they regarded as harsh discipline. The most that might be said was that among non-Bevanite members of Parliament there were some center and right-wing intellectuals who wanted conciliation rather than suppression. Their numbers were few and their potency almost nil against the decision to exercise a discipline agreed upon by the party leaders and their trade-union supporters.

However, moderate influences did have an effect on the Parliamentary Labour party's balloting, late in 1952, for members of Labour's shadow cabinet—the twelve members of Parliament who were to sit with the leader and deputy leader on the Opposition front bench. Enough non-Bevanites eventually voted for Aneurin Bevan himself so that he was chosen as one of the team from which he had resigned in 1951.[54] But this was hardly

---

53. London Times, October 24, 1952, p. 8.

54. Ibid., November 28, 1952, p. 8. This result was achieved only after considerable maneuvering, since the party leaders had in this instance fostered the adoption of a second ballot system of election which, while it turned out to have results rather like those that would have been accomplished by a single ballot, was nevertheless designed to prevent the Bevanites from concentrating enough votes on a few of their own members of Parliament to elect them while right-wing votes were spread widely over many candidates.

a Bevanite victory. Bevan was elected only as the twelfth man, and all his fellow-rebels were defeated, including the two most prominent ones whose selection, along with his own, had been the original hope. Consequently, the effect was to isolate Bevan from his supporters. As a front-bencher, he now had to speak for the official party point of view and only when charged with doing so by the non-Bevanites of the shadow cabinet. Outside Parliament, of course, the speeches of Aneurin Bevan could remain a rallying point for his movement, but in the Commons his left-wing leadership was temporarily cramped.

Even if Bevan could not be permanently separated from what were called his "Nye-dolaters," there seemed to be no present possibility for his movement to win the struggle for power within the Labour party. The opposition to Bevanism had politically solidified, within parliamentary ranks as within the Trades Union Congress. Continued support from the constituency organizations, which could not very well increase much above its 1952 level was not, in any event, going to outweigh the crucial union strength that was pitted against concerted rebellion. By winning occasional policy triumphs, the Bevanites were unlikely to affect the dominance of their opponents in the control of party machinery. In time, some of Bevan's most determined enemies might die or retire, but their successors, especially in the unions, were not the most probable converts to a left-wing political movement.

Although Bevanite chances of gaining control of the Labour party might thus be discounted, there were prospects that the left-wing ideas of the rebellious movement could succeed where the rebels themselves did not. This might be attributable not only to Bevanite agitation but generally to the party problem of framing a new program while out of office. Opposition-mindedness, especially if frustrated by firm trade-union reluctance to go forward with nationalization, might take shape around rearmament and foreign-policy issues. Here the force of Bevanite conceptions, if not of the Bevanites, could start a drift from the general acceptance of the terms of the Anglo-American alliance. The question that arises is whether there is a "natural" Labour position to which the party was to be pressed by its socialist dispositions. Might the inherent appeal of left-wing ideology, whether called Bevanism or something else, capture the mood of the party as it had during so much of the interwar period? That presumably would entail hostility not only to a large arms program but also to the leadership of the United States.

In 1953 the evidence with respect to any such opposition-minded
drift was still inconclusive. The Parliamentary Labour party had remained firm, except possibly on the special issue of German rearmament, and there was no sign that Bevanism, or anything like it, was
in the process of changing the minds of the majority of the members of
Parliament. Perhaps Labour members regarded themselves as representatives and not as delegates, at least not as delegates for the opinions
of the constituency militants who adopted radical policy resolutions on
foreign policy. These militants, while they were zealous party workers,
were of less consequence to a Labour politician than were the unions,
whose financial contribution carried with it considerable influence,
particularly in the selection of candidates in relatively safe Labour seats.

While a non-Bevanite Labour member of Parliament could derive
satisfaction from the fact that he was apparently on the side of the decisive
political forces within his party, nevertheless the magnitude of rank-and-
file socialist sentiment that had to be contained was something which no
observer of the 1952 Labour party conference was inclined to minimize.
The picture was of a leadership clearly resisting, less by persuasion than
by the unions' bloc vote, the pressures of a very large portion of the active
party membership. Those pressures, representing the traditions of the
Labour Left, might not always look so impressive as they did when gathered
under the Bevanite banner, but their existence, in one form or another, was
a permanent feature of Labour politics. Without being associated so spec-
tacularly with a factional bid for power like Aneurin Bevan's, the left-wing
socialist forces could exert an influence, no less potent because indirect,
over party policies during an extended period of Labour opposition. The
will and the ability to resist could diminish as the party leaders became
farther removed from the need to defend their own previous governmental
policies and at the same time more conscious of the need to unite their
followers for a campaign against Conservative policies. Thus the party
could continue, as it did in 1953, rejecting Bevanite resolutions and yet
in its official pronouncements accept, at least implicitly, some of the more
popular left-wing objections to American foreign policy.[55] To be sure,
such objections may also have reflected preferences which the moderate
party leadership always held but could not express while sharing the responsibility for maintaining harmonious Anglo-American relations.

---

55. See the reports of the 1953 Labour party conference in the London
      Times, September 29, 1953, p. 6; October 1, 1953, p. 2; and October
      2, 1953, p. 2.

With relatively few and diminishing exceptions, the volume and intensity of articulate objections to American foreign policy have been observed to increase markedly as one moves from right to left in British politics. Explaining the ideological basis for this tendency, and particularly for the concentration of hostility in the Bevanite movement, has been a principal aim of this study. In devoting a disproportionate amount of space to the socialist outlook, an attempt has been made to throw light on the process by which the most equalitarian political forces have, in effect, reversed nineteenth-century attitudes toward the United States and left the task of defending American intentions to relatively conservative elements (whose traditions, in some cases, ran counter to the social democracy of the United States).

But this polarization of opinion was not equivalent to the isolation of adverse criticism. Neither the Bevanites nor their predecessors of the left were sharply set off from the rest of the community. Operating as a substantial minority within a major party, their political pressure, at critical moments, had to be taken into account by a Conservative government only less directly than by Labour leaders. It could never be assumed that a movement based on hostility to American policy was incapable of gaining converts. In some respects, the postwar British environment was uniquely favorable for just such a development. Distrust of the foreign policy of the United States was at times so widespread that Bevanism might be viewed as but its most extreme symptom. Its extremity resulted from socialist preconceptions, but its existence as a political force owed much to the recurrent national uneasiness over the postwar American connection. Left-wing opposition to the alliance did, in fact, rise and fall along with the less sharp but nevertheless important shifts in other sectors of opinion. Thus Bevanite hostility only emerged when more general suspicions of the United States had been rekindled by Far Eastern events.

Basically, the Anglo-American disagreement over China brought to a head all of Britain's dissatisfaction concerning its role as a junior partner and an economic dependent. America's policy was disliked and

265

its consequences feared, and much of the time it seemed that Britain could do nothing to influence its dominant ally's crucial decisions. Non-Bevanites did not even have the illusion that it was possible for Britain to threaten to break the alliance as a means of getting its way. The more starkly realistic an Englishman was about his nation's dependence on American military and economic help, the more frustrated he was likely to be. The most he could do was to offer apparently unwanted advice.

The essence of the British advice was that the United States should exercise diplomatic and military restraint. Non-Bevanites, without believing that the United States was deliberately provocative and aggressive, did think that Americans were capable of creating the conditions under which war would become unavoidable. This British attitude flowed in part from the traditional disdain for American skill in international relations but also from a suspicion that the United States, while preferring peace, was less thoroughly determined in its preference than was Britain. On this basis, it was assumed that American leaders might take measures riskier than those which a British government would approve (if asked).

Another way of putting this point is to say that the fear of war was more obviously operative in the British consideration of world politics. A third world war seemed to endanger the very survival of the nation. The island home was conceived as peculiarly vulnerable ever since its subjection to German rocket bombs. The dreadful possibility of rockets with atomic warheads was deeply imbedded in the national consciousness, and the British expected, in case of war, to suffer the first and worst blows from the new weapons of mass destruction.

Englishmen could not believe that the United States appreciated their expectation of impending doom. One reason was that Americans often approached the prospect of war with an equanimity thought unseemly in Britain. From almost the beginning of strained East-West relations, talk about a preventive war, common enough in the United States, had been a British unmentionable. American speculation about when war with Russia was to begin and how it was to be fought conveyed an impression of callousness about Europe's prospective calamity. And it added to the fear, much played upon by the left, that the United States regarded Britain primarily as an unsinkable aircraft carrier and as a more or less expendable site from which to launch an attack on the Soviet Union. The presence of American atomic bombers on East Anglian bases served as a reminder of Britain's front-line position and as a stimulant to anxiety.

The feeling, shadowy though it was, that American policy might be founded on a lesser fear of war was potentially the most divisive factor in the alliance. If transformed by events into a settled conviction, it was the one thing capable of upsetting the calculation of national interest that underlay British acceptance, however grudgingly, of American leadership. Britain had welcomed American power not because it promised success in a war with the Soviet Union but because its presence provided the best chance of preventing the outbreak of large-scale hostilities. This was the heart of the defense of the alliance against both the Third Force alternative and the vaguer "go it alone" spirit of Bevanism. Fundamentally, being joined to the United States was justified as less dangerous than being exposed, in weakness, to the Soviet Union. When the risks of the former seemed, in British eyes, to approach the speculative hazards of an independent line, there was inevitably a re-examination and something like a great debate over the national commitment—however remote the likelihood of changing it.

In 1951 and 1952 what was thought to increase the risks was the prospect of the United States abandoning containment, whose promise of a largely peaceful coexistence based on mutual strength had been considered the most appealing feature of American policy. British opinion had never divided between the defenders of containment and those who wanted something stronger but rather between the proponents of the Acheson-Kennan position and those who preferred a weaker and softer approach to the Soviet power. American contemplation of a more aggressive policy tended to confirm the belief that the United States was motivated by an anti-Communist spirit which Britain did not share. This did not have to be imputed, in the left-wing manner, to a capitalist conspiracy for it to be regarded seriously. More often, it was spoken of as a reflection of an American moral fervor that might be thought commendable in other situations but which was deemed a dangerous quality to impart to the conduct of foreign policy. Its consequences had been feared most expressly at the time of the Truman Doctrine as well as after the Chinese aggression. Always an American crusade to destroy communism was antithetical to the very object of British postwar diplomacy: to be strong enough to deter Russian aggression while assiduously avoiding the slightest appearance of an aggressive intent.

Finally, in 1953, a wide section of the British public began to view the appearance of American moral rigidity as an obstacle in the way of achieving any more definite settlement with the Soviet bloc. During most of the postwar period this particular complaint against the United States had seldom come to the fore, since the chance of a general agreement was made remote by Russian intransigence. But after Stalin's death and the accession of rulers whose hostility was not so well established in the public mind, there was no doubt that Sir Winston Churchill spoke for most of his countrymen when he stated that "a conference on the highest level should take place between the leading Powers without delay."[1] It was characteristic of British opinion, in contrast to American, that following this Churchill statement of May, 1953, there was an increased pressure on the government to follow through on Sir Winston's suggestion.

Indeed, during Churchill's summer illness the Labour party (not just its left wing) sought to make political capital out of the failure of the Conservative ministers to secure American assent to a Four-Power conference.[2] Sometimes the Labour attack took the form of arguing that the ministers really agreed with the American reluctance to engage in a high-level conference, and at other times it was merely contended that British representatives had not been sufficiently insistent in persuading the United States Administration to take up Sir Winston's idea. Either way, Labour was seeking to mobilize popular feeling against what was widely assumed to be an unwise American policy—so widely assumed, in fact, that there was hardly any consideration of the Eisenhower-Dulles position on its merits. Labour had simply to draw upon the suspicions of American foreign policy which had accumulated in the previous seven years, but particularly in 1950-52. Similarly in the circumstances of the Korean armistice of 1953 the British propensity to believe American policy too rigid for success in a peace conference had its roots in previously created impressions as well as in contemporary announcements by the Secretary of State.[3]

---

1. 515 H.C. Deb. 897 (May 11, 1953). There were only rare public objections to the Prime Minister's preference, although the Economist (whose line at this point was much more sympathetic to the American position than was the independent press generally) expressed its fear that pressure for a Big-Four conference might cause a harmful display of Western disunity ("Magnificent—But Is It Policy?" CLXVII [May 16, 1953], 417-19).

2. 518 H.C. Deb. 211-337, 384-515 (July 21 and 22, 1953).

3. 518 H.C. Deb. 1547-1610 (July 30, 1953); London Times, July 31, 1953, p. 9.

Uneasiness about the policies of the United States was sharpened as the postwar loss of great-power status diminished the British sense of authority in what was now almost wishfully called the "Anglo-American alliance." In addition to the increasingly poignant appeals to British statesmen to take a firm stand against various American preferences, there was a growing tendency to make the United States serve as a large and convenient object of cumulative resentments and as the particular target of extremist political movements. Americans have had to get accustomed to a certain amount of British abuse. Much of it is implicit in the new relationship. The important point is that the fully developed left-wing critique should not become plausible to the great majority whose misgivings about the conditions of the alliance have so far been subordinated by generally favorable dispositions toward the United States and by an appreciation of the need for American power.

It is in building and maintaining the confidence of this wider public that there is room for American concern. No doubt, there are (and should be) limits, imposed by the calculation of our own national interest, as to how far American policy can be adjusted in order to earn British good will in any given matter. Sometimes, however, only the sound or the appearance of a policy has to be modified in order to reduce antagonism to ourselves and our interests. In order to maximize the willing participation of our British ally, it ought to be worth while to comprehend even those attitudes which, in our perspective, may seem unduly fearful, narrow, or wrong-headed.